LIFE LINES

Tales of Hope from Capernaum

Don Gee

insta
ap

First published in Great Britain in 2017

Instant Apostle
The Barn
1 Watford House Lane
Watford
Herts
WD17 1BJ

British Library Cataloguing-in-Publication Data
A catalogue record for this book is available from the British Library

This book and all other Instant Apostle books are available from Instant Apostle:
Website: www.instantapostle.com
E-mail: info@instantapostle.com

ISBN 978-1-909728-72-1

Printed in Great Britain

Contents

Prologue

Some are intent, on a mission to find a bargain. Others, less motivated, just want to go in, take what they came for and get out with as little fuss as possible. From the car park it's a short walk down the alley and into the market – but you have to push your way through crowds of people.

Some see it as a day out, a bit of a break from the normal routine of life, a chance to look around, and perhaps meet up with old friends.

Others drift.

Depending on the motivation, some are pushy, irritable and impatient; others laid-back and friendly, open for the unexpected.

A few wander aimlessly, killing time.

And you? Why are you here?

Grab a coffee from the vendor on the corner, and sit on the bench under the shade of the tree.

Now settle back and observe…

Over by the entrance from the car park there's a woman selling *The Big Issue*. She's slightly stooped and has a headscarf pulled down covering her forehead. Her coat's ill-fitting and has the look of having served previous owners better than her. A tired expression is on her face, but her dark eyes scan the people as they enter the market, looking for a potential buyer. Past experience has taught her the ones to avoid and those who will be her best chance of a sale.

Surveying a middle-aged man she holds out a copy and, with a smile, says, '*Big Issue*?' He diverts his eyes and turns in the opposite direction, pretending not to notice her, and hurries off.

She sighs and looks for the next punter as she shuffles her feet. It's mid-March and, although the sun is shining brightly, the air is still cold and the flat shoes she wears aren't designed to keep feet warm. Wiping her nose on the back of her mitten, she pushes a wisp of black hair back under her headscarf and, forcing a smile, holds out her latest edition.

Who is she? Where does she live? Why is she trying to sell *The Big Issue* to people who don't want to buy?

There's a bit of a commotion over on the other side of the market. A trader shouts at a small group of teenage boys who've just missed knocking over one of his clothes racks as they weave in and out, two on skateboards. Some mutter as the boys push past; others smile at their antics.

Suddenly the boys stop, change direction, split up and disappear out of the market. You look over to see why, and it's not hard to find the reason...

Two people in uniform are ambling between the stalls. Authority has arrived in the shape of two officers – one male, black, six foot three with size 12 feet, Constable 479; the other female, blonde, five foot four, PSSO.

Dave, the trader, still holding his clothes rack, gives them a mouthful. 'Did you see that? Almost knocked over my rack! Shouldn't be skateboarding here any time, let alone when the market's on. What you gonna do about it?'

The blonde PSSO gives him her best smile. 'Would you like us to slam them in the stocks for the rest of the day, Dave? Or how about you show me some of your new tops? I've a party tonight, and I need something to wear.' Her smile and feminine charm calm him down, and he gladly shows her what he's got. Her fellow officer winks at a bystander and chats to another shopper.

There's more than one way to exercise authority. Where do they learn when to be heavy-handed and when to defuse a situation with a soft word and a smile?

The bench creaks as someone else sits at the other end, eating a hot dog from the same vendor who sold the coffee. He appears to be in his twenties and is wearing a smart blue sweatshirt with designer jeans and trainers. He settles back and looks around, enjoying the sun and watching the crowd, giving the impression that he's waiting for someone – a girl, no doubt.

His blue eyes catch yours and he says, 'Great day, isn't it? Did you see those boys cut through over there?'

He's smiling. 'You have to laugh. Poor old Dave always gets in a strop over 'em. Same thing happens most weeks; I think they do it just to wind him up! I love the way that PSSO handled him; quick smile, distract him with the possibility of a sale and she has him eating out of her hand!'

The Big Issue lady's got a punter: a trendily dressed girl – slim with long dark hair and an infectious smile.

'Thank you, thank you,' sings *The Big Issue* lady, and smiles at her customer. The contrast between the two couldn't be more marked – 'Oxfam vs Selfridges'.

Our bench friend jumps up and calls out, 'Over here, Sophie!'

She glides over to join him, and greets him with a kiss and hug. 'Got your *Big Issue* then? Did you read the one you bought last week?' he teases her and, smiling, they sit down on the bench. Looking over at us, he says, 'Does it every week. Arrives late and buys *The Big Issue*, but I bet she never reads it.'

'Do too!' she says, in her own defence. 'But even if I don't, it gives her a bit of encouragement.' She takes his hot dog and bites off a big lump of the sausage.

'She does that every week as well – pinches most of the sausage and leaves me only the bread!'

'I'm worth it, aren't I?' She looks at us. 'I like to buy *The Big Issue* from her. I think it could be me over there, selling it. Makes you wonder – you never know, do you?' she says, thoughtfully, then continues, 'We've met up here for the last six weeks so I can go with this hot dog stuffer to have his chemo. Only two more to go, and then we get to find out how successful it's been.'

You never know who you'll meet at the market, do you? Or what the story is behind a face.

Any market, any time, any place. Unknown people – all with a story to tell.

Back to the car, and drive out of the car park…

…to arrive at another market, in another place, in another time…

Capernaum!

We dismount from a camel, and a quick walk down a dusty street takes us into the market square of Capernaum on the lakeside of Galilee in Palestine, AD 30.

Sit down on the wall with a cup of local wine, and watch…

I Touched Him!
The Weary Woman Who Reached Out

She walks into the market and sits down on a packing crate by the side of a display of spices and herbal remedies. Her clothes are of quality but now old and threadbare, her hair untidy. She's smiling to herself, but her face is lined and looks older than it probably is. Someone in the crowd recognises her, and comes over to greet her. Moving over to a fruit stall, the newcomer buys some oranges and offers her one. She takes it gratefully, and eats.

You get the feeling she hasn't eaten fruit as good as this in a long time.

Ruth is her name.

Her faded clothes are in a style that tells us she is a widow. Her story…?

Chapter 1

I remember it as clearly as if it were yesterday. I'd have been about eight years old at the time, and I recall my father returned home after a long trip away on business down by the Sea of Galilee. He arrived home in the early evening and I ran out of the house to greet him, expecting him to scoop me up in his arms and swing me round, as I had seen our next-door neighbour's father do to his daughter when he had come home from work. She was the same age as me.

I cried, 'Abba! Abba!' and jumped up into his arms.

But his arms didn't catch me.

Falling into an untidy heap at his feet, I noticed he had a visitor with him, a man I hadn't seen before.

'Child, is this the way to behave when I return with an important guest from an arduous business trip?' he asked. 'Return to your mother and inform her of our arrival, then tidy yourself up and present yourself in the proper manner after we have refreshed ourselves.'

I retreated to the house, hearing him apologise to his guest for my behaviour. Mother pulled me in and ushered me into the servants' quarters, instructing my maid to make me look 'presentable' while she straightened her own hair and smoothed down the front of her dress. Then she turned to welcome her husband and his guest into the home.

Adina, the maid assigned to care for me, drew me to herself and gently removed my dress, then washed my face and dabbed it dry with a soft towel. She slipped a clean dress over my head and sat me down so she could brush my hair.

'Try not to cry, my beautiful little one. He loves you very much, but sometimes, when men come home after a long trip, they have many very important things on their minds and don't show what they really feel like. You understand?'

I nodded, trying hard not to cry. 'When Tova's Abba comes home, she jumps into his arms and he lifts her up and swings her round with a big smile on his face.'

'But Tova's Abba comes home every night, so he expects her to run from the house,' countered Adina.

'Then my Abba should be even more happy when I run to him as he hasn't seen me for many weeks!' I exclaimed. My tears, no longer able to hide in the corner of my eyes, started to run down my face.

'Shush, little one, try to understand. Your Abba has so much on his mind because he has been away for a long time. Tova's Abba is able to leave all his worries behind every day and not bring them home all at one time.' She wiped my eyes and squeezed my face with both hands, then kissed my nose. 'Come, your mother wants you to go and greet your Abba and his guest. Remember, he is the head of this house and deserves your respect.'

I joined my mother in the hallway, and together we went into the main room. I walked quietly over to my Abba and bowed slightly. 'Welcome home, Abba, I'm sorry I was out of order earlier.' I stood with my head down.

'Look up, child', he ordered, 'That's better. We will say no more of it. This is Mr Amos Ben-Hadon, and he will be staying with us for this week.'

I bowed again and greeted Mr Ben-Hadon. 'Sir, welcome to our home.'

He nodded by way of acknowledgement of my presence, but said nothing.

'You may go and have your supper with Adina,' my Abba said. 'Your mother will see you once you are in bed.'

I left the room, disappointed at this lack of affection for me, but glad to get away from the stifling atmosphere of the grown-ups. Adina beckoned me into the kitchen and we sat at the table and ate supper. I looked across the table as she passed me a slice of lamb, then spooned fresh vegetables onto my plate.

After supper, Adina suggested that we take a walk down by the river. She knew I loved to go there, so as soon as we finished supper, we ran to the river.

I almost forgot the sadness of my father's rejection.

On the way back, I ran ahead and cut through the back garden into the house while Adina was still walking up the hill from the river. At that moment, I heard something that cut into my heart, making that day stand out so vividly in my mind.

There were voices coming from my parents' bedroom. My father was shouting loudly at my mother. 'I just can't believe you let that child run out like that in front of my client. Whatever were you thinking of?'

'But, Nathan, she is only a child and was so glad to see you back,' my mother protested softly.

'A child! I know she is a child! But children have to be taught that there is a time and place for everything, and that was neither the time nor the place! Why you had to give birth to a skinny girl, I do not know! If only you had given me a son, then I could lift my head up and proudly show I have a worthy heir!'

I didn't hear my mother's answer, as she replied far too softly, but I remember being rooted to the spot, feeling my world crumble around me. Adina came up behind me, but I didn't hear her. Laying a hand on my shoulder, she steered me away from the bedroom door and towards the kitchen at the back of the house.

I remember turning my head to look back. It felt like the bigger part of me was still standing there, while I, just a shadow of myself, silently drifted into the servants' quarters. Sitting on a stool in the corner of the kitchen, I spoke not a word. Adina stood in front of me with an anxious look on her face, as our eyes met. 'What is, it my beautiful little one? Did you not enjoy being by the river and running back? Why such a sad face?' she asked.

Staring back at her, I felt a tear coming into my eye. I blinked it away, and continued staring without answering any of her questions.

She tried again. 'Ruth, what is it? Did I say something to upset you while we were out?'

I shook my head and buried my face in the fold of her rough servant's clothing, refusing to cry. Gently but firmly, she again placed her hands on my shoulders and held me at arm's length, searching my face for an answer.

I gave her none.

Reluctantly, she led me to my bedroom and helped me undress for bed. Climbing in, I turned to face the wall as she covered me with blankets and kissed me on the top of my head. 'Don't worry, my beautiful little Ruth, it will be all right in the morning. Sleep well; may your angel watch over you. Your mother will be in shortly to tuck you in.'

The room had grown dark with the fading daylight, and I was still facing the wall when my mother came in. I didn't roll over to see her as she came closer to my bed and laid a hand on my shoulder. Softly, she whispered, 'Are you asleep already, Ruth?' I closed my eyes and pretended I was.

'God bless, and sleep well,' she whispered as she kissed my head.

She left the room – but I did not sleep.

From that day on I changed, keeping what I'd heard hidden deep inside.

I did as I was told, and tried to do all I could so as not to earn any more displeasure from my father, but he seemed not to notice.

Chapter 2

Amos Ben-Hadon did indeed stay for the week – and was to come back on frequent visits as he became more and more involved with my father's business. He didn't take to me, and for my part, I wasn't taken by him. I kept out of his way and was always glad when he left the house. Mother didn't seem to notice me withdrawing into myself as she was preoccupied with trying to please her husband. My father became more demanding, and the atmosphere in the home became ever more tense.

After I had turned ten years old, things changed within the household. Mother became pregnant again. Having been told that she would not be able to bear any more children after I was born, the news was greeted with much delight by my father. Perhaps this time he would have a son and heir, not a skinny girl.

Mother was like a different person and became more like the mother I had known in the past. She would sit and comb my hair instead of letting Adina do it; she would hum a little tune, with a smile on her face. The downside for me was that I felt it was the baby inside her that was making her happy, not me. My insecurity grew, and Adina became my only source of comfort. Then the fear of the baby not turning out to be a boy began to fill my mind. How would father react if it were another girl?

I was also afraid in case it turned out to be a boy. If it were a boy, I would become even more of a burden to father. What would he want to do with me?

Mother gave birth, and I had a baby brother.

How my parents rejoiced! Father threw a big party for all the neighbours of any standing, as well as his business associates. I helped Adina and the other servants in the household prepare the food.

Amos Ben-Hadon was there, and it was then that I felt something more than just not liking him. I felt uncomfortable in his presence, and I didn't like the way he looked at me.

The time for my baby brother's circumcision came, and he was given the name Hananiah.

I loved him!

Despite all the fear of rejection, I looked at my little brother and was smitten. He was a fat little bundle with masses of dark hair, and I was fascinated with his tiny fingers and toes. Mother let me hold him, and even my father didn't scold me. Maybe my little brother would be a way for me to gain some affection from my father.

Determined to do all I could to make it happen, the next year was one of my happiest. I was allowed to take Hananiah out and watch over him when he was in the garden. I loved it when he would grasp hold of my finger with his podgy little hands and kick his little fat legs and squeal with delight. When I came within his sight, he would give a big smile and his hands would reach out for me to pick him up.

It was near the end of my thirteenth year. Amos Ben-Hadon was staying for a few days while he worked with my father on some business venture. As was my habit, I kept out of his way as much as possible, and he didn't notice me around – or so I thought.

I was not such a 'skinny' little girl now. Caring for Hananiah had helped my confidence to grow and, with the tender attention of Adina, had enabled me to slowly develop into a young woman. Adina always paid close attention to my hair, which was now long and flowing.

She was particular about the way I dressed. Combing my hair, she would whisper in my ear the same way as she had when I was much younger: 'Ruth, my beautiful little one, you are becoming more beautiful each day. One day, a handsome young man will come and ask your father for your hand in marriage.'

I blushed at the thought, but there was the beginning of a yearning to know a man who would love me and show me affection.

Later that morning, feeling positive, I walked out through our back courtyard into the stables. One of father's horses pricked up his ears as I came over, and gave a little whinny, so I entered his stable and patted his nose. I felt happier than I had for a long time and, because of Hananiah, father seemed to be more affectionate towards me. I was whispering in the horse's ear when I felt a presence behind me.

Someone was standing between me and the doorway. A shadow fell across the floor and I turned around, feeling my heart beat faster in my chest.

Framed in the doorway stood Amos Ben-Hadon.

The look on his face put a knot in my stomach. The door was pushed shut and, as he walked towards me, I backed away, but there was no place for me to escape.

'Ruth, I do believe you are growing into a little lady,' he said, with an oily voice that sent shivers down my spine. 'Now I know you have never been Abba's little girl, but I think it would be nice for you to be Amos' little woman instead, wouldn't it?'

He now had me pinned up against the back wall of the stable, and I could smell his stale breath as he brushed my hair from my face. The next thing I knew was that I was flat on my back on the floor, and he forced himself on me. I tried to scream but he clamped his left hand tightly over my mouth as he hissed in my ear, 'Scream, and I will tell your father that you are nothing but a little slut who tried to expose herself to me. Relax, and we can have some fun together, little Ruth.'

When he had finished with me, he stood up, and pulled me up with him. Straw from the stable floor was stuck in my hair. With his face close to mine he said in a menacing tone, 'One word to anyone about our little secret and I will let your father know just what sort of daughter he has brought into the world. You've known all along that you are a big disappointment to him, and he has never had any time for you. He would never believe your word against mine, and he would have you banished from the house or even stoned to death for behaving like a common prostitute at such a young age. What a disgrace you would bring on his good name.'

His words went deep, and the picture they conjured up in my mind fuelled the dread that welled up within. He forced a kiss on my lips and walked from the stable with the parting words, 'Bye, my little one. Till the next time I am over on business with your father.'

Repulsion gripped me at what he was implying – that it was to be an ongoing abhorrence and torture for me.

Indeed, it was.

The pain in my body and the fear and revulsion in my mind made me so confused that I didn't know what to do. I stayed in the stable, huddled in the back corner, shaking all over.

After what must have been about an hour, I heard his voice as he shouted 'Goodbye' to my father, mounted his horse and rode from the stable-yard.

My mind cleared enough for me to realise that I must not let my father find me in the stable looking a mess. Pulling the straw from my hair and covering my shame with my crumpled dress, I crept to the stable door and peered out into the yard. A stable-lad was attending to two horses over the other side, and his back was towards me. Quickly and silently, I moved over the yard and slipped through the servants' door at the back of the house.

As I passed the kitchen, Adina looked up from her work, but I moved quickly before she had a chance to speak. Once in my room, I shut the door and pushed a chair under the latch so that no one could come in. Flinging myself on my bed, I sobbed into the blanket until I had no tears left.

Eventually, I got up off my bed and walked over to a bowl of cold water that had been left there from my morning wash. I splashed water over my face and then sat on the bed, slowly rocking back and forth.

If anyone had noticed me go up to my room they didn't come and ask why, and as my mother was occupied with taking care of my young brother, she didn't notice that I was not around. It was only later in the afternoon that Adina came and knocked on my door. 'Ruth, are you in there? We missed you for lunch. Are you feeling all right?'

I called out before she tried the door latch. 'I'm fine, Adina, just got a bit of a headache and wasn't feeling hungry. Don't worry, I'll go for a little walk and be back for dinner.'

'If you're sure, then I'll leave you in peace. Your mother will be back with Hananiah by mid-afternoon. Enjoy your walk.' I heard her retreating footsteps as she walked back to the kitchen.

I quickly changed my clothes, dabbed my blotchy face with some more water and brushed my hair. Then I quietly slipped out of the house and made my way down to the river. After every few steps I looked over my shoulder to see if I was being followed, then I took the path that ran beside the river.

Where the river was joined by another tributary I walked off to the side and sat in the shade of some trees in a spot where I would often come with Adina. My mind went back to the day when Father had first come home with Amos Ben-Hadon, the time when I had overheard him shouting at my mother about me being a skinny, useless girl.

My misery reached a new depth; my mind even turned to thinking how I could put an end to my life.

The sun moved round as the afternoon wore on, and I was no longer shaded by the tree. The warmth of the sunshine caressed my face, and a gentle breeze wafted the scent of some wild flowers over my tortured body.

It eased the pain and bade my soul be still.

Looking into the blue sky, I wondered where the God of my people was in all of this. Did he favour boys more than girls?

Returning home before mother got back with my little brother, I did my best to pretend that nothing had happened. Hananiah was now beginning to talk, coming out with so many words, and he was the centre of attention, so no one noticed my silence and my drawn face.

That is, no one except Adina.

After the evening meal, I slipped away and went to my room to get ready for an early night. There was a soft tap on my door and, before I could answer, Adina walked in. 'Ruth, my beautiful little one, you are not yourself, are you?' she asked with concern in her voice as she sat down on the bed beside me. 'While you were out, I remembered that your mother had instructed me to give your room a good clean since the housemaid is away this week.'

I caught my breath, as I guessed what was coming next. 'Ruth, under your bed I found some of your underclothes with blood on them.'

My eyes grew wide with alarm. What was I going to tell her, and would she believe me? But before I could speak, she went on, 'Ruth, don't be alarmed. It happens to all girls as they grow up. It is a natural thing that happens to us every month. I thought your mother would have talked to you about it before now, or I would have explained it to you months ago. You may feel a bit washed out for a day or two, but you will be all right, trust me.' She gave my shoulders a little squeeze.

I thanked her for her kindness, but didn't tell her that mother had indeed told me more than a year before, and I let Adina carry on thinking it was only my monthly period.

Chapter 3

Life returned to 'normal', and I tried to push my dreadful secret to the back of my mind. Father had begun to allow me to go into his vineyards and learn how to dress the vines.

Much to his surprise, I was quick to learn and soon became very competent at it. This earned me a small measure of respect from him, and I was allowed to go on my own to work on the vines. Being alone in the vineyards was like an oasis for me. I would leave the house as soon as it was prudent to do so, and allow myself to be submerged in the task at hand.

I didn't realise that this new-found talent was indeed making an impression on my father, so much so that he began to trust me to care for more and more vines without having to check on how well I was doing.

But the silver lining had a dark cloud on the other side. Soon, Amos Ben-Hadon arrived on his monthly business round.

Apparently, Father was so impressed with my ability that he told Ben-Hadon of my talent and sent him over to see for himself. The vineyard I was in that day was a long way from our house and was surrounded by a tall wall that protected the vines. As I was reaching up to prune one of the branches, he slipped silently behind me and slid his hands around me. Before I could cry out, he had covered my mouth with his hand and turned me round to face him. His hand moved from my mouth to the back of my head, and he forced his lips on mine.

My fate was sealed, and I knew it was pointless to struggle as I was pushed to the ground between the rows of vines.

When he rose to leave, he said in that oily voice, 'Your father was right, you really do have a talent for vinedressing. With a little help from me, you will be able to develop a talent for undressing!' A leery smile was on his face.

As he walked off, he reminded me that, should I tell, my father would never believe me and I would be stoned for immoral behaviour, lying and bringing disrepute to the family name.

For the next two years I endured this, and I saw no way of escape.

When I entered my sixteenth year, it was remarked that I should be married off, and Father began to raise the question with my mother. For mother, having me around was a help and a support: life for her was difficult because of the demands of Father. The novelty of having a son and heir was wearing off, as small boys can be troublesome.

Over one evening meal the subject was brought up again. 'It's high time Ruth was married. A pity that Amos Ben-Hadon is married; he would have made a perfect husband for her.'

I almost choked on my food, but just managed to control myself.

Mother came to my rescue. 'Are you really willing to receive a dowry for her at the moment? You have said yourself that she is one of the best vinedressers you have. She is much more of an asset to you still living with us in her single state than sending her off as a wife to someone who will use her vinedressing to their advantage.'

Money talks, so they say, and from my father's point of view Mother's reasoning made good financial sense, and the matter was dropped. I sat and listened, feeling as if I were a cow or donkey and they were summing up where best to stable me for the most financial gain. The one ray of hope in all this was that I had a good reason to escape to the vineyards for as much time as I could.

But, sometimes, dark clouds break!

Chapter 4

It was a strong wind that removed the dark cloud from my sky and allowed a ray of sunshine to break through.

It was the time of the month when Ben-Hadon was due for a business appointment with my father, and the inevitable diabolical rendezvous for me was about to come round again. I was resigned to my fate, and had found that compliance with his demands made the trauma of his actions less violent.

But he did not arrive.

For more than five days, I lived the nightmare of seeing his smirking face coming towards me. The month passed and he still had not come.

I was in the vineyard one afternoon, taking a rest from the midday sun, when Adina arrived with some food for me. I had forgotten my provisions for the day and she joined me in the shade, handing me a leather bottle full of fresh, cool water. As I took a drink, I sensed she had something to tell me but didn't know how to start.

'What is it, Adina? You have something on your mind, I can tell. Out with it!' I said, smiling.

'Ruth, my beautiful little one, I have some distressing news that I overheard your father saying to your mother. I didn't mean to hear, but I was working outside their window and couldn't help it.'

'What is it, Adina? You know I won't tell on you. You are the only person in the whole wide world that I can trust.'

'I heard your father telling your mother that there was a violent storm two weeks ago. Lightning struck a tree and it fell across the main road from Jericho. It crashed into two riders on horseback, and one of them was killed. That's why we haven't seen Amos Ben-Hadon this month. He was the one killed.'

Completely overwhelmed, I collapsed in an emotional heap into Adina's arms. Deep sobs welled up from within and I found it hard to breathe, while Adina held me tight and rocked me gently as she had when I was just a young child.

'Ruth, my beautiful little one, why has this news brought such deep emotion? I'm sorry I told you the way I did, but I had no idea that you were so fond of him, for I always felt you tried to keep out of his way when he came to stay.'

I sat up and focused through my tears, trying as hard as I could to bring the convulsions of my sobs under control. 'I – I – I hate – him! Adina – I – I – just – can't take in what you – have just said – I am free at – last!' and I threw my arms around the only person who really cared for me, hugging her so tight she had a job to breathe.

'Ruth, what are you saying?' She paused before going on. 'Did he take advantage of you – abuse you?' I nodded my head, and she stroked my hair and let me cry, asking, 'How long was it going on?'

I leaned back and whispered, 'Ever since the time you found the blood-stained clothes in my room, more than two years ago.'

She gasped in disbelief. 'Oh, Ruth, my beautiful little one, I'm so sorry. Why did you not tell me?'

'He said that if I told anyone he would tell my father that it was me acting as a slut, and Father would have me stoned to death for being a common prostitute. I was so scared that I have never told a soul until now. Father might still think I must have led Ben-Hadon on and it would have been my fault. Father trusted him as a business partner. Promise me you won't tell.'

Adina was shocked at my words. 'Ruth, my precious one. You are neither a slut nor a prostitute! You are the victim of an evil and wicked man who has now met his just reward!' She pulled me close to herself and rocked me in her arms, assuring me she would keep it to herself, and we sat together in silence for a long time, letting the full implication of his death sink in.

I was the one to break the silence. 'Adina, how can I ever marry? What would happen on our wedding night when my husband would find out that I am not a virgin? I could still end up being stoned.' Sadness was in my voice as I spoke.

Stroking my hair, Adina said, 'I think it would be good for you to concentrate on enjoying your freedom, now that Ben-Hadon has died. There will be time enough to worry about that. I'll try to think of a way to overcome this, when we have need to. But now my precious, you are free! Live today in your freedom.'

We stood up: Adina would have been missed if she had stayed any longer. She returned home while I went to work on a row of vines with a lightness and spring in my step that I had not known since I was a very young child.

I was free!

Because Ben-Hadon had been overseeing my father's interests in a business connection with another vineyard owner down by the Jordan, someone would be taking his place. It was of no interest to me, now that I knew that the man who had held such evil power over me was gone and could trouble me no more.

About two weeks later, while I was enjoying the freedom of being out in the vineyard, my father entered with two other men. One I had seen once before and knew to be the owner of the Jordan enterprise. The other was new to me. He was tall, a little younger than my father. When introduced to me, he took my hand and gave a slight bow. 'So very pleased to meet you, Ruth. Your father has told us how you are one of his best vinedressers, and the vines you tend produce more than those tended by others.'

I blushed with pride at his words and was taken aback to see that my father was smiling with pride over me. 'Thank you, Sir. Your words are most kind, but I'm sure that I do not deserve such high praise,' I replied, bowing back.

My father spoke up. 'Ruth, this is Joseph Ben-Jonah, whom I think you have met before. He is the owner of the largest vineyard over by the Jordan, and the master of the late Amos Ben-Hadon. God rest his soul. And this,' he said, as he turned to the stranger who had spoken to me with such respect, 'is Boaz, who is taking over Ben-Hadon's responsibilities.'

Joseph and my father walked down between the rows of vines while Boaz stayed to talk with me. 'Do you enjoy working in the vineyards, Ruth? I think you are the only female vinedresser I have ever met.'

'I love it, Sir. Being out here in the fresh air is the biggest blessing in my life,' I answered with enthusiasm.

His next question was not so easy to answer: 'Did you have much to do with my predecessor? It must have been a shock to you when you heard the news. A dreadful thing to happen to such a respected person.'

I felt the colour rise in my face and I lowered my head so that I didn't have to meet his eyes. I'd had too much to do with Ben-Hadon and there was only loathing in my heart towards him, not a trace of respect.

'You seem troubled by my questions. I'm sorry, Ruth, have I spoken out of turn?'

'No, Sir, you have not spoken out of turn. My father did all the business with Ben-Hadon; I was not part of their discussions,' I answered, as I desperately tried to think of a way to change the conversation. 'Sir,' I asked, 'your name is Boaz. Is that the same name as in the story of Ruth, the grandmother of King David? From all I have been taught, he was a wonderful man who showed kindness to a broken woman.' Even as I said this, in my mind I made a mental link between Ruth, the broken, outcast widow, and myself.

Boaz laughed. 'Well, I may be about the same age as Boaz, and I am unmarried. But I'm not sure that I live up to the qualities that he displayed to Ruth.'

I found Boaz easy to be with and contrasted him with the leering face of his predecessor. I found myself wondering whether it was really possible that there are men you can trust and who will treat women with dignity and respect.

Father returned with Joseph, and the three men left the vineyard together. Then, for the first time ever, my father said to me, 'Ruth, try not to be late for our evening meal. I would like you to join us at the table.'

That evening, I sat at the table in a daze. Instead of my father sitting there with a face like thunder every time he looked at me, there was almost a smile of approval. Instead of the leering face of Ben-Hadon, Boaz was there, acknowledging my presence as an equal. Joseph congratulated my mother for the fine family she had, and even my little brother was on his best behaviour.

After the meal, the womenfolk were excused from the room while the men sat and talked. Mother had set out a tray with the best wine and silver goblets. 'Ruth, please take this through for you father and his guests,' she requested, as she passed the tray to me.

I took the tray from her and went back to the dining room and placed it on the low table. Walking away from the room I heard Joseph say to my father, 'Fine young woman you have there. I'm surprised you haven't married her off before this. Why, if I were old Boaz here, I'd be asking you for her hand. What do you think, Boaz? It's about time you got yourself a wife.'

I hesitated in the hallway just long enough to hear what answer Boaz would give. 'That would be history repeating itself. An old Boaz with a young Ruth! I fear that I have left it too late, and wouldn't presume on Amos here to allow me to marry his beautiful and talented daughter. I am old enough to be her father.'

'Age has little to do with it, Boaz,' Joseph replied. 'Why, I am much older than my wife and it has never been a problem. In fact, it has its advantages: she will still be young enough to care for me in my old age!'

I didn't hear my father's comment on the conversation.

Joseph and Boaz left to return to their homes the next day. I hadn't seen them to speak to since the evening meal, so I never said goodbye.

Life was much better after that, and I relaxed, knowing that Ben-Hadon would not be preying on me every month. Boaz came in his place and he showed me only respect. He was kind and courteous and had the ability to put everyone at ease in his presence.

He took an interest in my work in the vineyard, but would not visit me there without the company of Adina and never let himself be alone with me. Here at last was a man I could trust, and who saw me as an equal and valued person. The memory of the abuse I had suffered at the hands of Ben-Hadon began to recede in my mind, and I felt some healing taking place.

Chapter 5

More than a year passed and I was at peace, enjoying the festivals that were part of our Jewish heritage. To visit the Temple in Jerusalem and stand in the Women's Court were highlights that I now enjoyed, as well as not having to look over my shoulder to see if Ben-Hadon were near.

It was after the Feast of Weeks that Boaz came on his monthly visit to my father. I was, as usual, enjoying myself working in the vineyard when Adina came through the gate, followed closely by Boaz. Leaving what I was doing, I went over to greet her. 'Adina, did I leave my water bottle behind again?'

She shook her head. 'No, Ruth, you have it with you. It's Boaz who wishes to speak to you.' She retreated a few paces back so that Boaz could talk to me. My heart skipped a beat. What might he want to say to me out here in the vineyard that he could not say at the table in the evening?

'Ruth,' he began hesitantly, 'I'm not very good at expressing my feelings and I don't know the right way to say this, but I feel I need to ask you if you would grant me permission to ask your father for your hand in marriage? I have wanted to do this almost from the first time I saw you. I felt I couldn't expect you to be willing to come and live with me away from your family. But now I fear that I have let too much time slip through my fingers, and I must know how you feel.'

That cold irrational fear surged up inside me, threatening to overwhelm me, so much so that I couldn't look him in the eye. My hesitation was not lost on him, and he interpreted it the wrong way.

Before I could get any words out, he spoke again. 'I understand, Ruth. I know I'm so much older than you; that's why I wanted to ask you before I spoke with your father. I didn't want him to make you do something you would not want for yourself.' His voice was flat as he spoke, and I could see the sorrow in his face as he turned to walk away.

Finding my voice, I called out, 'No, Boaz, you don't understand. It has nothing to do with your age. It's just that I can't. I can't marry you or anyone else.' Tears came to my eyes, and he turned back to me.

'Ruth, what is it? What's upset you so much? What makes you think you can't get married?' he questioned.

Looking over to Adina, I said, 'Adina, please explain it to him. Tell him what only we know, and help him understand.' Then I ran out of the vineyard and down towards the river. Finding the spot by the stream that was so familiar to me, I pushed aside some low-hanging branches beside the path, stepped through so as not to be seen by anyone passing by, and threw myself down on the grass and wept.

It wasn't long before I heard Adina calling out to me, 'Ruth, are you there? Please, Boaz is with me. He wants to speak with you. You have nothing to fear.'

As she was calling she pushed her way through the branches and held them back, so that Boaz could enter. They knelt down beside me, one on each side. Slowly and gently, Boaz bent over me and lifted me to a sitting position. 'Adina has told me what Ben-Hadon did to you. In my eyes, you are the virgin I want to marry. To me, you are innocent and pure, the victim of Ben-Hadon's lust. He

38

molested your body, but in your heart you are a virgin. I won't tell your father that you're not a virgin. No one will stone you or ever reject you again.' His face was streaked with tears and he spoke softly as he brushed my hair from my face.

I looked at him, and then at Adina. 'You told him everything, Adina?'

'Everything,' she replied.

'But Boaz, there is more,' I said as I looked at him. 'I won't be able to give you children.'

'Why do you say that, Ruth?' Boaz asked.

'Isn't it obvious, Boaz? He had sex with me every month for nearly two years and I was never with child. Whatever he did to me must have damaged me. I can never bear children. My periods are irregular and sometimes I go for months with none.' I closed my eyes with shame as I spoke, letting the tears run unchecked down my face.

Adina wiped my tears and stroked my hair. Then, after a pause, Boaz spoke again. 'That may be so, Ruth, but you have to keep in mind that it may be that Ben-Hadon was unable to produce seed to father a child. But either way, I come back to the question I asked you in the vineyard. Please, Ruth, will you give me your permission to ask your father for your hand in marriage? No one but the three of us need ever know the past. Children or no children, I want to take you to be my wife.'

I took his hand. 'Boaz, dear, good Boaz. You truly live up to your namesake. I can think of nothing else that I would rather do than to become your Ruth.'

He bent over and kissed me on my forehead. 'Then I shall go and speak with your father and lose no time in claiming you as my bride. Adina, I will leave you together. When Ruth is ready, please walk her back and help her to freshen up before the evening meal.'

As he left, Adina and I sat in the tranquillity of the stream and the promised security of a man who spoke of his love for me even as I was. I felt clean.

We were married the next month, and Boaz took me to his home beside his vineyard near the Jordan.

He was all he had promised to be, and would be so for the next five years.

I lived with peace in my heart.

Having no children was a big disappointment to me, but if it were so for Boaz, he never spoke of it. His love for me brought me comfort, and we were happy together.

After four years, it started.

I began to bleed, sometimes just for a few days like any woman in her monthly cycle, but then it became more and more prolonged until I was very rarely without blood loss.

Boaz did all he could for me, and would seek out the best doctors to try to find a cure. I was in the situation of being classed as unclean by the laws of purification and therefore unable to attend the Temple festivals or go to the local synagogue. The local rabbis would cross over to the other side of the road when I came along, for fear of being made unclean and therefore unfit for their duties. I saw this as further rejection by men, and it stirred up painful memories, both of my father's rejection of me as a child and of the painful abuse that I had endured at the hands of Ben-Hadon.

The love and acceptance of my faithful Boaz enabled me to keep going, as the blood loss weakened my body.

Was it because of my illness? I will never know, but Boaz's health too began to fail.

Following our fifth year of marriage, his condition worsened and he collapsed in his beloved vineyard. I did all I could to make him comfortable, and called the local doctor, but he was unable to do anything for him.

Two weeks later, my dear Boaz slipped away from this life. His parting words to me were that I should use all that we had to seek help to find a cure for my condition, and to assure me that in the last five years I had made him the happiest man on earth.

I grieved for him, my heart broken.

Why do men reject me, abuse me, walk the other side of the road to avoid me, or die and leave me?

Faithful Adina, whom Boaz had arranged with my father to come and be my servant, was the only one who kept me going. It was she who helped me pick myself up and try to move forward. She urged me to do what Boaz had made me promise: to look for doctors who could help me with my condition. We kept the vineyard going and it brought in enough income to give us a living. But medical treatment, such as it was, cost money.

Chapter 6

For twelve years, sometimes travelling many miles if we heard of a doctor who might have a cure, we did all we could, but both my money and my health slipped away.

All remedies failed.

I looked old for my age, and it became common knowledge that I was 'unclean'. None knew of my abuse, so many supposed that somewhere along the line I had lived a sinful lifestyle.

The vineyard had to be sold as, by now, I was unable to find the strength to keep it going. I sent Adina back to my parents' home; they were now getting on in years and needed extra help. It was a sad day to see her go, but I no longer had the means to keep her.

Over a period of a few weeks I began to hear talk of a new travelling rabbi being in the area. It was said that he had come from Nazareth, which, for many, made him a no-hoper, as it was generally accepted that nothing good ever came from there.

If only Boaz were still with me, I would have spoken with him about this new teacher. The stories were that he was not only a teacher but also a healer who had performed many wonderful miracles. I longed for this to be true. How I longed for my Boaz to hold me and touch me. I longed for men not to walk away when they saw me, especially the teachers of the law.

I so much wanted them to spend time and sit with me and explain how our God Jehovah had said through the prophet Jeremiah:

> I have loved you with an everlasting love;
> I have drawn you with unfailing kindness.
> I will build you up again,
> and you, Virgin Israel, will be rebuilt.
> Again you will take up your tambourines
> and go out to dance with the joyful.
> *Jeremiah 31:3-4 (NIV)*

I'd heard those words read at the local synagogue many times, and they had echoed round the void of my heart. Where was this loving kindness that had the power to draw? How I longed to be built up and to be one of Israel's virgins; oh, how I wanted to be His virgin and dance with joy before Him at the Temple.

But I was banished from there.

My financial state became worse, as I had spent a considerable sum on yet another doctor, and I was left with little to live on. The stories of this Jesus were being told all over the area, the most recent being that on the Sabbath day in Capernaum He had healed a man with a withered hand in front of all the Pharisees. They, apparently, were none too happy about it as they felt He shouldn't do that sort of thing on the Sabbath.

This Jesus, if what was said about Him was true, didn't stick with all the rules the Pharisees said we should. Some said He even ate with tax collectors and prostitutes – *and prostitutes!*

I felt so much like a prostitute, and the way the teachers walked on the other side of the road only rubbed it in.

I made up my mind – what had I to lose, as I had lost so much all ready? If nothing came of it, so what? Nothing had come of all the others I had visited, and I so wanted to just touch Him. To touch a man who sounded as generous and kind as my Boaz, yet was said to have God-given supernatural power! If He could heal a man with a withered hand, why could He not heal me?

Pulling my shawl around me and filling a bottle with water from the well, I set out for Capernaum. Having taken the road that went along the shore of Galilee, I noticed a crowd around one of the fishing boats. They began moving off towards the town, so I followed along behind.

At that moment, a well-dressed man came up from the direction in which the crowd was heading. He dropped to his knees in front of the man the crowd were following.

Then it dawned on me: this man in front of the crowd must be Jesus.

The crowd stopped, and a hush came over them as everyone was straining to hear what this newcomer wanted.

'Sir', he pleaded, 'my name is Jairus. Please help me. My little girl is dying. Please, please, come and place Your hand on her, so she can be healed and live.'

Jesus changed direction and went with him. The crowd pressed in, not wanting to miss anything. How I wanted Him to touch me and heal me so that I could live, really live. I quickened my pace and caught up with the outer edge of the crowd.

No one seemed to notice me.

So far, so good! But as we got closer to the town, my resolve began to waver. Who was I to approach a holy man, and I began to reason within myself…

I can't touch a holy man for I will make Him unholy.

Yet I could see Him, and I didn't think He looked like those other holy men. *I want to touch Him.*

But a holy man would cross to the other side, to preserve His holiness. *I can't touch Him.*

I still want to touch Him. What if I came up from behind and just reached out and touched the edge of His robe?

What if people could see what I was doing? Then what would they say?

But I so want to touch Him.

There are a lot of people. His disciples are around Him and they seem to be trying to keep people away from Him.

I must touch Him. He is a different sort of holy man.

What if nothing happens?

At least I will have tried, but He healed the man's hand.

Oh, that well-dressed man has His attention, I don't stand a chance against him. He's important; I'm just an unclean woman.

Wait a minute, though; everyone will be focused on him and whatever he wants, so this could be my opportunity. If I walk fast and round the outside of the crowd, I can stand by that tree up ahead where the road narrows. Everyone will be looking at that man and Jesus. I can squeeze into the crowd, reach out my hand and touch Him. No one will know.

I've made it to the tree before the crowd. A bit out of breath, but I'm here. Now they're level.

Hold it, hold – now!

I'm in the crowd, no one has noticed me; must push through these next few people…

That one was a bit offended, but I'm not stopping now.

Only that man in the way and I can reach Him; someone else has pushed past me.

I have got to do it…

Squeeze in here, reach out… reach out.

I can't, I'm scared; what if He does see me? I'll have defiled Him and He won't be able to go to the meeting at the Temple.

But He's not going to the Temple. This may be my only chance.

Push… reach. Got it! Touched His cloak. Let the crowd move on; stay still. I can't; I'm trembling so much.

I feel something has happened… I feel clean!

It's worked! I can feel myself being filled. I can…

The crowd has stopped moving, and Jesus is looking around. *He knows what I've done!*

I keep still, hoping He can't see me among all the people. The disciples are almost laughing at Him, because He said someone touched Him. With all these people around, they know many people have touched Him.

Jairus is looking more anxious, and he wants Jesus to keep moving.

Silently I pray, *Please move on, Jesus, don't notice me.*

He turns right round, and looks straight at me. I can't stop shaking and blurt out, 'Jesus, I'm sorry, it was me. You see, I've had this problem for twelve years *(I can hear myself talking, I can't seem to stop myself, the words just tumble out of my mouth; I feel such a relief)*. Lord, I have spent everything to get it sorted out, but nothing has – I…'

'Daughter…' – that's what he said to me. Oh, to hear a man call me 'daughter'! Daughter – I'm accepted, I'm forgiven, I'm cleansed, I'm free!

'Go', He says, 'Your faith has healed you. Go in peace; be free from this suffering.' I touched Him… or is it more that He touched me?

He's not like the other men I have known, apart from Boaz.

He has not rejected me, abused me, avoided me or left me.

He called me 'Daughter':

I have loved you with an everlasting love;
I have drawn you with unfailing kindness.
I will build you up again,
and you, Virgin Israel, will be rebuilt.
Again you will take up your tambourines
and go out to dance with the joyful.
Again you will plant vineyards
on the hills of Samaria;
the farmers will plant them
and enjoy their fruit.
Jeremiah 31:3-5 (NIV)

(Matthew 9:20-22, Mark 5:21-34 and Luke 8:43-48 give the biblical account of the woman.)

On the Mat!
Through the Roof to See Jesus

Chapter 1

At the other end of the market is an area set aside for what could be called the 'job market'. Those looking for casual or seasonal employment on a day-to-day basis gather, hoping that others who are looking for labourers will offer them work on a 'pay-by-the-day' arrangement. The system works well, and first thing in the morning this area is busy. Employers are looking for strong men to help with the barley harvest.

As the day wears on, a few of the less able are still standing about, hoping there may still be the chance of employment for what's left of the day.

Through the middle of this dispirited bunch run a gang of boys let out of the synagogue school early. Their enthusiasm is in stark contrast to the despondent mood of the 'less than hopefuls'.

Angry words rend the air as boys push thoughtlessly past the stationary men, their sights firmly set on getting to the lake and jumping in for a swim.

The voice was distant and indistinct. Almost inaudible but not quite, like something from another world – yet it had a certain familiarity about it.

Then, suddenly, it exploded into a very present reality. 'Ezra, are you listening?!'

Ezra's head shot up from its position of sagging forward so far that his chin was resting on his chest. He spluttered, 'Yes, Sir, of course I am, Sir.'

'Tell me then, Ezra, which one of the commandments did Moses say was the most important?' his teacher challenged, standing directly in front of him.

Trying desperately to awaken his brain, he teetered back on his stool, then lost his balance and fell backwards, landing with his back against the wall with the stool shooting forward, just missing the feet of his instructor.

There were stifled sniggers from the rest of the class of boys, quickly silenced by a menacing stare. Not allowing Ezra to arise from his embarrassing position, the teacher demanded an answer to his question: 'Well, boy! Which commandment is it?!'

'Err, to love the Sabbath as your neighbour's wife… No, I mean, to love yourself as unto the Lord your God… I can't remember, Sir,' Ezra finished lamely.

There was a twitch under the teacher's left eye as he kicked the upturned stool towards the beleaguered boy, still crumpled up against the wall. He tried to keep his composure while towering over him and, after a long pause, he turned on his heels and walked to the front of the class.

Then he lost it, and roared with laughter, 'Love the Sabbath as your neighbour's wife!' He clutched the edge of his desk as he allowed himself to sink down onto the chair. Removing a handkerchief from his robe he wiped the tears from his eyes and repeated Ezra's answer again, 'Love the Sabbath as your neighbour's wife… Oh, I like it.'

Clearing his throat, he jumped to his feet and addressed them all in a voice like thunder: '"You shall love the Lord your God with all your heart, with all your soul and with all your strength." 'That is what Moses taught as the most important thing for us to do. But today, on a hot afternoon, it might seem more important for some of us to go outside and run down to the lake and have a swim in the water!'

He thumped his fist on the desk top, and all heads shot bolt upright and turned in his direction – except Ezra, who was still trying to get his stool the right way up so he could sit down again.

'As Moses parted the waters of the Red Sea, I suppose it wouldn't be so out of place for you boys to try to do the same. Get out of here, the lot of you!'

There was a howl of delight as the gaggle of boys jumped to their feet and ran from the room down to the lakeside.

Ezra hung back, then slowly walked over to his father. 'I'm sorry, Abba, I didn't mean to embarrass you by not paying attention in your class.'

His father placed his hand on the boy's shoulder. 'I was young once, son. I can remember what it's like trying to concentrate on the rabbi droning on and on, on a warm day. Love the Sabbath as your neighbour's wife! I love it! Go on and join the others, but don't be late back for supper.'

Ezra gave his father a quick hug, and ran to catch up with his classmates.

Watching him go, Jairus shook his head. 'Oh, to be young and have no responsibilities. Lord, keep your hand on that one; he seems so easily distracted.'

It was the beginning of the harvest season and the synagogue school was about to finish, so the boys could help in the harvest fields. As Capernaum was situated at the edge of the Sea of Galilee, it was only a short walk from the synagogue through the marketplace, and down to the shore.

Jairus sat on the edge of the desk. Teaching a class of boys between the ages of ten and thirteen was not his idea of a pleasant way to spend a day. He would much rather have been working at his building business. He had only agreed to take the class for the rabbi who had an important trip to make to the Temple in Jerusalem. As Jairus was the ruler of the local synagogue, he felt it his duty to help by teaching the class. Placing some scrolls back on the shelves, he picked up some business papers and made his way back to his house on the wealthier side of town.

Ezra ran through the market and down to the water's edge. Most of his classmates were already swimming or splashing about in the water, and he sat down on the shingle and began to undo his sandals so he could join them.

Before he had time to take the second one off, he was once again knocked off balance. This time it was his best friend running over and jumping on top of him, then pinning him down by sitting on his chest and grabbing his wrists with both hands.

'Good one, Ezra!' shouted Obed, 'Your old man's all right – for a synagogue ruler and a stand-in teacher! I thought he was going to tan the hide off you for falling asleep while he was teaching, but instead he let us all out early for a swim.'

'Yah, he's not bad, is he?' Ezra panted, struggling to get his breath. 'He's not much good at teaching, and, with the sun shining, I just couldn't keep my eyes open. I thought I was in for a hiding, too. I think he's in a good mood because, after all this time since having me, Mum's going to have another baby. He's always wanted to have more kids. He thinks another boy would be great, as it would be a sign of the Lord's favour, but secretly I think he'd love to have a daughter.'

Obed lost concentration for a moment and Ezra took the opportunity to twist his body, roll over and get out from under his friend. Obed tried to gain the upper hand, and after a short wrestling match, both boys sat up, grinning at each other as they were joined by three others who collapsed down beside them, dripping with water.

Samuel, his twin brother Solomon and Jonah had started at the rabbi's school at the same time as Obed and Ezra, and they had become close friends.

Jonah overheard what Ezra had said about the possibility of having a sister, and felt it his duty to warn his friend. 'A sister! You don't want one of them!' he stated emphatically. 'I've got one who is older than me, and she's a right bossy thing, and then I've got one younger, and she gets all the attention. I can see why Moses said that boys showed the Lord's favour, 'cos sisters don't! You don't want to have a sister, Ezra.'

'Don't think I have any choice in it, do I? Nor my father, come to that. Anyway, it won't be for a while yet, but if it keeps him in a good mood thinking about it, I'm all for it.'

Jonah rolled his eyes with the grown-up wisdom only a twelve-year-old boy can have. He lived on the north side of Capernaum, with his mother and two sisters. His father was the manager of a large vineyard and winepress. Jonah was gangly with an angular face, and feet that sometimes wanted to go in different directions to each other. He was the joker of the bunch.

Samuel and Solomon were identical twins and, for those who didn't know them, it was difficult to tell them apart. Their father was a fisherman and owned two boats that were beached further along the shore. In contrast to Jonah, they were well built for their age, and agile. As they often helped on the fishing boats, they were always ready for action, and could sail the smaller of their father's boat by themselves. When they had first started at the school, they would trick the others about their identity, but as their friendship drew them closer together, the others in the gang knew which was which.

Ezra found it hardest to be at school, not just because he was slow at learning, but also because his father was the ruler of the synagogue, and on days like today he sometimes became the stand-in teacher. Ezra felt he was expected to behave better than the others, and Jairus pushed him to try harder. He was a good student and could hold his own, but had a chip on his shoulder because of the expectations placed on him. He helped in his father's building-yard, and enjoyed working with the carpenters. When left on his own, he would try whittling shapes with bits of discarded wood.

Obed was undoubtedly the leader of the pack. He was about the same height as Jonah, but not gangly. His mother had died when he was only six and his father had brought him up on his own. A neighbour kept an eye out for him when his father was late home from work. From a young age, he had learned to fend for himself, and now was well able to prepare meals and sort out the day-to-day household needs. He was close to his father, who was employed in general labour, and would turn his hand to almost anything that came his way. Obed was streetwise and resilient, quick-witted, and the natural leader.

In the pecking order of this bunch of boys, Obed was the leader, Ezra came next, with the twins Samuel and Solomon close behind, and Jonah at the bottom of the pile. But their friendship was not going to finish with their schooldays.

Obed dreamed that someday he would be more than the son of a labourer living on the poorer side of town. He dreamed of having a place of his own, becoming someone whom people looked up to and did not feel sorry for because he had no mother. He dreamed of having money – and enough of it so his father didn't have to take on any job that came his way to make ends meet.

Obed dreamed.

Most of his dreams were not empty fantasies, and even in those schooldays, he was looking for ways to better himself and thinking up schemes to bring them to a higher standard of living. He was happy to play with the gang and get up to things that boys of that age tended to do, but his wits were tuned into what was going on around, looking for the realisation of his dreams.

Sometimes in his night dreams, he was falling, falling from the heights he managed to climb, and ending up at the bottom again. After the nightmare, he would resolve to make it happen. He would climb and achieve more than others of his social standing ever thought possible.

And he wouldn't fall!

Chapter 2

But he was falling!

The rope he was holding suddenly fell slack. He snatched at a protruding rock but missed, his arms flailing wildly and his feet standing on thin air. He somersaulted backwards, out from the cliff face and into the darkness of the night. A terrifying scream escaped from his mouth a split second before he hit the large boulder at the bottom of the cliff. His body bounced once like a half-empty leather water bottle, then came to a sudden stop on the rocks and shingle. He lay still, like one dead.

Jonah, standing in the moonlight a few steps away, was so shocked he couldn't move, and from his wide-open mouth no sound came. He stood there, rooted to the spot. Two bodies lay motionless in front of him. One had fallen right from the top of the cliff, and he knew it to be that of Marcus, who had planned this escapade with Obed. He had to be dead because Jonah knew you couldn't fall all that way and crash onto the rocks and live. But the second was Obed, his best friend from schooldays. Obed had only climbed a bit of the way up... perhaps he wasn't dead?

Jonah's mouth closed, and he forced himself to move. He didn't run towards Obed but in the opposite direction, away from the cliff and towards the water's edge. With his heart beating wildly in his chest, he ran for all his worth. After a few minutes he saw the silhouette of Ezra, standing and looking in his direction.

Ezra was near the water and had heard a cry, then, seconds later, another. He'd stopped walking away from his friends. Then he heard someone running on the shingle towards him, and he peered into the shadows. Jonah came panting towards him. 'Ezra, Ezra, please come back. Obed's fallen from the rope and he's lying in a heap at the bottom of the cliff.'

Without waiting to be told any more, Ezra raced to where the broken body of his friend lay, beside the large boulder. A few steps away he could see the shape of the lifeless body of Marcus. He turned back to Obed. His back was bent in a funny angle and one leg was pinned under him. Obed made no sound and Ezra could see, even in the half-light of the moon, a gash on the side of his head. Feeling his neck, Ezra found a pulse. Jonah stood beside him almost hysterical, trembling like a leaf.

'Pull yourself together,' Ezra muttered, then louder, 'He's not dead. Get to the water's edge, and see if you can see the boat coming. When you do, get Samuel and Solomon to bring something we can lay Obed on, and we'll get out of here by boat. *Move*, Jonah!'

Jonah ran to the water's edge, and he could see the twins' boat bearing down towards him. Waving his arms frantically, he waded up to his waist in the water. The brothers leaned over the side, and pulled him in.

Between gasps and sobs he managed to tell them what had happened. 'We – we – we need something to carry Obed on. Ezra says – he's not dead! But we need – to hurry in case some palace – some palace guards come.'

Solomon rummaged in the stern of the boat and pulled out a piece of old sailcloth. 'We'll lash this to two oars and make a stretcher to carry him on. It should work.'

The boat scraped on the shingle and stuck fast. All three jumped into the water, waded ashore and ran over to Ezra, who was gently trying to straighten Obed's body. Samuel, being the quickest at lashing sails, did the best he could to lash the old sailcloth to the oars. They half-lifted, half-slid Obed onto the stretcher and then, as fast as the shingle would allow, made their way back to the boat.

Jonah thought he heard voices coming along the beach from the opposite direction, so they broke into a run and, without stopping, rushed straight into the water. While Jonah took both oars of the stretcher at one end, Solomon jumped into the boat. Then he leaned over, reached down and took it from Jonah's hands. Jonah climbed aboard as Samuel and Ezra pushed the stretcher forward into the boat, and jumped in behind it.

'I'll see to Obed while you three get us out into the deep water before we get caught,' ordered Ezra, but Solomon was already back in the water and, with his shoulder under the bow of the boat, was pushing with all his worth to get her free of the shingle. Samuel was trimming the sail with Jonah's help, and Ezra manned the tiller.

Samuel turned the sail and, mercifully, a gust of wind sent them out into deeper water. Crouching low on the inside of the boat, Jonah peered over and informed them that he could see three or four men on the beach, but they seemed to be walking towards the cliff rather than out towards them.

Supporting the makeshift stretcher in the middle of the boat with a wooden plank, Ezra managed to make it steady. Once the sail was set, Samuel and Jonah joined Ezra in the boat.

'He's in a bad way,' Ezra said. 'I think his back could be broken and he has a nasty gash on his head. I've held my tunic on it and the bleeding's stopped. His breathing is steady now, but I'm no doctor and I'm afraid we might still lose him.'

Jonah almost collapsed beside Obed. 'You can't die, Obed, do you hear me?! You can't die.' He started to sob. 'It's all my fault. If I'd stuck with you, Ezra, we would have left long before we got into this mess.'

Samuel took control of the situation in a manner not typical of him. 'Jonah – shut up!' he said, decisively. 'We were all in this together. Obed made his own choice, and he wouldn't blame any of us for this.'

This shocked Jonah out of his despair and he tried to pull himself together. He stared wide-eyed at Ezra. 'Do you think he'll make it?'

'He's strong, so I guess he's got as good a chance as any.' Ezra looked closer at Obed's face, 'I think his eyes flickered just then.'

The other three crouched down lower to get a closer look. Obed opened one eye and a low groan escaped his lips, but that was all.

'At least we know he's alive,' whispered Jonah, somewhat relieved.

Obed sensed a dim light at the top of the deep hole he felt he was in. In his mind, he was reaching up to try to pull himself towards the top of the hole so he could climb out, but it was beyond his reach.

Was that Jonah's face peering down at him, blocking out most of the light? He remembered Jonah peering over him, recalling a long time ago when they sat together at school, and he was trying to read what Obed had written on his slate.

He blacked out and lost contact with the outside world.

With the increasing wind, the boat cut more quickly through the water and rocked from side to side on the waves. Obed became aware of the movement, and his eyes opened again. Jonah was still looking at him, with an anxious expression on his face.

In his confusion and jumbled thoughts, Obed fixed on the idea that they were back at the hostel that Jonah had persuaded him to go to when they were about sixteen. Only, it was he who was looking over Jonah slumped against the stone water trough Obed had just ducked Jonah's head in. In his 'black hole' he had a vivid flashback to that time…

Chapter 3

Jonah had called in at Obed's home after work and found him alone, as his father was working away for the week. Jonah's parents were also away and he was fed up with being in the house with his sisters, so he was looking for something to do. He'd heard about the hostel over on the north side of town. It was now being run by new owners who brewed their own beer, and word was that it was good, strong stuff. Jonah wanted to look, and suggested to Obed that they could go and find out.

'I've not much of a taste for beer, Jonah,' Obed could hear himself replying to the invitation. 'My father's not keen on my drinking too much fermented stuff. But I've nothing else to do, so I guess we could give it a try.'

As they were reaching the hostel, Jonah slipped in a question: 'Obed, what do you think of women?'

'What do you mean, "What do I think of women?" You're the one always moaning about your sisters, not me. And when I did meet your sister, I couldn't see what was wrong with her. She looked all right to me.'

'You fancy my sister, then? Obed, you've got to want your head seen to,' Jonah exploded.

'I didn't say I fancied your sister, only that she didn't seem like what you've always said about her. I think she's quite good-looking, that's all,' retorted Obed.

'So you do fancy women then, Obed?' questioned Jonah again.

'Well, I suppose I do. That's all part of growing up, isn't it?' Obed said, trying to look mature, 'Look, if you must know, I think my father is seeing someone he likes. He's mourned my mother for a long time, had a job to get over losing her. I think part of this time away, he might be seeing someone.'

Jonah hesitated. 'You don't mind? I mean, if he brought another woman into your home, how would you feel?'

'Wouldn't care. He can do what he likes, can't he? Anyway, if he did get another wife, I could always move out. I quite fancy a place on my own. Jonah, what's all this about women all of a sudden? Have you got a girl that you're seeing on the sly?'

'No, nothing like that! It's just, well, it's just that I've heard that there's not only a good brew here, but there are women too. You know, women who let you sleep with them,' Jonah answered.

'You old devil, you!' Obed exclaimed. 'You wanted to come here for the women, not the beer! I should have known. I've seen you looking at the girls as we go through the marketplace. Well, you can try the women if you like, but I'll stick to trying the beer tonight. I think that'll be enough for me.'

'No, you got me all wrong, Obed; I've come for the beer,' protested Jonah. 'I just thought I'd mention about the women before we went in, in case they came up to you and you weren't expecting it. Didn't want you to be embarrassed and make a fool of yourself, that's all.'

'Very considerate of you, I'm sure. But now we're here, are we going in or not?' With that, Obed pushed open the door of the hostel.

The place was dark, with only a few oil lamps burning. There was a long table down one wall with two big men standing ready to serve, or, as Obed recalled, ready to throw out anyone who caused trouble. There were low tables with benches and a few travellers sitting, either drinking or eating. An elderly woman came from the room at the back and dumped a bowl on a table in front of an Egyptian-looking man. He grunted and pulled the bowl towards himself, and began to spoon whatever was in the bowl into his mouth. Jonah stood in the doorway, looking very out of place, while Obed casually made his way over to a table and sat down.

He beckoned Jonah over. 'Sit down, idiot, and stop staring around. You'll have everyone looking at you.'

Obed kept his own head down, so as not to draw attention to himself. Jonah followed him and sat down with his back to the room, facing Obed, who was leaning against the back wall.

A hand touched Jonah's shoulder, and he could smell the heavy scent of cheap perfume. 'What can I get you, young man?' asked the soft female voice. 'If you two are lonely, I have a friend who could join us.'

Obed rescued Jonah as the colour ran up his friend's neck. 'Thank you, no. We've walked a long way and need to be off early in the morning. Just two jugs of your beer, and some lentil soup would be enough.'

'Another time then, perhaps.' She bent down and kissed Jonah on his cheek. 'I'll get your food and drink.' She bent even lower in front of Obed, so that he could be in no doubt about what he would be missing, while making a pretence of wiping the table.

Obed looked at her and let his eyes meet hers. 'Thank you. Should we change our minds, we'll let you know.'

She smiled at him, gave him a wink, then went to the next table. Jonah's colour returned to normal.

'Good job the light isn't too bright in here, Jonah, it hid your blushes. I think you made a hit with her,' Obed teased.

The lady brought their food and drink and left them to it, as new travellers arrived. Obed ate the soup and bread while Jonah tried the beer. It was stronger than any he'd had before, but he liked the taste.

'You need to try this, Obed,' Jonah urged, as he took another long drink from his jug. Obed watched his friend and lifted his own jug to his lips. He didn't care for it and thought he would need to keep a clear head, as Jonah drained his jug and beckoned to the elderly woman who was just passing their table. She took the jug from him and refilled it quickly, leaving them to drink.

'Don't think that one fancied you, Jonah. You must be losing your touch,' Obed taunted him.

Jonah kicked him under the table. 'Leave off, Obed. Are you going to drink your beer or not?'

Obed took another swig then pushed it across to Jonah. 'You can have it if you like, but you've had almost two jugs already.'

'No problem. Working on blending the wines at the vineyard has given me a taste for good fermented stuff. I can handle it.' And he downed all that Obed had left, and then ordered another for himself.

The drink was beginning to influence Jonah, and when the first girl came along, he slapped her on the bottom as she passed by.

She quickly turned and came back to their table. 'Getting frisky, are we? Sometimes it takes a few jugs to get you lads in the mood. Want to come out the back with me, then?'

'Don't mind a do, don't do if I do.' Jonah slurred his words as he spoke. Pushing his bench back, he tried to stand, but his head was spinning and he toppled towards the girl. She took a step back and let him fall to the floor.

'If you can't take your drink, you can't take me!' she said, and walked off while seasoned travellers laughed at the hapless heap on the floor.

One of the big burly men came over, looked at Obed and said, 'Get your friend out of here, or I'll throw him out myself.'

Bending down, Obed got hold of Jonah and pulled him to his feet. With Jonah's arm round his neck, Obed half-walked, half-dragged his confused friend out of the room.

'Don't come back unless you can make better use of the facilities,' shouted the man as they went through the door, much to the amusement of the other patrons.

Obed dragged him round to the stable-yard at the back. He got him as far as the horse-trough and stuck Jonah's head in the cold water.

Jonah spluttered and sank down to the ground, leaning his back against the stone trough.

'Can take your drink, can you?' Obed muttered. 'Thanks for a great night out, Jonah.'

'Think nothing of it, my friend, pleasure's all mine,' slurred Jonah.

'Well, it's no pleasure for me and that's for sure!' exclaimed Obed, somewhat frustrated. 'How am I going to get you home in the state you're in?'

Jonah's head cleared a little. 'Home. Oh no! What will my sisters say? They'll blab to my parents when they get back, and life will be hell.' He staggered to his feet and voluntarily stuck his head back in the trough. Standing up, he shook the water off, just as a dog shakes itself when it's been in the lake.

Despite himself, Obed had to laugh. 'Come on, doggy, I'll get you back to my place.' And with Jonah's arm round his shoulder, they staggered off towards Capernaum.

As they stumbled along in the cool night air, Jonah became more coherent and could walk on his own, only tripping every now and then. The moon was bright, so they could see most of the potholes in the road, but it still took them a good two hours before they arrived at Obed's house.

Pushing the door open, Obed guided Jonah towards his own bed and let him collapse onto it, without bothering to take his clothes off. Then he slumped on his father's bed and pulled a blanket round himself.

Early the next morning, when the sun streamed in, Obed awoke. He jumped up quickly and shook Jonah. 'Get up, you oaf, we need to get you home before your sisters realise you've been out all night.'

Obed pulled Jonah to his feet and splashed water over his face. Jonah held his head in his hands and groaned, 'What'd you do that for? My head hurts. Obed, what are you doing in my house? My sisters won't like it. You been here all night?'

Obed slapped his face. 'Get a grip, Jonah! You're at my house. And if we don't get you to your place before your sisters wake up, you really will be in trouble.'

Jonah looked around wildly, then sank back on the bed. 'Oh no! Now I remember. I'd better get a move on. How late is it, Obed?'

'You're in luck because it was the early morning sun that woke me,' Obed answered. 'Pull yourself together and get home. If you go round the back of your house and up onto the roof, you can crash out there and your sisters will think you've been there all night. Tell them that when you got home last night, it was such a lovely moonlit night you decided to sleep on the roof under the stars. Can you make it on your own?'

Jonah mumbled that he could, and stumbled off to his own house hoping that his sisters wouldn't notice. Obed gave himself a wash and had a bit of bread and some goat's cheese for his breakfast. Sitting outside in the sun, he began to see the funny side of their night's escapade, and laughed to himself.

'Some drinker,' Obed remembered, while at the same time recalling how he did fancy that girl a bit...

Obed's 'black hole' closed in on him, as he lay in the bottom of the twins' boat.

Chapter 4

Solomon shouted from the stern of the boat, stirring them into action. 'We'll be back at our landing place soon. Trim the sail, Samuel, and Jonah, get ready with the rope. When I say "jump", jump over the side and pull us ashore. Ezra, you hold on to Obed in case we ground hard and he slides off the stretcher.'

Everyone jumped to fulfil their orders and, with little trouble, the boat was grounded. As gently as they could, they lifted the broken body of their friend out of the boat and put him down on the shingle.

'What now?' questioned Solomon, looking round at the beleaguered band of friends.

'I think we should carry him to his father's house.' Ezra looked down on the unconscious form of Obed. 'He told me his stepmother wanted him to come and stay. Besides, where else can we take him?'

Everyone agreed, and slowly, each carrying a corner of the stretcher, they skirted Capernaum and headed to Obed's childhood home. It was a walk of about two miles, but, stumbling along in the moonlight, it became a never-ending journey. Once, as they paused, Obed's eyelids flickered again and he uttered a low groan. It was feeble, but enough to spur them on, so with renewed hope they picked him up and moved on at a slightly quicker pace.

Daylight was beginning to appear over the horizon as the house came into view.

Nearing the end of their strength, they struggled to the door and virtually collapsed. Ezra knocked loudly and, after what felt like an eternity, a bleary-eyed Enoch slid back the bolt and stared out. What met his eyes dispelled any remnant of his sleep and he shouted out to Hagar, his wife, Obed's stepmother, 'Come quickly, the boys are here with Obed on a stretcher!'

She was with them in an instant and, taking charge, ordered them to bring Obed inside. With their remaining strength, he was moved inside and they carefully lifted him onto his old bed. Enoch helped his wife remove Obed's torn and bloodstained tunic and wash his wounds clean. Bruising was beginning to show, and his whole body was marked.

'What happened?' Enoch asked nervously, half-afraid to hear the answer.

'He fell while climbing up the cliffs, near Herod's palace. Solomon and Samuel were just off-shore with their boat, so we brought him back on the boat, then carried him here.' Ezra said, giving just enough details to satisfy Enoch for the time being. A fuller explanation would have to come later.

Enoch could see they were exhausted, so he asked no more but left Hagar to finish dressing Obed's wounds while he brought them something to eat and drink. He passed them some pressed figs, and they sat in silence while they ate.

Hagar held a cloth soaked in cold water on Obed's head, and he showed signs of coming round. His eyes opened, and he focused on the face of his stepmother. She gently wiped his face and let water from a clean cloth refresh his mouth. Moving his hands slowly, he took hold of hers and gave it a weak squeeze. His lips parted, and in an almost inaudible voice he whispered, 'Am I home?'

'Yes, Obed, you're home. You have some wonderful friends who've carried you a long way to get you here.'

His eyes closed but his grip on her hand was stronger, and then he whispered again, 'Is Ezra here?'

'Ezra is here.'

Hearing his name, Ezra got up and walked over to the bed. 'I'm here, Obed. You're safe now.'

Eyes wide open this time, Obed reached out his other hand towards Ezra, who quickly clasped it in his. 'Ezra, I'm so sorry, I should have listened to you… I could have got us all killed.' He shut his eyes again and a big sigh escaped from his lips.

Leaning close to his ear, Ezra spoke softly, 'We were all free to make up our own minds, Obed. Don't worry about it now, we're all safely back. You just rest and get yourself better.'

All the others had joined them round his bedside, and again it was Hagar who brought direction. 'Come, boys, we need to leave him to sleep now. Enoch, sit with him while I get the boys something more to eat.'

She moved out to the back of the house, the 'boys' following her, and she began to prepare bread for the oven. 'Jonah, put some more wood on the fire and get the oven warm, would you? Solomon, Samuel, do you know where the nearest doctor is who might be able to help us?'

Ezra answered her, 'At the synagogue, my father has a friend who is highly thought of; perhaps we could get him to come?'

'Sounds promising, if your father trusts him. When you've all had something more to eat, would you be willing to try to find him for us? We have enough money to pay him.'

Ezra nodded. 'I could go now.'

'No, it's still very early. Stay and rest a while, then, when the bread is ready, eat some breakfast before you go. You all need to recover from your long night of hard work in bringing Obed back. Another hour is not going to change his condition very much.'

What she said made sense, so they sat down with their heads resting on the table. Despite all the emotional trauma they were experiencing, their bodies were fatigued and weariness began to overtake them.

Jonah had almost nodded off when they heard movement in Obed's room. All four jumped to their feet and hurried to his bedside. Enoch had his hands on his son's shoulders, pinning him down, because he was thrashing about and in danger of hurting himself. He had a wild and frightened look on his face, and he grabbed at his father's arms, gripping them so tightly that his fingernails dug into the skin and drew blood.

'My legs! I can't feel my legs! Abba! My legs, what's happened to my legs?!'

'You fell down the cliff, son, and have hurt your back. Stay still now, and we'll get a doctor to come and look at you as soon as people are up and about,' his father tried to reassure him but, in his confusion, Obed screamed out in fear.

'I'm going to find the doctor now, Enoch,' Ezra insisted, and Jonah was keen to go with him. Without waiting for breakfast, they left the house and headed back towards Capernaum.

Hagar didn't try to stop them, but was glad the twins stayed back. They all tried to soothe Obed, but he was so disoriented and confused he didn't know what he was doing. Gradually he calmed down again and drifted back to sleep. Hagar took the bread from the oven, and they ate as he slept.

'So tell me, boys, what really happened out there last night?' Enoch asked between mouthfuls. 'How come your boat was there at the same time as the others were climbing that cliff? What was the point of it all, anyway?'

Samuel looked at Solomon before he spoke. 'We were sailing down that way before going fishing. Obed, Jonah and Ezra were going to walk along the shoreline to the cliffs and we were going to join them when we got there by sea.' He didn't add more as he wasn't quite sure just how much he ought to say, and he didn't know all that had gone on at the bottom of the cliff.

Solomon picked up the story. 'We were going to pick them up after their climb and then they were going to sail with us over to the other side of the lake.'

It was enough information for Enoch and his wife not to ask more questions, and they sat back from the table. She offered the twins some curdled milk and they drank it down, glad not to have to say any more.

Enoch checked on his son and found him sleeping peacefully, so he left him to rest. Solomon and Samuel felt so tired that, as they leaned back against the wall, both dropped off to sleep. Enoch motioned to his wife and left them to it. They went to sit out at the front of the house to await the arrival of the doctor.

It was mid-morning before Ezra returned. He had the doctor with him but had persuaded Jonah to go home and rest, as his mood was doing nothing to bring calm to the situation. Enoch stood up as soon as he saw them coming, and hurried to meet them.

'How is he at the moment?' the doctor enquired, as Enoch reached them.

'Sleeping,' was all he said.

'Ezra's told me what's happened,' the doctor said, 'and I have to tell you now, if Obed's condition is as I think it is, there'll not be much I'll be able to do.'

Enoch nodded his understanding. 'Try your best, doctor, that's all I'm asking.'

They went inside and Hagar took Ezra to the back room, while Enoch went with the doctor to see Obed.

As they removed the covers, he stirred and looked at the doctor through half-opened eyes.

'Some fall you've had, son,' the doctor said softly as he ran his fingers down each side of Obed's ribcage. Obed winced as a finger touched a badly bruised spot. 'Broken rib, I think,' commented the doctor.

Gently, with the help of Enoch, the doctor rolled him onto his side. Starting at Obed's neck, the doctor ran his fingers down his spine. When he pressed on the spot halfway down, Obed groaned a little, but didn't cry out.

'Let's have you on your back again, so I can look at your legs, Obed.' Taking a sharp pin, the doctor pricked Obed's toe. 'Feel that, son?'

'Feel what?' answered Obed.

The doctor pricked the other foot, and Obed didn't respond. The doctor moved the pin up to his calf and pricked again – no response. The pin went in at his right knee – no response; left knee – no response. Looking across at Obed's father, the doctor slowly shook his head. He tried higher up – still no response.

'Let's look at that cut on the side of your head,' he said, as if to change the subject. 'Nasty cut there, old son, but your mother has dressed it well. If she keeps that up, it will heal in no time. Now you have a rest. I have something for you to drink that will deaden the pain, and I'll come back to see you tomorrow.'

Before Obed could gather his wits enough to ask anything, the doctor had left the house and was talking to Enoch outside the door.

Worry was written all over Enoch's face and the expression on the doctor's did nothing to reassure him, or give him any hope. 'No easy way to say this, Enoch. His back is broken. He has no feeling in his legs at all. I'm afraid your son will never walk again. He is paralysed from the waist down. The only positive thing is he can't feel any pain. If he could, it would be unbearable. The broken rib and bruising on his body and head will heal well enough, but his back is way beyond any medical cure. I'm sorry, I can do nothing for him.'

Although he had expected the worst from the moment the friends had brought Obed home, the doctor's words crashed like a thunderbolt in his ears. He murmured his understanding of what the doctor had said, but couldn't trust himself to speak. His body trembled with emotion, and tears forced their way out of the corners of his eyes and trickled down his face into his beard.

The doctor put his hand on Enoch's shoulder. 'Do you want me to tell your wife, Enoch?'

Choking back a sob, Enoch managed to speak. 'Thank you, doctor, but I need to do that. How much do we owe you for coming all this way?'

The doctor shook his head. 'Nothing, Enoch, you're going to need all the money you've got. I'm just sorry that I can't give you more hope.'

'False hope is worse than no hope, doctor. I thank you for being straight with me. And thank you for attending with no charge. Would you like a drink before you go?'

'No thanks, Enoch, I think you need the time with your wife. If you feel you need me again, Ezra knows where I live. He's a good man.' With that, he walked off back to Capernaum.

Enoch turned to go back into the house, almost colliding with Ezra and the twins. 'Sir, we didn't mean to overhear what the doctor said, but the door was not properly shut. I can't take it in. Only a few hours ago, we were striding along the shore full of fun and ready for a climb...' Ezra's voice trailed off, and he could get no more words out.

Solomon added what they all wished to tell Enoch. 'We want you to know that we are willing to do all we can to help look after Obed – and I'm sure Jonah will say the same. We've been friends since we were in school ten years ago, and won't drop him now when he needs us the most.'

Samuel added, 'We'll leave you now with your wife, but can we come back tomorrow to see how Obed is doing?'

Hagar heard them getting ready to leave and came to the doorway, her face etched with disbelief, having heard what the doctor had said. She embraced each of them, kissed them affectionately on their cheeks, and let them go. Standing in the open doorway with her husband, she held his hand as they watched the three young men walk slowly from their home, until they went round the bend in the road and were lost from sight. Then they could hold it in no longer and collapsed in a heap together on the doorstep, and sobbed.

The sound of a weak cough came from the bedroom, and they dragged themselves to their feet. How would they tell Obed? was the question uppermost on their minds as they entered his room.

Obed's eyes were still closed as they entered, so they returned to the kitchen and made themselves busy tidying up, saying nothing, each lost in their own thoughts.

Obed woke up a few times in the afternoon but, for the most part, slept. With the light fading, Enoch sat in a chair in Obed's room, and Hagar went to bed. Deep breathing indicated to Enoch that his son was sleeping soundly, so he closed his own eyes, pulled a blanket around himself, and slept in the chair.

Chapter 5

The next day, being the Sabbath, Jairus had the surprise of seeing his son, Ezra, enter the synagogue.

Ezra hadn't gone home to ask his father where the doctor lived, as he had remembered from his last visit to him, so the previous morning he had gone straight to his house. This meant that Jairus knew nothing of the events of the last two days, so seeing his son enter the synagogue was a great encouragement to him, and he saw it as an answer to his prayers.

After the scriptures were read, the rabbi sat down to teach. For the first time in a long time, Ezra paid attention to what was being said.

The rabbi retold the story of Joseph and how, after many years, things that had seemed a disaster to Joseph and his father, Jacob, turned out to be the source of blessing.

In an unexpected way, the rabbi's words gave a tiny spark of hope to the battered mind of Ezra. Was it possible that the disaster they had just witnessed could somehow turn into a blessing?

The gathering ended, and people made their way out of the synagogue. Jairus pushed his way over to his son, who remained sitting as everyone else walked off. Jairus sat down beside him, and it was obvious Ezra was deeply upset. He remembered the wise words of his wife about not being hard on their son and said nothing, but placed a hand on his boy's shoulder.

At the touch of his father's hand, Ezra buckled and fell into his father's lap, as he had done as a young child. Jairus slowly rubbed his back and rocked his baby boy once again. Miriam, Ezra's mother, seeing it all, walked from the women's side of the synagogue and sat down on the other side of Ezra.

Eventually, Jairus spoke. 'Will it help to talk about it?'

Ezra sat up, his face tear-stained. 'The night before last we went down to Tiberias. Obed was climbing the cliff, and he fell. His back is broken – he'll never walk again.'

His mother asked, as gently as she could, 'Why were you climbing the cliffs in the dark, near Herod's palace?'

Turning to face her, and worn out with trying to hide the plan behind the trip, Ezra poured out the whole story…

'It was about a week ago. You'll remember it because we had a row over me not attending the synagogue over the last few weeks. You felt that Obed was a bad influence on me, so when I'd finished the job I was on, I left the yard and went over to Obed's house to catch up with him. He could see I was upset, and suggested that we do something more than just sitting and talking, something a bit physical and a bit daring. I was all for it, as I wanted to let off steam and forget our row.

'It was going to be nearly a full moon that night, so there would be enough light for us to see what we were doing, even in the dark. Obed had this idea to take the coastal road down to Tiberias, then walk along the beach until we came to the cliffs near Herod's palace, and then climb them. The daring bit was to be at the top. We were going to scale the palace wall and put a flag on the top – all in the dark.'

Jairus glanced at his wife but said nothing. The thought that their row had led to this hare-brained scheme troubled him deeply.

'I loved the idea. I'd never climbed rocks before, but as you know, I've climbed up plenty of buildings onto the roofs. The bravado of doing it at Herod's palace in the dark made it a bigger challenge, and I couldn't wait to get going.

'We gathered a few bits together – a rope, a couple of water bottles and some dates to eat – and set off southwards on the road to Tiberias. By the time we got there, the sun was beginning to set and we turned off the road on to the shingle on the shoreline. It was an effort as the shingle was deep at that point, but we were soon round a small outcrop of land and came to the beginning of the cliff that rose higher, the further south you went.

'We stopped near the foot of the cliff, about half a mile along the beach. By this time, the shadows were lengthening and some of the boulders that lie up against the cliff looked a bit like a haphazard graveyard.

'Obed took the length of rope from his bag and asked me who should go first. I was keen, so I jumped at the chance. I grabbed the rope and scrambled over a large boulder that rested up against the foot of the cliff. It gave us a good boost to the start of the climb. Standing on the top of the boulder, I reached up, feeling for the handholds.

'With the moon rising and casting shadows, the footholds were fairly easy to see. I found a crack in the rock, jammed my hand in, and was soon up on a small protruding ledge.'

Ezra was looking at his feet as he told his story, his voice gaining strength as he got into it. Adrenalin began to pump through his veins, like it had with the thrill of climbing.

'Obed was watching me from the top of the boulder, and I think he was impressed with the way I was getting up the cliff. About a third of the way up, I found a large ledge that went back into the cliff, almost like a small cave, so I sat down, lowered the rope over the edge, and whispered to Obed to use it to climb up to me. He was glad to have the rope, as he wasn't much of a climber. But he was soon sitting beside me on the ledge.'

A smile almost came to Ezra's face as he recalled Obed's comments. 'Obed said he thought I was like a wild monkey, and was really impressed with the way I climbed. I was enjoying it, and was pumped up to get to the top. He passed me the rope, and I was off! The face of the cliff was an easy climb, with small ledges, fissures and crevasses. The moon was now higher in the night sky. Soon I touched the grass on the path at the top of the cliff and pulled myself up onto it, then lowered the rope down for Obed, having threaded it round the trunk of one of the trees by the palace wall. Obed grabbed it and made his way up, following the route I'd taken.'

Miriam, listening in disbelief at her son's story, found her voice. 'You must have been worn out by then. And didn't it hurt your hands – all that climbing? You could have fallen and killed yourself.'

'I know it sounds stupid now, Mum, but I didn't think about falling – just getting to the top. It did cut our hands a bit, but with the thrill of getting to the top in the dark, we didn't notice it. We rested for a few minutes at the top. The bushes and shrubs were dense along the wall, and reached almost to the top. I found one thick enough to bear our weight, then climbed up to peek over the wall. Obed had a makeshift flag made from a rag and a stick. I could see soldiers leaning against a stone building inside the palace walls, and climbed down, and Obed went up to have a look for himself before we started the climb down to the lake.'

Jairus gripped his son's shoulders at the thought of him being seen on top of the wall of Herod's palace, but Ezra continued…

'The grass was long on the cliff top, and I suggested that we leave the rope tied to the tree trunk for another time, in case we came back with the others. So we pulled the tufts of grass back, dug a channel with our hands and hid the rope in it, then covered it up again. By the time we'd finished, the rope was invisible to anyone walking by. Obed went down first, lowering himself over the edge. It only took a few minutes, and we were both standing on top of the boulder on the beach. We hid the rope ready for another time, and went back to Obed's house.'

'But that was a few days ago, Ezra. I remember clearly you coming in for work and saying to me that you were sorry for your part in our row. You were in such good spirits. What changed? What happened last night to Obed?' asked his father.

Ezra was quiet for a moment. Miriam passed him a cup of water and he drank it down in one go before he continued…

'Obed had met this man called Marcus. He is some sort of businessman who buys merchandise from abroad and ships it over here. Among other things, he does a lot of buying for King Herod. Anyway, Obed started to do a bit of trading for Marcus, and as it turns out, not all of it was honest. I didn't know that last week and only found out the other night. The cliff-climbing was part of a plan that Marcus and Obed had come up with to remove valuable stuff from Herod's palace and get it across the lake to sell on. I thought it was just a fun thing he wanted to do and so we went again, this time with Jonah coming along, and the twins were going to meet up with us after their night's fishing. When we got to the place we had left the rope the week before, he told us about his dealings.

'We had a row over it, as I'm not into stealing, especially from King Herod. So I left them to it and walked off back to the shore. I'd only been away a short time when I heard this terrible scream, followed quickly by another. Then I heard running footsteps on the shingle, and Jonah shouting for me to stop and come back to help him.'

Ezra looked up, and his eyes focused on the Ark of the Covenant which contained the scrolls of the laws of Moses. He knew the words by heart, as he had often recited them at the synagogue school: 'You shall not steal.' A shudder went down his spine as he finished his story...

'Obed was lying in a crumpled heap at the foot of the cliff, and a little way off we discovered the body of Marcus. Jonah was in a state, and I sent him off to see if the twins had arrived with their boat, as that was part of Obed's plan. While he was looking out for them I tried to make Obed comfortable by gently moving his legs from under him. He had blood all over his face from a gash in his cheek, and I did my best to stop the bleeding.

'It seemed forever before Jonah came back with the twins and a makeshift stretcher. We got Obed on it and carried him back to the boat, then sailed back here. There were some men walking along the beach as we left, but they didn't spot us in the moonlight. When we got back we carried Obed to his father's house, then I went and fetched the doctor. Abba, his back is broken – he will never walk again!'

Ezra broke down and cried, while his mother hugged him close to herself. Jairus buried his face in his hands at the thought of the ramifications of what his son had just told them – attempting to rob Herod, the most hated and ruthless tyrant around. Where would this leave Ezra, if what had happened were to be traced back to them? He groaned inwardly at the thought.

Wiping his face with the back of his hand, Ezra said, 'Obed and I fell out over it and I walked off. If I'd stayed, I would have been the one on the end of the rope! I would be the one paralysed now. How I wished I'd have stayed and made Obed see what could happen.'

'God probably wished you all would never have gone! But you were not wrong to walk away from what was happening, Ezra. The commandments teach, "You shall not steal," and you were obeying them,' said his father.

'That's not much help to Obed now, is it? What are we going to do now?' Ezra looked at his feet as he spoke.

'We? In what way, do you mean?' Jairus asked.

'Well, we can't just walk away from Obed, can we? How is he going to make a living? Somehow we must support him – myself and Jonah, Solomon and Samuel. We were all in this together.'

Miriam, despite the stupidity of their actions, was proud of her son. Many would have run and left the others to their own fate. He had tried to stop them, walked away from the wrong they were doing, then went back at great risk to himself, so he could help the friend who had rejected him. 'I think you'll do the right thing, son, but we have to take one step at a time.'

'That's more than Obed can do,' Ezra answered bitterly.

'Then you'll find a way to take those steps for him, won't you?' was her soft reply.

They left the synagogue.

Miriam went over to the group of women who had taken charge of Ezra's little sister – now eleven years old. They had seen that her parents were in some sort of crisis with her big brother. Jairus and Ezra, instead of following them and walking home, wandered down to the lakeshore. As it was the Sabbath, the boats were beached and left ready for the next day's fishing – apart from the smaller boat belonging to the twins. This was beached, but left in the chaotic state it had been in when they had landed with the comatose Obed in the makeshift stretcher.

The breeze blowing from the lake helped Ezra clear his head. Jairus felt for the first time in a very long while that he was at peace with his son. They ambled along, Jairus with his arm over Ezra's shoulder, kicking the odd stone, and just being father and son.

'I'm proud of you, son.' Jairus' voice was choked with emotion. 'You stood your ground on what was right, but you also stood with your friend in his desperate need. Obed is blessed to have a loyal friend like you.'

He pulled his son close to him, and Ezra put his arm around his father's waist as they stood looking out over the lake.

Jairus continued, 'Obed quickly adjusted to leaving school and stepping out on his own when you were both only twelve years old. I think, if anyone can cope with this devastating accident, he will.'

'I hope you're right, Abba, but I'm not so sure.' Ezra looked at the chaos that was left inside the twins' boat. 'He was the one who took control, was out in front, the organiser, the natural leader. Now he won't be going anywhere unless we carry him.'

'He'll be able to tell you where to carry him. If he comes to terms with where he is, he can still use his sharp mind to see how to move on, and get things done.' Jairus wondered if he was trying to convince himself more than his son. 'It'll take time, but who knows, he might even be able to help me organise some of my building projects. I spend a lot of my time planning jobs, to make sure the right materials are in place at the right time for the builders to use. If he can get his mind around his disability, he'll be able to earn a living.'

Ezra was somewhat comforted by his father's words, and he could see it was possible, but it still remained a daunting prospect for Obed.

Chapter 6

As the Sabbath day ended, four sober young men made their way to the home of Obed and his family. Hagar, having seen them coming, was at the door to welcome them.

'Come in, boys. Obed will be glad to see you. He slept well and has eaten food today. But I must warn you, he is still confused at times, and doesn't always make sense. He keeps asking about someone called Marcus, I've never heard of a Marcus. It's always been the five of you, so I don't know where this name comes from.'

As she talked, they walked towards Obed's room. 'Enoch has gone to Tiberius to see a contact about work for tomorrow, so please go in and see Obed. I'm glad you've come.'

They entered the bedroom and Obed looked anxiously up at his friends. His expression was wild and his eyes staring. 'Am I glad to see you?! Marcus – what's happened to Marcus? I can still hear him screaming. I saw him in the moonlight – he flashed past me – but I don't remember what happened! What happened, Jonah?' he reached out his hand and grabbed Jonah's arm, almost pulling him on top of himself.

Jonah was fearful and didn't know how to answer.

Ezra answered for him. 'Jonah ran and got help, Obed. You fell from halfway up the cliff and have damaged your back. We carried you to the boat, sailed round to Capernaum and carried you here.' He paused, took a deep breath and went on softly, 'Marcus fell, or was pushed, to his death from the top of the cliff. I saw his body on the boulders. He's dead, Obed.'

Obed lifted his head off the pillow and opened his mouth, but said nothing. He searched the faces of the group round his bed, then closed his eyes and let his head flop back on the pillow.

'Don't take the blame for what happened to him, Obed. He knew the risk he was taking, and he nearly dragged us all down with him,' Solomon stated, with little emotion in his voice. 'Messing with Herod is like playing with fire, and Marcus got burnt – and you almost got killed at the same time.'

'Did the palace guards find him?'

'We didn't stay to find out.' Solomon was watching Obed's face. 'By the time we had you in the boat, we heard voices coming towards us and pushed off as quickly as we could.'

'The guards found him, and, yes, he was dead.'

For a moment, everyone was struck dumb, and the statement hung in the air like a frozen fork of lightning. Enoch had entered the room, his presence undetected by the friends, and had heard the end of their conversation.

'In Tiberias, I overheard traders talking in the market. I heard them say that one of Herod's most trusted servants had double-crossed him and he had been pushed over the cliff by a palace guard. They found him later at the foot of the cliff, killed by the fall. All the things he had stolen from Herod were still intact on the ground at the top of the cliff. There was talk of him having an accomplice at the bottom, but they found no one. So if he did, whoever it was must have run away.'

Enoch looked at the broken body of his son lying on the bed, and his four friends standing round him. 'I think it's time someone told me just what was going on that night, don't you?'

Ezra caught Obed's eye, but before he could speak, Obed opened his mouth and told his father the whole story, as the others looked on. As he came to the end, his voice was almost a whisper. 'Abba, I've been a fool. Marcus dead, me a cripple for the rest of my life, and my friends here could have been executed.'

'If anyone connects your past association with Marcus, the time of your accident and the day of the death of Marcus, it could still happen, and the rest of your life as a cripple could be very short,' was his father's cold response to the end of his story.

Hagar had come into the room and, having heard what her husband said, gave a sharp intake of breath. She pushed her way to Obed's bed, dropped to her knees, laid her head on his chest and sobbed. Jonah, for once, didn't react in a panic-stricken way but examined the facts as he saw them: 'We only met Marcus once or twice. He was not seen by many in this area, apart from when he travelled through on Herod's business, and if any knew of him, and who he worked for, they tended to keep out of his way.'

Everyone looked at him as he continued, 'Obed didn't tell anyone what was going on – he didn't even fill us in until we were at the foot of the cliff. We got him into the boat and sailed away before anyone saw us and, at the end of the day, nothing was taken – Herod got it all back – and the one responsible for it is now dead. We haven't stolen anything, and if anyone had recognised the boat they would have been knocking on our doors by now.'

Hagar stopped sobbing, and the alarm on Enoch's face subsided. Obed closed his eyes, but it was obvious that he was shaken by the possible consequences of his involving his friends as well as the potential threat to his own father and stepmother. Silence invaded the room as each person present took in the gravity of the situation.

The twins looked at each other and a slight smile came to the corners of Samuel's mouth. 'But we got away, didn't we?!'

This broke the tension, perhaps more because it was 'sensible Samuel' who said it, and despite the condition of Obed, a more positive outlook pervaded the group.

'What's done is done,' Ezra said. 'We have to think how we'll go on from here.'

Obed cut in, 'You must think how you'll move on from here, but I won't be moving anywhere, will I? I wish I were dead!'

Ezra shot back, raising his voice slightly, 'I said "we" and I meant "we"! And that includes you as well, Obed. *We* will move on and *you* will be moving on with us!' All eyes were on him. 'We carried you on a makeshift stretcher in the dark over rocks and into the boat, when you were out of it. If we could do that then, we can easily carry you about if we set you up with a proper movable bed. You can use your upper body to help. You have your brain and the use of your arms and hands. Together we can overcome this.' He said it with more conviction than he felt, but his speech galvanised them all into thinking how they would implement what he said.

From that moment on, despite the bleakness of Obed's position, five young men were drawn closer together in a common goal to make life for Obed as good as his abilities would allow. Together with Enoch, they built a stretcher-bed that enabled them to carry Obed around, and when they rested him on the ground, he could pull himself up into sitting position.

Sometimes, especially at night when all were asleep, Obed would be wide awake and stare out of the window into the darkness. A feeling of despair would creep up and begin to suffocate him. He was in that black hole again, and the daylight was even further away.

After one particularly trying day when he had rolled off his bed while trying to do things for himself, he was watching the stars in the night sky. His pulse quickened and panic welled up. *What's the point of living? I'm just a burden to my friends and family.* This blackness covered him like a blanket; he felt as if he were in the bottom of a boat, adrift on a stormy sea with waves threatening to engulf and sink his fragile ark.

A cloud covered the silver of the moon, and the darkness felt deeper as he shivered on his bed. It was then that he noticed that, as the sky grew darker, so the stars shone brighter. One in particular was very bright, and he called to mind being out on the lake sailing with the twins, and how they would use the stars to guide them.

'I could do with a star to give me some direction now.' He spoke aloud, and somehow it was of comfort to him. 'The sky is so vast and there must be millions of stars. Which one should I look at to know the way to go?'

There was no answer, just the darkness, but he felt that the threatening waves had subsided somewhat, and he managed to turn on his side and drift off to sleep.

Chapter 7

Enoch had remarried three years before this happened and Obed had felt that that was the right time for him to move out on his own. His dream of attaining position and power had not left him, and the thought of having a place of his own felt like a step in the right direction. His small enterprises had earned him enough money to purchase land and buy all the materials he needed to build himself a house. He enlisted Ezra's help, and together they had constructed a reasonable property. It had become a gathering place for the 'gang of five', and Ezra often stayed there with Obed, as did Jonah, to escape his sisters! Obed hadn't moved out because he disliked his new stepmother but because he wanted to take control of his own life.

It had only been a week earlier, when he was finalising the plans with Marcus for the 'removal of Herod's surplus', that he'd called back at the family home.

His stepmother greeted him warmly as she invited him to sit at the table and have some of the fresh bread she'd just brought from the oven. The smell was so inviting that he hadn't needed to be asked twice.

'You seem on top of the world today, Obed. Things are going well for you?'

He replied with a mouthful of bread, 'Mmm! Really good – and this bread makes it even better!'

He knew people said that the way to a man's heart was through his stomach; he also knew that the way to win favour with a woman was to compliment her on her cooking.

'Fresh every day, Obed. You'll always be welcome to have some – you do know that, don't you?' she would always look for opportunities to make it clear to Obed that she had never wanted him to feel that he should leave home because his father had remarried.

'I know, and thank you. I assure you I didn't leave home because you came into my father's life. I was, and am, glad that he found a new wife after losing my mother. I just wanted to do my own thing and felt it best all round that I move out. But now, tasting fresh bread like this makes me think that maybe I should have stayed!' He stuffed another large lump into his mouth and munched on it, with a big smile of contentment on his face.

'Your room is still empty, so any time you're passing you can stay for the night, should you be working this way,' Hagar added.

He simply said, 'Thank you. I promise I will. I'd better be going as I have a few things I need to get done before the day's over. Thanks again for the food,' he paused, 'and for your welcome and friendship – Mum.'

That one word touched her heart more than a thousand others could ever do, and she threw her arms round his neck and kissed him.

'Thank you, Obed! I'm so glad you called in this morning. Don't leave it so long before you do it again, will you?' She let him go, and he walked off, feeling even more on top of the world. He did a little skip as he walked around the corner, just like he used to do when he was a young boy, walking along with his mother.

Little did either of them know how soon it would be before he was back in his old bed!

Chapter 8

Four weeks after the accident, the sound of his father going off to work woke Obed, and he pulled himself up so he could lean his back against a stuffed bolster that Hagar had put in place for him. 'Abba,' he called out softly, in case Hagar was still sleeping. 'Have you a few minutes to spare?'

Enoch, dressed and ready for work, entered his room. 'Sleep well?'

'Not really, but I have a question. Do you think I could go back to my own house? It's not fair on Hagar to have to look after me. You both need time for yourselves.'

Sitting on the edge of the bed, Enoch looked at his only son. 'You're my son, Obed. Don't you feel welcome here? Hagar loves you as if you were her own. We're happy for you to be here with us.'

'I know she does, Abba, and I do feel welcome, but I left home three years ago, and I hate putting on you both. If there is a life for me, then I need to do something to make it happen. Just lying here won't change anything. I have to try.'

'But something is happening. You're getting stronger and you're finding ways to get around the house. It's only four weeks since your accident,' Enoch reasoned. 'It'll take time, Obed, but you are making progress.'

'That's the point, Abba, I am feeling stronger. But also more frustrated, and I need to be doing something. I can't just lie here; I need to get moving.'

'I understand, but how would you manage in your own house?'

'I don't know, but I need to try. If the gang calls by, I'll ask them to take me over to look.'

Enoch kissed him on his forehead and left for work. It was still early and few people were about.

The conversation with his father spurred Obed on. He gritted his teeth and pulled the bedcovers off his legs. Leaning forward, he used his hands to lift one leg at a time and managed to pull himself to the edge of his bed. Then he found that this didn't help, so he let his body flop back onto the bed. By pulling on the side of the bed with both hands, he rolled his shoulders over the side of the bed, and his lower body and legs followed him into an untidy heap face down on the floor. With both arms under himself he managed to push his shoulders up and, using his hands and elbows, dragged himself across the floor into the living area.

Hagar was still sleeping, and with adrenalin pumping through his body and determination flooding his mind, he pushed, dragged and rolled himself over to the storage jars near the table. Pushing up with one arm and reaching with the other, he pulled a wooden bowl off the table. Rolling over a couple of times, he was near enough to reach into the jar of flour and pull a handful out.

Unknown to him, Hagar had heard noises in the room and got out of bed. She peered round the door just in time to see him searching for the oil, spilling the flour from the bowl at the same time. Her instinctive response was to rush over and help him, but she had the presence of mind to stop herself, and let him struggle on.

Having hold of the jar of oil, Obed refilled the bowl with flour and began to mix some dough. The fire was heating the stones as his father had made it up before he had left for work. Working a lump of the dough into a flat pancake, Obed dropped it onto the stone and rolled another. Hagar watched with tears running down her face and pride rising in her heart. Her boy was not going to be beaten; he was going to make a new life!

She quietly pushed the door shut and washed herself in some cold water. She took her time to comb her hair and get dressed, as the smell of the bread wafted its way in from the cooking area.

'Enoch! What are you doing, cooking bread? You'll be late for work!' she exclaimed, as she pushed the bedroom door open and entered the room.

Obed was sitting, leaning up against the wall, with the first real smile she had seen on his face in four weeks. He had a plate on his lap with fresh, stone-baked bread piled on it. 'Not your husband, Hagar, but your son. I've cooked you breakfast!' The thing that blessed her most was that he called himself her son. She rushed over to him, and dropped down in front of him, and they hugged for a long time.

He pushed her away gently. 'Come, Mum, enough of this display of emotion. The bread will be getting cold.' Then he pulled her back for another embrace. He lost his balance and slid to one side with Hagar still in his arms, and the plate with the bread rolled onto the floor. They lay there laughing, both unable to get up. Hagar disentangled herself from her stepson and, while still on her knees, picked up the plate and the bread.

Rising, she placed the plate on the table and turned back to Obed. 'Do you want me to help you, or can you manage on your own?' she said softly, fully understanding what was on Obed's mind.

'I'll try on my own.' He pushed his legs to one side with his hands, then, lying on his front, pulled himself over to the table. Rolling over using both arms, he then pushed with his right and pulled with his left hand, and sat himself up with his back against the wall.

Hagar passed him some of the bread with a portion of goat's cheese and then handed him some milk. 'The bread's good,' she said, with her mouth full. 'You'll make it, Obed, I am confident you'll make it.'

They ate in silence for a few minutes, each lost in their own thoughts, when they heard voices approaching at the door.

Ezra's voice called out, 'Anyone up or are you all having a lie-in?'

Hagar flung the door open, her mouth full of bread. She beckoned them in, pointing to the food in her mouth, then pointing to Obed. 'He's baked me some bread!' she spluttered, spraying crumbs over Jonah and the twins. Swallowing, she added, 'Sorry – shouldn't speak with my mouth full! But Obed got up before me and baked bread!'

Solomon was the first to help himself from what was left on the table, and rammed it into his mouth. He chewed it a few times, and then said, 'It's good! Sam, try some.' Both Samuel and Jonah took a piece and began to eat.

'It's been on the floor, boys, but I think it gives it a nutty flavour!' Hagar teased them. 'Ezra, want some?'

'If the fall from the cliff didn't kill him, I guess this should be OK,' he replied, and joined the others. 'You really did this on your own, Obed?'

Obed nodded. 'On my own.'

'Then you must be ready for us to take you down to the lakeside. Are you up for it?'

'More than you'll ever know, Ezra. Let's go!' was Obed's eager response.

'Not so fast, boys', Hagar interrupted. 'There's the small matter of ablutions to attend to. You men pack some food, enough for you all, and fill the water skins while I help Obed get ready – if that's all right with him?'

'Thanks, Mum, I need a bit of help,' he replied, humbly.

With Obed tidied up and the food packed, Obed rolled himself onto the stretcher-bed and, with one of his friends at each corner, he was hoisted up and marched off towards Galilee. 'Could we call at my house on the way?' Obed asked.

'Already on our plan,' Jonah answered. 'We thought you'd want to see your place.'

As they approached the house, Obed lifted himself up on his elbows and strained his neck to see. It seemed another life when he was last there. The gang of pole-bearers grew quiet as they sat Obed down outside his own door, and waited for his reaction.

They'd been busy. The path along the front had been freshly swept, and on the door hung a laurel garland, like the ones that would be placed around the necks of athletes when they won a race. Obed reached over and pushed the door open. He could see that the inside of the house all was clean and tidy, and there was even a basket of food on the table. Pointing to the door, he said, 'Forward, my good men, forward!' and, at his command, they picked up his bed and marched inside.

It was then that he noticed his table was lower than it had been. Instead of a bench, there was a stuffed bolster against the wall, and space beside it to place his stretcher-bed.

'Lower!' he ordered, pointing to the spot.

They lowered him and took a step back, bowed and said in unison, 'Your every wish is our command, Sir!' Then they laughed!

Obed rolled off his bed and hoisted himself onto the bolster. Tears glistened in his eyes, and his voice came out in a hoarse whisper. 'I don't deserve this, fellas. You have to be the best friends anyone could ever have. I'm at a loss for words.'

He reached out his arms and they responded in a group hug that ended up the same as the hug Obed had with Hagar – and more laughter followed. 'I only spoke with my father this morning and said I wanted to see if I could live on my own in my own house.'

'Why on your own?' Ezra asked. 'Jonah and I could move in with you – if you wanted us to?'

'And we can come around after night-fishing and help carry you about,' Solomon added on behalf of himself and his brother.

Jonah reached for a flagon of wine that he'd left on the table, ready for this occasion. He quickly filled five cups and handed them round. 'To Obed! May you go from strength to strength!' He raised his cup in the air.

'To Obed!' they all echoed.

'Ready for the lake, Obed?' Ezra asked, and he received an enthusiastic nod. He rolled himself onto his bed, and was hoisted up and carried towards the lake.

Chapter 9

Zebedee was sitting by his boat, mending nets, as they approached, and he rose to his feet as he saw them. 'Good to see you, Obed. The twins told me about your accident – real sorry to hear about it.'

A shadow crossed Obed's face, but he managed to put on a smile and shook Zebedee's hand. 'Thank you, Sir, but with friends like I have here, I think I'll be able to have myself picked up!' They all smiled at his joke, as he went on, 'No James and John about today? And I see Simon and Andrew's boat is unoccupied.'

This small group of fishermen had been one of the gang's favourite spots when they had been let out of school. The twins' father, along with Zebedee and his two sons James and John, and the other brothers Andrew and Simon were in a fishing group together. Simon was the one who would liven things up, and all in the 'gang' had been thrown overboard by him at one time or another.

'They'll be back in a few days, I expect, Obed. They left me with some hired help,' Zebedee replied, but he looked somehow older as he spoke.

'They went off with this new Teacher who's around the area. He was a carpenter and used to live in Nazareth. A week or so ago, he walked to the Jordan where a bit of a prophet has been preaching. Something of a wild man by all accounts, called John the Baptist. He's been drawing crowds of people, telling them to "repent" and get ready for the Messiah who is coming. He doesn't mince his words and tells people just what he thinks of them. Managed to upset a few of the Pharisees – not that it's hard to do!'

Zebedee looked out across the water. 'Anyway, apparently this carpenter from Nazareth comes along and wants John the Baptist to baptise him. Funny thing is, so I've been told, John didn't want to do it, even though he had baptised so many others. But the carpenter persuaded him, and John baptised him in the Jordan.'

'People who were watching say that as he came up out of the water, a dove flew down and sat on his head, and then a voice like thunder said, "This is my son, hear him!" John said this was the long-awaited one from God.'

Obed was intrigued by Zebedee's story. 'So James and John have gone off with this carpenter? What's his name?'

'Jesus. He'd spoken to Simon and Andrew first, then he walked up from their boat and called out to my boys, and they joined them. I don't think they'll be away long; the pull of fishing will lure them back.'

Ezra was listening intently; he had heard his father mention the name of Jesus. 'Jesus? My father was talking to the other synagogue rulers about him. They weren't impressed with what they heard. Sounds like he has no time for the laws of Moses; he breaks the Sabbath rules and has generally upset the Pharisees.'

Zebedee laughed. 'Anything upsets the Pharisees! Maybe this Jesus will be able to teach my boys something, if that's the case! Perhaps going off with him may be no bad thing. Simon said that Jesus spoke about fishing for men.'

'Simon says! Simon is always saying something. What sort of bait will he use to catch men?' Jonah laughed. If Simon wasn't already married, I could see him following someone who would show him how to catch women!'

The twins laughed. 'Can't see Simon becoming a disciple of a travelling rabbi. He's too quick to open his mouth and say the first thing that comes into his head,' Samuel joked. 'But I hope he gets over this Jesus thing quickly – I'll miss his banter when we're mending the nets or are out fishing at night.'

Shifting his position in the boat, Zebedee's gaze scanned the path he had last seen his boys and Simon and Andrew walk along with Jesus.

'It's quiet here without him, I'll give you that, Samuel, but will they be back soon? I'm not so sure. The carpenter had a manner about him – a style – well, something. I can't put my finger on it. But something that draws you. I must admit, I wouldn't have minded going myself, and I'm not one to jump on the next boat that floats by. I've seen enough rabbis and so-called messiahs in my time, but he wasn't like them. Sort of powerful but not pushy, sure of where he was going, but not arrogant or overbearing. I wasn't too worried about James and John going with him.'

Obed rolled off his bed and, by pulling and pushing, managed to prop himself up against a pile of old nets and floats. 'The synagogue hasn't been my scene for a long time, as you all know. Couldn't see the point of worshipping a God who let my mother die, and a religion that was run by a lot of Pharisees who told you what you could or couldn't do but did nothing themselves to really help anyone. But the other night, I was looking at the stars and was thinking I needed something or someone to guide me, now I can't make it on my own. Your carpenter, Jesus, sounds interesting; I'd like to meet him.'

'When I hear from them, Obed, I'll let you know where they're going, so you can meet him.' Zebedee looked at the broken form of the young man who, a few weeks before, was focused and sure of himself, and was now propped up on discarded fishing tackle. His heart went out to him. 'You could do worse, son. If he really is the Messiah, then you couldn't do better than to follow him.'

'To do that, I'd need four others to carry me,' Obed mused with a mixed expression on his face – a wistful smile with a hint of despair.

'We'd give it a go, Obed, if Jesus walks slow enough for us to keep up,' Ezra said

Jonah chipped in, 'And we could get back in time for me to do a bit of wine-tasting at home on the vineyard.'

The sky was changing, and they knew enough about the weather in Galilee to know a storm was brewing. Solomon moved first. 'Obed, we need to get you back before we get caught in the storm. Are we going to your house or the house of your parents?'

'My place is closer, and anyway I was half-hoping that I could stay at my place tonight – if any of you are free to stay as well?'

Ezra stood up and helped Obed back onto his bed. 'I was planning to, if you were happy about it. I wouldn't mind staying with you long term, but we can talk about that later.' The twins stood, one on each side by Obed's feet, and Jonah joined Ezra on the other side of Obed's head.

'One, two, three, lift!' ordered Obed, and they all lifted together and walked back off the beach towards Obed's place.

Chapter 10

They arrived before the storm broke and soon had the fire going, ready to cook the food they'd left there that morning. Jonah was a good cook, and soon the smell of fish frying, mingled with that of fresh bread, filled the house. They sat down on the floor to be at the same level as Obed and, like a group of schoolboys, began stuffing food into their mouths as if there were no tomorrow. A sense of relief filled the minds of Obed's friends. This could work!

They joked and drank the wine Jonah had brought and, for a while, it was as it had always been – 'the gang of five' enjoying each other's company!

Their party was pleasantly interrupted later in the afternoon when Enoch, on his way home from work, saw the smoke rising from his son's house and heard the laughter. He turned off the path and knocked on the door, before pushing it open. 'Is this a private party, or can a weary worker join in?' he asked, with a smile.

His eyes met those of his son, who was propped up against the far wall, opposite the door, and they misted over. Never had he been more proud of his boy. Here he was, back in his own house, entertaining and being entertained by his friends. He knew deep inside that somehow, Obed would make a go of it.

Samuel jumped to his feet and pulled a bench over for Enoch and then poured him a cup of wine. 'Please, enjoy!'

Enoch was pleased to and downed the wine without stopping. He placed the cup on the table and wiped his mouth on the back of his hand as he smacked his lips. 'Good drop of wine – supplied by Jonah, no doubt?'

Jonah bowed slightly from where he was sitting. 'Glad you approve, Sir, care for more?'

Enoch picked up his cup and pushed it across the table for Samuel to refill. 'Boys, I don't know when I've been more proud of you all. I had my misgivings when I left for work this morning when Obed said he was thinking of coming back here. But, seeing you all here now...' – he looked round the room catching each eye as he did so – '... seeing you here like this – Obed, you have my blessing. I won't try to persuade you to come back with me. But you must promise me one thing...'

'And that is?' Obed asked.

'You must promise me that you'll come and stay with us any time you feel you need extra support or these lovely friends of yours are not available to help you. And, boys, you must, you really must not let guilt prevent you from following your own dreams or plans for your lives. Hagar and I will always be willing to take over.'

Softly, Obed replied, 'Abba, thank you. I promise I'll do as you ask.' He looked round at his friends. 'And I agree totally with my father. None of you must let caring for me prevent you from doing whatever you feel is the path for yourselves. I got myself into this mess, and it must never stop you getting into whatever mess you want to get into!'

Laughter!

'Who knows, Jonah,' Obed continued, 'despite your trials with your sisters, you might even want to find a woman for yourself.'

Jonah's face coloured slightly. He changed the subject and they all had another drink.

Enoch walked across the room, knelt and gave his son a hug. He whispered in his ear, 'I love you, son, and so does Hagar. Take care now.' He stood up and made his way home.

While it was still light, and because the storm had passed, Solomon and Samuel left to prepare for a night's fishing. Jonah left to be home before dark, and Ezra helped Obed wash and get ready for sleep.

As they were sitting, staring into the embers of the fire, Obed looked through the open door at the night sky. The storm had cleared the air, and the night was warm. 'You feel tired, Ezra?' Obed asked.

'Not particularly. What's on your mind?'

'When I was a kid, Abba and I sometimes used to take our sleeping mats and climb the stairs onto the roof and sleep under the stars. We'd lie there in the starlight and watch them, as we talked together. I'd love to do that now. What do you think?'

'Do you think we can make it up there, Obed? I'm happy to try, but how could we get you up there?'

'If I get on my stretcher-bed and you get behind my head, you should be able to drag me round to the steps.'

'That's not a problem. It's when we get to the steps, Obed, I don't think I could drag you like that all the way to the top.'

'One bit at a time, Ezra. Drag me to the steps and then, if I roll over onto my front and you take my feet. I could go up feet first! You carry my feet and I'll get so I can lift myself up with my hands and arms, and then I can climb the steps backwards.'

'We must be mad, but let's give it a try,' Ezra responded, with a bit of apprehension.

The first part was easy. Ezra had little trouble lifting the 'head end' of the bed and letting the other end drag as they made their way round the side of the house and to the foot of the steps that led up to the flat roof. He dragged Obed past the last step so that his feet were level with it. Obed then rolled over and hitched himself up until he his head and shoulders were hanging over the end of the bed.

Ezra stood on the first step, bent down and lifted the foot of the bed and Obed's feet. Obed pushed himself up with his arms, and began walking backwards on his hands as Ezra went up the stairs. When Obed's hands reached the first step, he stopped for a rest. 'As soon as I push myself up, Ezra, you move up another step. If I don't stop, keep going and we'll be up there in no time.'

He took a deep breath and pushed himself up on his hands. Right hand first, and then quickly followed by the left, and he was on the first step. 'Keep going,' he muttered through clenched teeth as he mounted the second step. With a grunt, he did the third and fourth, then sank down, panting for breath.

'Six more to go, Obed. Do you think you can make it?'

'I'll do the next four, and by then half of me should be on the roof. Then perhaps I can roll up and over the last two.'

Taking another deep breath, Obed straightened his arms and, with a Herculean effort, made his hands climb the next five steps before he collapsed and rolled over onto the roof, exhausted but jubilant.

Leaving him to recover, Ezra went back down and gathered up enough bedding for himself and Obed, and took it to the rooftop. He made Obed comfortable and then went back down for some drink and a couple of stone-baked loaves. The sky was clear, and there was only a sliver of moon. The stars were so bright, and the expanse of the sky was awesome.

They both lay there on top of the roof, saying nothing, just looking.

Ezra broke the silence. 'I had to smile when you said to Jonah about getting a woman. He coloured up and changed the subject quickly, didn't he?'

'Do you know where I met Marcus, Ezra?'

Ezra shook his head, 'No, I don't, Obed. I was going to ask you one day, but didn't like to dig it up, seeing where being with him got you.'

'Well, indirectly, it was through Jonah. A while back he talked me into going to the hostelry the other side of town. He'd heard that they brewed their own beer, and wanted to try it. We went, and he had too much and got drunk and I had to almost carry him home.'

'So much for our hardened drinker, then,' Ezra said with a smile. 'But Jonah never mentioned meeting Marcus before.'

'He didn't. But we did meet a woman! She served the drinks, and also served men in other ways, if you know what I mean.'

'A prostitute?'

'Yes, she was a prostitute. She made eyes at Jonah and he nearly fell off his bench. I saved him and told her we only wanted drink, but she was attractive. Her name was

Abigail, and when Jonah couldn't stand up, she let him fall and we got out of the place as quickly as I could drag Jonah through the door.'

'Poor old Jonah, couldn't take his drink and couldn't get the girl,' Ezra smiled.

Obed lifted himself up on both elbows and focused his eyes on his feet. 'No, he didn't get the girl, but later I did.' He glanced at Ezra. 'I went back a few weeks later. You and the others were out somewhere, and I had nothing to do and started thinking about her. She had given me the nod that night, so I knew she would be happy for me to come back. So I did. I'm not proud of it now, Ezra, and I feel ashamed telling you.'

'You don't have to tell me, Obed.'

'I feel I do! I want you to know how this all came about. I went back and slept with her. Then, a week or two later, I went back again. That was when I met Marcus. It was in the early morning, as I was about to leave, that I overheard a conversation between a couple of traders.'

'Look, Hadad, you know this is good stuff. You won't find better anywhere this side of Rome.'

'I know, Marcus, but that's what's worrying me. Where did you get it? How can I sell it on when the quality will draw attention?' was Hadad's answer.

'Where it came from is my business. The quality will sell it for you. You could make a very good profit at the price I'm asking.'

Hesitating, Hadad asked, 'Let me try another sip.'

Marcus obliged and poured some wine into a cup and handed it to him.

'It's good, very good. But I still think it's too good for the market where I sell, and with the trouble I've had with tax collectors recently, it will draw too much attention. No, it's good, but not for me this time, Marcus.'

'Your loss will be someone else's gain, my friend. You'll be kicking yourself next week,' Marcus said as he returned his merchandise to the saddlebag of his pack mule.

'I watched Hadad ride off and followed Marcus round to the stable area. I went up to him and said, "Excuse me, Sir, but I couldn't help overhearing your conversation with the other gentleman. I might be interested in your wine, as I know where I could possibly sell it on, no questions asked."

'He looked me over without saying a word, then continued to walk away from the hostel. I followed, but said nothing. The pleasure of the evening filled my mind, and I smiled as I tried to persuade Marcus. We walked on for almost a mile before Marcus stopped and turned around.

'"What's your game, boy?" he questioned me.

'I stood my ground and mocked his challenge. "They have old boys where you come from, do they?"

'A smile slowly came to his lips. "Fancy yourself as a dealer, do you? Marcus is the name. Where do you come from, and what do you get up to most of the time, when you're not sleeping with the girls at the hostel?"

'I managed not to blush, and with a steady stare I looked Marcus in the eye. "If you stay on this road you'll come to my place in about half an hour. My name is Obed, I live on the outskirts of Capernaum, I work at anything that brings in money, but my passion is doing a good deal and trading for profit. Oh, and if you must know, I'm twenty years old."

'Marcus liked what I'd said and stuck out his hand. "Good to meet you, Obed. I think we may be able to do business."

'We arrived at my place and discussed business, but it wasn't until a month later that he decided he could take me into his confidence. I had a good eye for opportunities to do a quick turnaround in whatever "merchandise" Marcus came up with. I took a few risks, but they were calculated – nothing stupid. Well, until the one that's left me in this mess.

'It was then that he came up with what he wanted to do at Herod's palace – to climb the cliff and ship the stuff over to the other side of the lake. Most of what happened next was my doing. I persuaded Solomon and Samuel to ship it for me without them knowing what it was, when they were out for a night's fishing, and Jonah was easy to talk round.

'You were the only one I was worried about, because I knew what you had been brought up to believe in. But I knew you weren't happy with you father, so I hoped you'd join in, to prove you were your own man. I hate saying this, Ezra, but that's how low I'd sunk, even with my friends. I guessed you'd love the idea of climbing the cliffs in the dark, so it was easy to put it all together.'

Obed looked Ezra full in the face and, for a brief moment, he smiled, 'You should have seen yourself climb up the cliff! You were like a monkey!'

His face fell again, 'That's why I was so angry when you backed out when I told you what we were really doing. If only I had listened to you, I wouldn't be stuck like this for the rest of my life.

'Marcus worked for King Herod, and Herod trusted him to buy the best of everything for him. It was easy for him to buy a little extra here and there and cream it off on the side. I told him I thought it was a big risk. I'd heard how people lose their heads if they get on the wrong side of Herod. He just laughed and said you just had to make sure you kept on the right side.

'I loved the sound of taking something from right under Herod's fat nose and him not even knowing it, and I guessed it clouded my judgement.

'You know the rest.'

Obed flopped back onto his bed and stared into the night sky.

Ezra thought over what he'd heard, and realised again how close they had all come to losing their heads by the swords of King Herod's guards.

Propping himself up on his elbows once more, and looking towards Galilee, Obed said, 'That one', as he pointed, almost losing his balance. 'It's so bright. If you were out there on a boat, it would look like you could almost reach up and catch it.' His voice was soft as he spoke.

Ezra followed the direction of his finger and watched the star he'd pointed out. 'Your guiding star, Obed?'

Dropping back onto his bed, Obed paused before answering. 'It was good today, Ezra. And I appreciate everything you have all done for me, but…'

'But?'

'But it's at this time of night when everyone's either gone home or sleeping, I begin to sink. This dark blanket rolls up from over my feet and I feel so helpless. When I try to lift my hands, they're trapped under this blanket as well, and I want to scream out... Then it passes and I'm left covered in sweat.'

Ezra was on his side, looking at his friend in the twilight and was at loss as to what to say.

'Who are we kidding, Ezra?' Obed continued. 'I'm never going to make it, am I? I'll always be dependent on someone, and it's not right. I had a dream of pulling myself out of the lower end of society and making something of myself. I dreamed of having money, enough so I could make it, so my father didn't have to take any job that came along. I wanted to be somebody who had power and influence. Once, when I was out with my father while we were still at school, a Roman soldier made him carry his stuff for a mile. As it was the orders of Rome, he could do nothing about it, so Abba picked up the soldier's bags, hoisted them on his back and got on with it. I walked behind, seething! I vowed that one day I'd somehow have the power to get my own back for my father.'

He shifted his position. 'Now, look at me, Ezra! I don't even know until I smell it that I've relieved myself! When it first happened, Hagar cleaned me up, but I was still too confused to really take it in. Then it was embarrassing. She should never have to do that for a twenty-year-old man! I know you've been willing to help me, but it makes me feel so useless, a waste of space, inadequate.'

Ezra broke in. 'But look at what you achieved today, Obed. And look where we are. On the roof! It takes someone with guts and determination to do what you've just done. If you can climb up steps onto a roof, you can do anything you put your mind to.'

'There's truth in what you say, but when it's quiet, something comes over me and I just feel as if I'm kidding myself. I'm a paralytic. I'll never walk again. I'll never be able to do a proper job. I'll never marry.'

Ezra passed some of the leftover wine to Obed, then he sucked on a few grapes, trying to think of what to say, but he couldn't put his thoughts into words. He realised that Obed's accident had damaged more than his back, and knew a few well-meaning words wouldn't solve anything. Standing up, he took a few paces to the edge of the roof and looked over, with his back to Obed.

Draining the last of the wine, Obed cleared his throat and began speaking again. 'But above it all is this crushing weight – call it guilt, self-pity – I don't know. But it was my bravado that got me into this mess. What I've done has affected so many others. I know you all say you don't mind helping me, and I believe you mean it. And my parents – their lives have changed because of me.'

He reached down and moved his left leg to free the bedding that was caught under it. 'That night, down on the beach, you were the only one with the guts to turn away and leave me in my stupidity. And then you came back to help me. It could have cost you your life, Ezra. If Herod's men had found us, your head as well as mine would have been severed. That's the guilt I carry.'

Ezra paused while he tried to think of something to say. 'They didn't find us, and we all have our heads.'

'But by only thinking of myself, my foolishness has had this knock-on effect. Whatever you may say, Ezra, what I did has affected your life.'

Neither spoke for a while, then Obed began again, 'If what I did that night influences your life and my parents' lives, then so all the other things I've done affect others too.'

'Like what? Come on, Obed, you're being too negative now. What else have you done that has hurt anyone else? We've all done things that maybe we shouldn't have – that's just life. No big deal. It's not like you've murdered anyone, is it?'

'Do you believe all that stuff they teach at your father's synagogue? That's even scarier – more condemning! Does your God like what I've done? I remember the Ten Commandments the rabbi and your father taught us.'

'Well, you haven't broken all of them, have you?' Ezra protested.

'What's the pass mark, Ezra? Six out of ten?'

Silence followed.

'Then there's Abigail,' Obed whispered.

'Abigail? What's a prostitute got to do with it?'

'Yes, she's a prostitute, Ezra, but saying that just shows up my hypocrisy and dismisses my personal responsibility. Abigail is a person, a human being, not a thing to be used. But I used her like a plaything and left her feeling less than a person.'

Even in the darkness, Ezra could see tears on Obed's face, sparkling in the faint moonlight. 'I can't undo any of this, can I? I can't mend my back, I can't remove the scars

I've inflicted on others, on Abigail, and especially on what the rabbi said about God.'

More silence.

'I thought we came up here to watch the stars and go to sleep?' Ezra ventured. 'I can't answer your questions. I wish I could. But today – we did have a good day, didn't we? We laughed like the old times.'

'I know. And yes, you're right, we had a good day. But because you, out of all the boys, came back for me, I feel I can talk to you, and I needed someone to unload to. Sorry, Ezra, it's just at night I can't shake off this guilt. I think when we have a day like today, all is well. But then it comes back to haunt me. I might have got away from Herod and we could argue that I took nothing from him in the end, but the guilt remains. And I feel crippled by that even more than the loss of my legs.' He rolled over to face Ezra, 'It's helped to talk, Ezra. You're a good friend.'

They settled down and eventually went to sleep.

Chapter 11

The singing of birds woke up the roof-sleepers very early and they found it easier to get down than they did to get up – gravity helped. Ezra saw that Obed had all he needed nearby and at his level, so after having some of the leftovers for breakfast, he left for work, leaving Obed to fend for himself. Because of the early start to the day, much to the delight of his father, Ezra arrived early for work. Jairus asked if he thought Obed would be all right on his own for the day.

'I left him all he'll need, Abba, and he's managing to do a lot for himself now. I think he needs the challenge to help him stay focused,' Ezra said. 'When the others left last night, we made it up onto the roof and slept under the stars. That's when he finds it the hardest, at night. By the way, Abba, have you heard any more about the new rabbi, Jesus?'

Jairus sat back in his chair. 'He's been stirring things up around here, that's for sure! I've heard talk of healings and how he finds it easier to mix with the underclass – prostitutes, tax collectors and beggars. The Pharisees don't like him and say he's an impostor. Why do you ask?'

'Zebedee told us yesterday that James and John, as well as Simon and Andrew, have become his disciples. They've been good friends to us, and I just wondered what they were getting themselves into.'

'You know Jesus came to our synagogue a couple of weeks ago. Broke the Sabbath laws by healing a man. It wasn't well received by the Ruling Council.'

'But what do you think? Is he the Messiah sent from God?'

'He's from Nazareth, Ezra. What comes from there hasn't been any good, let alone the Messiah.'

Ezra let it drop and, after learning what his father wanted him to do for the day, he gathered up the necessary tools, loaded some sawn timber onto a handcart and, with the help of a hired hand, made his way to a large property on the lakeside of Capernaum. It was the type of work that he really enjoyed, and so he set to it with a positive attitude. The property was built around a courtyard where three sides had a second storey. The fourth side was one storey high, a large room that opened on to the rest of the courtyard, with steps leading up to the roof from the outside. Part of this roof had fallen in and needed new timber joists, then it had to be covered over with lath and mud plaster.

The day was warm and, with the hired hand's help, the old rotted timber was soon removed and cleared away. The new timbers were cut to length and spliced into the solid existing wood, and then pegged together to give a strong joint.

They took a short break for a drink of water, then they set the laths in place and mixed up a large quantity of mud and straw. It was heavy work, lugging buckets full of this mix up onto the roof, but the labourer was strong and had a will to work, so while Ezra spread it into place, the labourer fetched more from the ground. By mid-afternoon the job was finished, and they spread a piece of sailcloth over the new mud and tied it down, so if a storm came before it was completely dry, it wouldn't be washed away.

Towards the end of the day, Jairus visited the site. He called his son over. 'Would it be possible for Jonah to live with Obed for the next two weeks? I've secured a big job down south of Tiberias and I'd like you to oversee it, at least for the first week or two.'

Ezra knew this meant that his father now fully trusted him, and he felt proud to have been asked. 'If Jonah is free, I'm sure Obed would cope. I'd love to go! Thanks for the opportunity. As we've finished the roof job, I could go over to Jonah's now and see if he could do it?'

Jairus was only too happy, so Ezra made his way to the vineyards and found Jonah. 'A couple of weeks without my sisters! Yes, Sir! I'll make it, no problem,' was Jonah's ready response. A hefty thump on the back and the arrangement was made: Jonah would move in with Obed the next day, and Ezra would be off to Bethpage.

Jonah was good to Obed, but lacked a few graces. Obed, though grateful, was glad when Ezra came back. In only two weeks Ezra could see that Obed looked stronger, his upper body was visibly heavier and his arm muscles more pronounced, but Ezra could tell that Obed's mental attitude had taken a downward turn.

'Fancy a night on the roof?' Ezra suggested. 'The moon's full and the sky's clear.'

Obed knew at once what his friend was saying, and he sighed with relief. Jonah's answer to most things was to have another cup of wine, and that didn't help Obed's frame of mind. 'That'd be fantastic. You take the bedding and I'll get up there on my own.'

'Sure?'

'Sure. I can pull myself round there with my new sliding mat! I got Samuel to bring me a torn sail and cut it into a mat with holes at the top. I put my arms through the holes so the mat stays with me as I crawl forward on my arms, dragging my useless legs along behind. The sailcloth is strong and covered with wax, and it slides over the ground. I haven't tried it up the steps yet, but can't see why it wouldn't work.'

Bundling two lots of bedding together, Ezra wrapped a belt around them to keep them together, and hoisted them on his shoulder. By the time he was around the side of the house, Obed was halfway up the steps. His dragging mode of motion worked, but it was hard on the front of his legs. The fact that he had no feeling or sensation in them meant it didn't worry him, but Ezra could see they would have to watch Obed's skin in case it became broken or cut and he remained unaware of it.

Chapter 12

The beds were rolled out, and they settled back to watch the stars in the moonlight. 'Your body looks stronger, Obed, but you're not OK, are you?'

'Shows that much?'

'Not to everyone, but after our night on the roof, I understand more of how you feel, so I guess I'm more sensitive to it,' Ezra said, softly.

'Jonah was great, but you know how he is. A drop of wine solves everything. Trouble is, when it wears off I feel more desperate than I did before I drank it. It gets worse, Ezra. I'm not full of self-pity; I just can't get the guilt off my mind. If I could, I think I'd go back to the synagogue and see if that helped. What do you think?'

A star shot across the sky and they both saw it. 'Could do with a shooting star, couldn't we? I asked my father about Jesus, after we talked last time. He was non-committal because Jesus did things at the synagogue he felt could have been done on another day, and not the Sabbath. But that was then, Obed. He's changed his mind radically since!'

Obed rolled onto his side so he could look at Ezra. 'What do you mean, he's radically changed his mind? What's happened?'

'While I was away, my little sister, who has just turned twelve, suddenly went down with a fever. She was delirious and in a bad way. They called the doctor – the same one who came to see you – and he was unable to do anything about it. Said she might pull through, or she could die. My father was frantic, and he sat by her bed and realised she was slipping away. Her pulse got weaker, and she went all limp. My mother was crying, and there was nothing they could do. Then my father suddenly got to his feet and ran out the door. One of the servants asked him where he was going, and he shouted back, "I'm going to find Jesus. They say he's healed many people, so perhaps he can heal my little girl."'

'And by the look on your face, he did?!'

'He did more than that! Before my father could find Jesus and return with him, my sister died. When they arrived at our house, the women were wailing and mourning, and my mother was overcome with grief. Jesus went in with my parents and shut the mourners out, took my sister's hand and said, "Little girl, get up." And she did!'

Obed flopped back on his bed, 'That's something else! He really did that? Your sister had really died?'

'My father, as you well know, is not given to sensationalism. Ask him! Mother said it was the first time she had seen him literally jump up and down. She said he scooped my sister off the bed and danced round the room, throwing her up in the air so high she hit her head on the ceiling. Jesus told them to give her something to eat.'

'A miracle worker with a practical outlook! I like that,' Obed said with a wistful expression on his face. 'What's he like with backs?'

Ezra laughed. 'You'd better ask him.'

'Will you take me to him?'

'You bet! Wouldn't that be great?! You walking again?'

It was more than the shadow cast by the moon, but as Obed lay there, a shadow spread over his face. His eyes were closed tight, but Ezra could see a tear squeezing its way out. He said nothing, but waited for his friend to speak. The tears made their way down the sides of Obed's face, but he didn't speak.

'What's the problem, Obed? Don't you think Jesus could heal your back?'

Eyes still closed, Obed replied, 'Oh yes, I believe he could do that. If he can bring your sister back from the dead, then a broken back shouldn't be a problem to fix.'

'So?'

'Your father is the ruler of the synagogue, an honest man. Of course a holy man would help him. But look at me, Ezra. I left the synagogue and all that it stood for twelve years ago, the same time as your little sister was born. I deserve what I've got. No holy man is going to want to touch me.'

'You haven't seen the crowd Jesus hangs out with, Obed. He has this group of women who go about with him; at least one of them was a prostitute. He talks to tax collectors and even touches lepers, so I've been told. Solomon said he saw Simon the other day, and Simon says that he spends more time with the poor and the misfits than he does with the so-called "holy" people.'

'He really has an ex-prostitute among his followers?'

'A real live one, Obed.'

'Not Abigail, is it?'

'I don't know. I've no more met Jesus than you. But I'll tell you this, Obed, everybody's talking about him. Wherever he goes, huge crowds quickly gather.'

'Would you really take me to see him?'

'Solomon and Samuel are coming round after their night's fishing. If we can get hold of Jonah tomorrow, we'll find out where Jesus is and carry you to him – and then you can walk home!'

'Wouldn't that be something?' Obed mumbled, as he closed his eyes and let the thought penetrate his mind. *If only...* 'Imagine having power to heal people, Ezra. I've dreamed of having power, but the power to heal is something else. Where does he get it from?'

'I think it has to be from God. Who else could do that? That soldier who made your father carry all his stuff got his power from Rome, but it was used to keep us under. Your friend Abigail used the power of seduction to lure you into her bed. The power that Jesus has must be the power of Love. You must love people to want to help them and heal them, even when others look down on them. Simon says that one of his disciples is Matthew, who used to collect taxes right here in Capernaum.'

Chapter 13

They both woke up early, and Obed made an ungainly descent from the roof. Ezra prepared some breakfast while Obed struggled to sort out his personal washing. Leaving him to eat, Ezra hurried off to find Jonah, so that when the twins came they could carry Obed to Jesus. The news on the street was that he was still in Capernaum.

Jonah was just about awake and objected to being dragged off before he had time for a leisurely breakfast. By the time they got back to Obed's, the twins were already there, engaged in a spirited conversation with Obed.

'... And Simon said that Jesus shut the Pharisees up by telling them that the one with no sin could throw the first stone!'

Samuel added, 'And Simon said that they all began to walk away till only Jesus was left standing there, with the poor half-dressed woman kneeling at his feet.'

'What did he say to her?' Obed asked. 'I mean, if she really was caught in bed with another man, I remember enough of the commandments to know she could be stoned.'

Solomon finished the story, 'Simon said Jesus reached out his hand and gently helped her to her feet, kissed her on the forehead and told her to go home and sin no more.'

'Simon said!' blurted out Jonah. 'Simon said a lot of things.'

Solomon cut him short. 'Jonah, you haven't seen him lately. We went fishing together last night and he's still the old Simon in one way, but he's different as well. And Andrew backed up every story he had to tell. It has to be true, and what with Jesus healing Ezra's sister – I can't wait to get Obed to Jesus.'

Jonah bent down and took hold of one corner of Obed's stretcher-bed – 'What are you waiting for, then?' – and he started to lift Obed, almost tipping him off the bed.

'Hold on, Jonah, all together now,' Obed cried. 'Lift!'

Carrying him feet first, Ezra and Samuel led the way, with Jonah and Solomon carrying the head end.

It was easy to find where Jesus was, as everyone seemed to be going the same way. A few streets into Capernaum, Ezra knew where they were heading: to the large house with the courtyard he'd worked at only a few weeks earlier.

As they rounded the corner, their faces fell. There was such a crush of people spilling out of the courtyard and into the street that it would be impossible to get near Jesus. They rested Obed on the ground and Jonah, being the tallest, pushed his way to the entrance of the courtyard. He could just see someone he assumed to be Jesus standing in the open room at the far end, under the shade of the roof.

Pushing his way out again, he came back to the little band of men. 'There's no way we can get Obed in there! There have to be three or four hundred people in or around the place.'

The twins showed their disappointment, and sat down on the ground beside Obed.

Ezra laughed, 'Oh yes, there is! I worked on this house only a couple of weeks ago. I repaired the roof, and the mud will still be reasonably soft. If we find some rope, we could climb the steps around the side and get up on the roof, and lower Obed through, right in front of Jesus.'

The idea of making a hole in the roof appealed to the boy inside the men. Obed was a little nervous at the thought of being lowered down in front of all the people, but wasn't about to dampen the enthusiasm of his friends. The twins found some rope hanging in an open stable-yard, so they 'borrowed' it. Taking their places round Obed, they carried him, almost at a run, around the side of the house, and up the steps onto the roof.

The patch of new roof was clearly seen and Ezra, knowing where the timber joists were, began working his hand through the straw and mud until it came out on the underside. He was then able to pull up his hand, making a hole big enough to get his other hand in. Jonah, kneeling the other side of him, pushed his hand through, and, together, they pulled up a large part of the roof.

Below, Jesus was speaking to the crowd, with some of the Pharisees standing in the front asking questions about his authority to teach. A shaft of sunlight suddenly burst through the ceiling, lighting up Jesus' face. The Pharisees and the owner of the house looked up, and were shocked to see a large hole that was getting bigger by the minute. The crowd laughed, and some standing in the courtyard pointed to the five men on the roof.

Jesus took a step to one side as a few bits of straw and mud dropped inside the room. He looked up, and the crowd went quiet.

The hole was now more than six feet long, and the width of the gap between the joists. The sun was momentarily blocked out as the four friends moved Obed's bed over the hole and, slowly, they lowered him to the ground by the feet of Jesus. Four faces peered through the hole and watched. Silence pervaded the crowd.

Moving a step closer to the bed, Jesus looked in the face of Obed.

Obed suddenly felt sick. The crushing weight that came upon him descended with full force. He looked at Jesus, but couldn't hold eye contact. Tears ran down his face and he tried to turn away from such purity. He felt dirty, and wanted to crawl into a corner and hide. He felt dirty – he knew he was a sinner!

Jesus spoke. 'Take heart, son; your sins are forgiven.'

The words shot through Obed life a thunderbolt. *My sins are forgiven! My sins are forgiven!*

He believed it! The black crushing weight lifted from him, and he felt as if he were hovering two feet above the ground. His paralysis was forgotten; the stifling darkness was gone. Jesus had said it – his sins were forgiven!

The Pharisees muttered to each other, but Jesus turned his gaze towards them and said, 'Why do you entertain evil thoughts in your hearts? Which is easier to say: "Your sins are forgiven," or, "Get up and walk"? But I want you to know that the Son of Man has authority on earth to forgive sins.' Turning back to Obed, he said, 'Get up, take up your mat, and go home.'

For Obed, as he explained it later, it was not that he felt he had to struggle to his feet, but just that he lowered his legs to the ground and stood upright!

Jesus simply smiled at him and whispered, 'Pick up your bed and go home, son.' Obed bent down, rolled the two carrying palls together and swung them over his shoulder. He glanced up at the grinning faces peering over the hole and said to Ezra, 'I'm free!' and jumped up in the air.

The crowd cheered, clapped and parted as Obed danced his way through the middle of them and out of the courtyard. The palls of his bed almost hit one or two of the tallest people in the crowd, but that only added laughter to the spirit of rejoicing, particularly as one of them was a Pharisee!

Few heard it, but Ezra called out from his perch on the roof to the owner of the house, 'I'll be back tomorrow to repair your roof for you, sir – at no cost.'

The owner shook his head and roared with laughter. 'See you in the morning.'

Jesus smiled. 'Take heart, son; your sins are forgiven,' He said.

(Mark 2:1-12 gives the biblical account of Jesus forgiving and healing the paralysed man. Mark 3:1-5 gives the account of the restoration of the man's withered hand on the Sabbath day, and Mark 5:21-24 and 35-42 is the account of Jesus bringing the little girl back to life).

Power and Authority
The Centurion and His Servant

The crowd in the market parts to make way for a small band of Roman soldiers led by a centurion. His face is clean-shaven but his dark eyebrows give an appearance of strength and rugged good looks. The red plume on his helmet is matched by the red cloak draped over his broad shoulders. He walks as one on a mission, but there is a softness to the corners of his mouth. The soldiers who accompany him keep an eye on the crowds and another on their leader. There's no question of who is in authority here. One or two of the local people greet the centurion warmly, not as one would expect, seeing as he represents the dominant power of Rome. A ruler from the local synagogue walks up to him and engages him in conversation. Roman and Jewish leaders talking amiably together...?

Chapter 1

'I swear that I shall faithfully execute all that the Emperor commands, I shall never desert the service, and I shall not seek to avoid death for the Roman state.'

Eighteen-year-old Julian's voice rang out with the rest of the new batch of army recruits. They'd all heard the motivational speech of the *Legate* (commanding officers) and were fired up for service, dreaming of action, victory, glory and all the other benefits of being part of the Roman army.

It wouldn't be long before many of them would become disillusioned as they faced the rigours of army training. Twenty-mile marches in full kit weighing somewhere between sixty and ninety pounds that had to be completed in five hours was no picnic. Julian took it all in his stride – this is what he lived for, what had driven him for the last six or more years.

Enlisted but liberated, controlled but confident. He could endure the humiliating taunts of his commanding officers; they spurred him on with even greater determination. Start up at the bottom, and you will be ready to climb up!

And he anticipated climbing.

He had been just twelve when his father had taken him to the Saturnalia celebrations. It was a wild occasion of revelry, and his father was eager to introduce him to it, as it was his favourite festival. Gladiators fought to the death, and other forms of depravity were on public display. Watching the brutality, as the gladiators killed to the roaring of the crowd, had had the opposite to the desired effect his father wanted for his boy. Instead of instilling in him a lust for blood and killing, it produced repulsion. But even at that young age, Julian knew better than to let his true feelings show, and he mimicked the shouting and adulation of his father – he'd learned young how to survive in a dysfunctional family.

His father roared louder than most. He was responsible for training some of the most successful and deadly contestants. An ex-gladiator himself, he had gained his Roman citizenship by his many victories.

As brutal as his training regime was, so was his management of the home. 'Titan' was his nickname, and he revelled in the adulation his 'trade' brought him. Home life had to replicate the same ethos. Love and compassion were unknown virtues; kindness was seen as weakness. The property that was called 'home' was substantial; Titan's success in the arena was bringing in large rewards. He had servants and minions who, out of fear, did his bidding.

Three women, who were wives, concubines or expendable entertainment, depending on his mood or degree of sobriety, attended to his 'needs'. Children, mostly unwanted by-products, numbered five, with Julian being the second oldest, but the eldest son. Julian's elder sister, whom Titan called his 'Venus', was six years older than he was. She was the only one from whom Julian had ever received anything that could be called affection. In the six years between them, other children had been born, but they had either died at birth or had not survived one of Titan's drunken frenzies.

Julian survived because he was a strong and healthy baby, and Venus took care of him when his mother was negligent. Titan somehow saw the potential in this baby, and began to view Julian as his protégé. To say that Titan nurtured him would be a statement wide of the mark; it was more that Julian was teased, tormented or cajoled into responses that Titan saw as appropriate for his son.

Out of sight of his father's gaze, one of the servants, who was given the responsibility for his well-being, did treat Julian with the attention that was more befitting a young child. This, along with the limited affections of his sister, registered within him as a warm shadow that was to lurk somewhere at the back of his mind.

With the arrival of other 'by-products' – three of whom survived – Julian, in his growing-up years, was never really sure which of the three women in the house was his birth mother.

Without a doubt, Titan's god was Bacchus – the god of wine and party! A shrine dedicated to him was prominent in the home. But with three women from vastly different backgrounds, other 'lesser gods' were also given space.

On the day of the Saturnalia celebrations, Titan offered his oblation to Mars and, with an extra flagon of wine, set off early to the arena with Julian running behind, trying to keep up. Venus, now almost eighteen, pushed a cloth bag containing food into his hands, knowing that her father would not think of Julian's need for food all day, as he would be drinking and revelling with the others. She gave him a quick peck on his cheek, saying, 'Keep your head down and you'll be all right. Shut your eyes if you don't want to see.'

Little did he realise, but that would be the last he ever saw of Venus.

As the gladiators fought and the wine flowed freely, Titan became less and less in control of himself. This gave Julian a break, but, heeding his sister's words, he kept his head down, remembering to shout enthusiastically each time his father stood up, roaring at the fighting.

Two things happened that day that set a resolve in Julian's mind, and they would never change.

The first was the sight of between four and five hundred Roman soldiers marching into the arena, fully armed and decked out in their full plumage. The discipline as they marched in tight formation, not one out of step, fired his young imagination. At the shout of a centurion riding majestically on a horse, they changed direction as one man. Such military precision thrilled him – the contrast of the dysfunctionality at home, the order and form, the pride and the glory. The climax of this military display was the formation of thirty legionaries into the famous *Testudo* (or 'tortoise'). They locked their shields tightly together, with the row at the back placing theirs on top of the others, forming a protective 'shell'. From the far end of the arena, a one-horse chariot, driven by a centurion, drove straight at them, rode right up and over them and down the other side. The crowd cheered as the soldiers lifted up their shields, and shouted, 'Hail Caesar!'

Julian was sold on the dream of becoming a centurion in the Roman Imperial Army.

The second thing that cemented his mind was the result of a drunken gamble. Titan gambled with a fellow trainer from another part of the Roman Empire, and lost the bet.

Venus, his eldest daughter, was to go with the winner to be his concubine. Julian found out the next day, after she had been drugged and carried away forever.

He did not cry, but fixed his mind on joining the army as soon as he was able to. He would join the glorious Legions of Rome and fight to bring justice and order to every corner of the Empire.

Chapter 2

Schooling was secondary in Titan's mind; gladiator-fighting skills came first. At fourteen, Julian was taken daily with his father to the training compound and exposed to the harshness of their training. Using dummy weapons, he was encouraged to watch and mimic the actions of battle-scarred gladiators. Mercifully, he was spared the whip and rod that were used to beat the real trainees, but all the other rigours were his to endure. Titan was impressed with the boy's ability, and Julian was rewarded with a rare smile, as he felt Julian was following in his footsteps, not knowing the direction in which his son's mind was set.

Home life didn't change, at least not for the better, and when not forced to be at the gladiators' school Julian drifted around Rome, sometimes spending time in the Pantheon, learning about the gods. Mars, the god of war, was to be feared and, because of his desire to fight for the Empire, needed to be revered. Minerva appealed, as she was the goddess of wisdom, learning, art, craft and industry. Her symbol of an owl stood out in contrast to the thunderbolt in the hand of Jupiter, the master of all the gods. Venus he gave little attention to, believing that had his sister not been so shapely and beautiful, she would never have been part of a wager. If Venus had endowed his sister with her beauty, then she would have been better off without her!

When he turned eighteen, Julian needed no permission from his father to go and join the Legions. In the weeks before his eighteenth birthday, he spent time near the garrison, making himself known to the enrolment officer. Because his father was well known, Julian was looked upon as good 'army material', and there was no problem with him signing up. Discreetly, Julian explained to the officer that it would be better that his application was kept out of public view, as his father wouldn't take it well. The officer was only too pleased to comply, and all was set.

The day after he turned eighteen, Julian got up early, packed a few belongings in a leather bag, and slipped out of the house before the others awoke. A few hours later, he was standing in line with the other recruits, declaring the military oath.

For all its downside, his upbringing had toughened him up, and he could embrace army life with enthusiasm. His enthusiasm soon earned him the attention of his centurion. Whether running or doing weapons training with weighty dummy weapons, the snarl of the centurion's orders to 'move faster, jump higher, thrust deeper' was relentless. Training exercises where the recruits had to pitch the heavy leather tent in the gathering gloom of the pelting rain, and then with eight others crowd in to sleep, were make-or-break time.

Those who didn't break found themselves forged into a band of men with the camaraderie that would see them through many life-threatening skirmishes with the enemies of Rome.

This was the life Julian had craved. The army was his salvation, and hope of a better life. Here he could prove himself, climb the promotional ladder, and end up with a good salary and posting in some far-flung corner of the

Empire. Rome itself had no appeal to him; he craved adventure and distance from his dysfunctional family.

He was quickly promoted to lead a *Contubernium*, a group of eight men. Ten such groups made up a *Centuria* overseen by the centurion.

The short *gladius* sword became a lethal extension to his right hand. He could lock his *scutum* (curved shield) with his fellow soldiers to form the almost impregnable human 'tortoise' he had seen demonstrated in the arena, when he was twelve. Clad in his armour and with his layered leather boots on his feet, the soles covered with heavy metal cone-shaped hobnails, he felt he could overcome the world for the sake of the glorious Roman Empire.

Julian's first real posting was to quell an uprising of a renegade army in Philippi. His centurion was impressed with his performance, and he began to climb up the promotional ladder.

In battle, his motto, along with his fellows in the *Contubernium*, was 'We take no prisoners', and their fighting style demonstrated their commitment to the Empire. The only downside for him was being shipped from one port to another. He was a good soldier, but definitely not a sailor!

After two years in the province of Iconium in the city of Lycaonia, and only five years after he had signed up, Julian was promoted to the rank of centurion. By this time, he found that the best way to get the most from his men was to treat them fairly, work them hard, give no room for insubordination, show them that he was able to do all he asked of them, and reward them well. He took time to get to know his men, and learn about their individual strengths and weaknesses. By the end of his sixth year, he had a band of men who were willing to die for one another.

A centurion had the privilege of riding a horse, and, with the distinctive armour and staff, he was easily recognised. The staff, a rod about four feet long, was used by most centurions to beat their men and keep them in check, some very brutally. Because of his childhood upbringing, Julian disliked this practice and found he got more from his men without being so heavy-handed.

He had regard for them and they, in turn, respected him.

Chapter 3

Five years in Athens gave him more experience, and then Julian was posted to Bithynia for another five years.

Near the end of this posting by the Black Sea in Bithynia, a rebellion needed quelling over in Pontus. Julian and three other centurions were sent with their men to quell this uprising, and to restore order to the region. Guerrilla fighting took a heavy toll, and Julian took it personally, as a failure in his ability to correctly deploy his men. He doubled his offerings to Mars, but the god of war did not seem to respond to his requests. They regrouped and, with a concerted effort, made inroads against the insurgents. With a final push, the rebels were defeated, and Julian rewarded his men with extra pay and rations.

In the mopping-up operations, while clearing out isolated guerrilla fighters, one of his *Contubernia* found a ringleader hiding out in some disused farm building. Three other fighters, as well as his woman and her twelve-year-old son, were with him. The *Contubernium* quickly dispatched the three fighters and took the ringleader prisoner. With the fighters safely out of the way, one soldier held the boy and the others gathered round to enjoy the woman as part of their spoils.

Hearing the anguished cry of the boy and the scream of the woman, Julian turned his mount and rode into the farmyard. His voice cracked through the air like a whip. 'Cease! Bring the boy and the woman to me – *now!*'

They jumped to obey.

Seeing the three dead bodies, and the captured ringleader, he sized up the situation quickly. 'You've done well – very well! He looks like the one responsible for our many losses. The boy? I think he has the misfortune of being fathered by the wrong man, and I know what that's like.' He had never before given his men any reason to know that he had any negative thoughts about his home life.

He looked at the terrified woman and thought of his sister, Venus. Perhaps the woman had likewise suffered at the hands of this pig. 'Abuse her no more. You will be rewarded for your work today, but take the woman and her son back to my tent and have them guarded until I finish my surveillance.'

They saluted him, gathered up the prisoner and led the boy and his mother towards the camp.

On his return, Julian found the woman and her son standing in the enclosed area that demarcated his official officer's quarters. Two soldiers stood and saluted as he arrived, and then took a step back. The auxiliary who took care of his personal belongings and food brought him a flagon of wine and a cup. Taking them from him, Julian ordered him to fetch an extra cup, then dismissed both the auxiliary and the two soldiers. He poured wine into both cups and handed one to the boy. 'Give this to your mother.'

The boy handed it to his mother, who took a drink, then handed it back to her son,

'He may drink too?' she asked, looking at Julian.

'He may drink also.'

He watched them both, wondering what life had been like for them. The lad reminded him of the day his father had taken him to the arena, the day he last saw his sister, the only one who had ever given him any affection.

In a quiet voice that was barely audible, she spoke again. 'Sir, if you have saved me for your own pleasure, would you not use me in front of my son? I ask for nothing else.' Her speech was that of a defeated woman, but she stood with a bearing of dignity. She would not grovel or beg for mercy; neither had she used her body to try to bargain with him by seduction. Her only request was for the well-being of her son.

Taking a step towards him, she could see a nerve twitching in his neck. He reached out his hand that held his cup, and offered it to her. Taking it, she drank, then handed it back, trying hard to read what this powerful man might be thinking. Her breathing became heavy, as his movements were unpredictable, and she feared what he might do to her.

Turning to the boy, he said, 'Boy, see the stool over there?' He pointed to the corner of the enclosure. 'Fetch it over for your mother to sit on.'

The boy moved instantly, and quickly brought the stool and sat it down by his mother.

'Please, sit,' Julian said to her.

She did so, her eyes not leaving his face.

He in turn sat down on the ground and beckoned for the boy to do the same. Her breathing became steadier because of this show of kindness from a man who had the power to do whatever he wished, with both her and her son.

'In one sense you're right. I have saved you for my own pleasure.' She caught her breath, but he continued, 'But my pleasure is not to use you or your son for my own sexual gratification.' He let his eyes scan her body. 'Truly, Venus has blessed you with beauty, but my pleasure is much deeper than that. My desire is for you to be restored to what you were born to be, and for your son to know a mother's love.'

She was speechless at his words; her mouth opened but she closed it before she could say anything. He continued, 'Is the man who is my prisoner your husband? Tell me how you met him. If I am not mistaken, you are of Jewish heritage?'

Finding her voice, she replied, 'My father is Jewish, my mother Greek. We fell on hard times, and to pay off the debts we offered ourselves as domestic servants. Your prisoner promised my father that he would take care of me like his own daughter, and treat me well as long as I served him in the home with the general housework and cooking. He lived in the next town, his property was well cared for and his household seemed respectable. My father agreed a sum, and I became one of this family's servants. For a time all was well, his wife was kind and I enjoyed working for them. I missed my own family, as I only saw them if we were at the market at the same time.'

'So he is not your husband?'

'All was not as it appeared on the surface. His respectable front was a cover for subversive activities. He, along with others, plotted rebellion against Rome. When they felt the time was right, in the dead of night they left Tarsus and headed off through Cappadocia and Galatia to Bithynia, taking me with them.'

A shudder went down her spine as she spoke. 'My life changed, and he used me as his woman, because he had left his wife back in Tarsus. I was beaten and abused, and within a short time I became pregnant. When he knew, he did treat me with a little less hostility and life became more bearable. My baby was born and he called him Leon, because he said this was his lion cub. Bearing him a son improved my status, and I was shown some measure of respect, and even kindness.'

'And your name?'

'My name is Hannah.'

'He has kept you and your son with him all these years?'

'Yes. Life has been hard, as we have moved constantly to avoid detection by the Roman authorities. But his treatment of us could have been worse. What will happen to him now?'

'My superior officers will have a tribunal and decide his fate. I have authority to administer what happens to you and Leon, and, as I have already said, my desire is to restore you to your family home. Do they still live in Tarsus?'

She shrugged her shoulders. 'It was more than twelve years ago. I have never been back and have heard nothing.' She lowered her head, and there were tears in her eyes. 'Why are you being so kind to us?' she whispered, fearing that voicing it might cause her to lose it.

'I had a sister. When she was about the age you would have been when you were parted from your family, my father lost a wager while he was drunk. She was the only one in our dysfunctional family who showed me love.' There was a trace of anger in his voice. 'He was a drunken, selfish fool! Leon needs the stability of a mother's love, and you need to be given back what you have lost. That, in my book, is what Roman justice is all about.'

He got to his feet, and Leon began to rise with him. 'No, boy, stay with your mother.' He called for his auxiliary. 'Erect a tent for this lady and her son within my enclosure. See to it that they get food and water. I plan to have them repatriated to Tarsus. It will be your personal responsibility to see they have what they need and that they are not molested by anyone. You understand?'

The auxiliary, Gallus, bowed his head. 'I understand fully, Sir.'

'Good. See to it.'

Gallus left to obey his orders. Hannah rose from her stool and dropped at Julian's feet, and held them with both hands. 'The God of Abraham, Isaac and Jacob be praised! Thank you, thank you for your kindness beyond all that I should receive from your hand. You are like an angel of the Lord. How can I ever repay you?' Her tears were now flowing freely, falling on his feet.

'I believe in justice. You need not fear for yourself or your son; my position is your guarantee of safety. As for repaying me? Perhaps one day you can tell me about this god you have just praised. I've seen your synagogues in various cities and have often wondered about the god you Jews worship. We have many gods, and I sometimes wonder what good they do to us. Come, Hannah, up on your feet, for whatever else I might be, I am not a god to be worshipped.' He bent down and helped her to her feet. 'I have duties to attend to. When Gallus comes back, direct him as to how you would like to have your space set up.'

He left her and went into the main garrison to attend the tribunal. Celsus, the prisoner, was standing between two soldiers, and it was apparent by the bloody state he was in that some form of retribution had already been meted out to him, unofficially.

The trial didn't last long, as there was nothing the prisoner could offer in his defence for his insurrection. The commander passed the sentence: 'Celsus, for your leading of insurrection and murder of Roman soldiers, you will be flogged and crucified. Take him away.'

The wretch of a man was dragged away for flogging, while a cross was prepared for his crucifixion. Julian was glad he was not the only centurion in the garrison, so he didn't have to oversee the punishment.

As he left the courtyard, one of his fellow centurions, Claudius, walked alongside him. 'Coming to watch the show, Julian? After all, it was your men who caught him.'

'I'm glad he's been caught, and I'm proud of my men for doing so. But watch the show? No, I believe deeply in Roman justice, but to my mind crucifixion betrays it. It's barbaric and undermines the laws of humanity.'

'You feel he should be released after all the trouble he's caused? Come, Julian, that can't be right. I hear you have his woman at your quarters – have you gone soft because of her?'

'Quite the contrary, Claudius. I've stood on the Tarpeian Rock overlooking the Forum in Rome, to administer executions by throwing criminals to their death. Crime has to be punished – and crime against the state, particularly. Capital punishment is a necessary evil, and should be administered quickly and efficiently. Crucifixion is neither of these. It is far from quick, and is totally inefficient. It's brutality for the sake of brutality, and does Rome a disservice in my opinion.'

'And the little woman has nothing to do with it?' taunted Claudius.

'She is a victim of that man's crimes as much as our own Legions are. For Roman justice to be complete in this instance, as much as he should be executed, she needs to be repatriated to where she comes from.'

'And you will see this "justice" carried out?'

'In as much as I am given authority to do so, I will.'

'You have a point, Julian, but I wouldn't shout about it too much. I'm not sure our commanders would agree with you. As for me, I'm going to watch him die, and I hope the birds pick the flesh off him, the scum!' He spat on the ground as he spoke, then slapped Julian on the back. 'Fear not, Julian, I will tell no one of your views. Enjoy the little woman.'

Walking the long way back, Julian let his mind relive some of his childhood memories. In place of his own face, he saw the face of Leon, and he hoped he could give the boy the stability he had never had.

Chapter 4

Another month was spent at Pontus, then Julian and his men were ordered back to Bithynia. Hannah and Leon accompanied him. Gallus was only too pleased to have them along, as he was able to pass on some of his duties to both mother and son. Leon was eager to please and quick to learn, and Hannah was a better cook than Gallus was! If she grieved over the death of her 'husband', she didn't show it. For Leon, any sadness he may have felt at the death of his father was overcome by his admiration of the Roman centurion who had shown them mercy.

At Bithynia, they were billeted within the garrison of the Legion, and life was more orderly than Hannah had ever experienced since leaving her father's household. Leon thrived in it, and became very useful to Julian.

An auxiliary was being sent to Tarsus on official business, and Julian was able to send letters to Centurion Cornelius, by whose side he had served the year before. He asked if Cornelius could possibly make a search in the area to see if any of Hannah's family were still living there. He included all the details Hannah had given him, and they waited to see if anything came back.

Bithynia was stable, with little trouble for the soldiers to sort out, so their main job was one of escort duties. Julian's men were now all seasoned soldiers, so ongoing training was at a minimum, and they used the time for maintenance and taking extra leave.

One evening, Julian was relaxing by the shore of the Black Sea when Leon slowly walked up to him. 'Sir, may I speak with you?'

Julian looked up at the lad silhouetted against the sea and the setting sun. 'You may, Leon. What's on your mind?'

'Sir, we have been under your care for almost three months. I have never seen my mother so much at peace. I've watched you. Why are you so strong, but also kind? Your men do what you tell them, but I have never heard you shout at them like the other centurions do. Why is that?'

'Sit down, Leon, and I'll try to explain. Some people think that to be strong, they have to be tough and mean, and that strength comes from their muscle and their ability to overpower others physically. To prove it, they put on a front, and act cruelly. My father was like that: he was hard, cruel and brutal. At your age, I feared him and hated him. I hated him for what he did to the women in our household. I hated him for how he treated us children, and most of all I hated him for what he did to my sister. I wanted to get away from home as soon as I could, and in the army I saw order, loyalty, trust and justice. The army became the family I never had.' As he was talking, he dug his hands into the sand and let it run through his fingers.

'Yes, you have to be tough at times, but you can do that without cruelty or humiliation. You have to command respect, but you can do that by showing respect and shouldering the load along with others. It's worked for me, so why shout when you can save your voice?' He smiled at the boy as he spoke, and a deep concern was born in him for this fatherless child.

Leon pulled his knees up to his chin, and he hugged himself. 'Is it true you were a gladiator?'

'No, Leon, I wasn't a gladiator, but my father was, and he made me train like one. That wasn't all bad, as it helped me as a soldier to move and duck and dive better than most. But I didn't want to kill for the sake of killing, and for the pleasure of others who watched. My father may have won many fights in the arena, but he lost his soul. And a man without a soul is less than half a real man; in fact, I wonder if he is a man at all.'

'Could I be a soldier, Sir?'

'Do you want to be a soldier?'

'I don't know. I don't want to be like my father, but somehow he did think he was doing right. He wasn't like your father – he wasn't all bad. He just felt it was wrong that Rome took all our money in taxes and stole the crops from our fields. He said that the Romans should be in Rome and should let us do what we liked. He was fighting for what he thought was right. You are the first Roman I have got to know, and you have been kind to us. But some of your soldiers were going to rape my mother, before you stopped them. Why did they do that – that can't be right, can it?'

Julian looked at the boy sitting beside him. He couldn't give an honest answer to his question, or at least an answer that satisfied him, let alone this boy. He was about to say something, but Leon spoke again. 'Sir, was my father crucified? Did you crucify my father?'

Diverting his eyes from the boy's, Julian stared out at sea, and felt sick inside. A loathing began to well up, almost like the feeling of becoming physically sick. He loved army life, but he did not love what it sometimes stood for. How could he tell this child that his army 'family', this wonderful glorious Roman army, had derived pleasure from driving nails through the hands and feet of his father, then stood laughing as they watched him die? How could he say that he stood for truth and justice when he was part of a nation that gloried in despicable cruelty?

Leon repeated his question, his voice barely a whisper: 'Sir, did you crucify my father?'

Julian forced himself to face the boy. If he was any sort of a man, he had to face this child. 'No, Leon, I did not crucify your father.'

As he spoke, this battle-hardened Roman centurion had a tear in his eye. 'Your father was crucified, Leon, and I have to admit to you that I am part of a system that thinks it was right to kill him that way. You said I was strong, but I am not strong enough to stop what I believe is a barbaric act. I wish with all my heart that it was not so, and I am truly sorry that your father had to die in that awful way.'

Julian was shocked at himself, for he could not stop the tears flowing down his cheeks. He had not cried since he was half the age of this fatherless boy in front of him. He cried: he cried for his sister, for his other brothers and sisters he had not really known, for the woman who had been his mother. He cried because he was angry with his own father, angry with the system, angry with himself and perhaps – and this surprised him most of all – he was very angry with the gods!

The fatherless child, kneeling on the sand, put his skinny arms around the broad shoulders of this strong man who was crying like a baby, and he cried too. Julian enveloped the boy in his strong arms, and they held on to each other for a very long time.

Eventually, Julian moved and held Leon at arm's length. 'Forgive me, son,' was all he could say.

'Please forgive my father, Julian Sir', replied the child. The question in Julian's mind was, who was the most grown up?

'Leon, I will do everything within my power to restore you to your mother's family, and maybe one day I will be able to answer your questions. Perhaps it has something to do with the gods, I don't know, but until then, I promise you on my soldier's oath that I will defend both you and your mother.'

'Thank you, Sir.'

They sat a while longer and watched the sun go down over the sea, then Julian got to his feet and pulled Leon up with him. 'Young lion, I think it's time we went looking for food – and I hope it's cooked by your mother, and not Gallus!' They both laughed.

Chapter 5

At the garrison, Hannah had indeed prepared food, and they sat on benches at the table in the courtyard. Gallus was not around, and Julian remembered he had let him take some leave. Hannah was surprised when she saw her twelve-year-old son walk into the house side by side with a Roman centurion more than six feet tall, talking to him as if they were old comrades. In the shadowy half-light, she noticed that Julian's face was blotchy and wondered if he was going down with some common bug, but said nothing.

She brought a stew to the table, placed it beside a plate of rye bread, and sat down and waited for Julian to help himself first. When he didn't move, she looked at him enquiringly. 'You want me to dish yours out, Sir?'

'No, Hannah, I want you to ask your God's blessing on the food before we eat, if you don't mind, then I will be only too pleased to help myself to what smells wonderful.'

'You want me to pray to my God for you?'

'Yes, Hannah, I want you to pray to your God. He is one I don't know, so I don't know how to address Him.'

'Back home, my father would ask a blessing on our food. When he did so he would cover his head, either with a cap or with his right hand.'

Leon took the lead and placed his right hand on his head and shut his eyes. Julian did the same, and Hannah remembered the blessing her father had used more than thirteen years before. 'Our praise to You, Eternal, our God, Sovereign of the Universe, who brings forth bread from the earth. Amen.'

Julian and Leon joined in together, 'Amen.'

Hannah had tears unashamedly running down her face as Julian took the ladle. 'Hannah, can I help you to some of this wonderful stew?'

She lifted her plate towards him, as more tears followed. Never, since she had left home, had she been treated with such respect – and by a Gentile.

'Leon, can I help you?' Julian asked.

Leon brought his plate close. 'As much as you like, Sir!' he said, with a mischievous grin.

Filling his own plate, Julian took a wedge of the rye bread and filled his mouth with the food. For him, it felt like he was at the table with the family he had never had.

Having lit the oil lamps after the meal, Leon put himself to bed, leaving Julian and his mother together at the table. The flickering lamplight sparkled in her dark eyes, as she sat at the other side of the table from Julian, and a contented smiled lingered at the corners of her mouth. Julian's blue eyes reflected the light, too, but his focus was on a knot in the wood of the table top.

She dared to speak. 'Sir,' she started, but he interrupted her.

'When we are on our own, please call me Julian.'

She started again; he was still studying the knot in the table. 'Julian, if I speak out of place, please forgive me, but when you came back this evening with Leon I thought your face looked as if you were unwell, and then... well, I mean, and then you asked me to say a Jewish blessing on our food. I don't understand.'

He looked up, and his heart jumped at the light in her eyes. 'No, I wasn't sick. Well, not sick in the way you were thinking. The truth is, Hannah, your son made me cry.' He smiled as he said this, to reassure her that Leon had done nothing wrong.

'He made you cry?' She couldn't believe what she was hearing from this mountain of a man who had authority over soldiers. How could her skinny son make him cry?

'It was the first time I have cried since I was about six years old. I learned at a young age that it was better not to cry, for it only brought punishment and anger. Today, down by the sea, Leon asked me questions which I found difficult to answer. I hated the truth I had to tell him. He is a fine boy, Hannah; you can be rightly proud of him for who he is, considering the life you have had to live.'

'What question did he ask you, that made you cry?'

'He asked if his father had been crucified, and whether I did it.'

She was silent, and a flicker of fear crossed her face. 'He asked you that?'

'Yes, he's a brave boy to dare to ask that of those who hold power over his life.'

'How did you answer him?'

'Truthfully. Yes, his father was crucified, and no, I didn't do it.'

'And that made you cry?'

'I hate crucifixion! It's barbaric and an insult to all that's just. I remember my own father, and he lived a barbaric life. When I was Leon's age, he took me to watch brutal sport and then lost my sister in a wager. But one barbaric act does not make room for another. Lawless barbarism does not excuse legal barbarism! I wept today for my sister, Leon's father and the father I had. Why, in whatever god's name, does it have to happen?' There was fire in his eyes, and it wasn't just the reflection of the oil lamps, and he thumped the table as he spoke.

'And the request for a Jewish blessing on the food? Was that because of what you felt today?'

'When I was weeping, Leon put his arms round me and we wept together. I embraced him, and it was like a father and son should be – holding each other, even when you don't understand life. Knowing you have someone to stand with you, and you're not alone. Your boy turned my little world on its head today, and I figured if this half-Jewish boy could do that, then a blessing from the Jewish God wouldn't go amiss!'

Hannah looked at his hands as they rested on the table. Large, strong, battle-scarred hands. Yet they were hands that had held and comforted her son, the son of the enemy of this man. Hands that had gently pulled her to her feet when she had bowed before him, and hands that had just served her with dinner rather than being served.

Slowly she moved her own hands over the table to cover his. He did not move his away, as she searched his face with her eyes. 'Thank you, Julian. I have never received such kindness, even from my own kinsmen. You must have been sent by God to rescue me.'

He turned his hands over and held hers. 'You may be right, but if so, He did it without my knowing. So from here on, we must be careful how we tread; perhaps there is more at stake than just our own lives?'

He squeezed her hands and released them, as he rose from the table. 'Sleep well, Hannah. May your God be with you.'

'I shall pray that He will be with you too.'

Julian walked to his room, leaving her sitting in the lamplight, her heart beating faster than normal.

Chapter 6

Another month passed before any word came from Tarsus. Cornelius had done some searching, and he was as sure as he could be that an old man and his wife whom he had found fitted the details Julian had sent. If they were her parents, they were living near the docks at the south end of the town. It sounded as if they had got themselves back on their feet and were able to provide for themselves in their ageing years. Cornelius, being discreet with his enquiries, had not disclosed to the couple that he knew anything of their daughter, but he did find out that they had lost a daughter about the time Hannah had been abducted.

A posting for centurions in Caesarea on the Mediterranean coast was coming up, and although centurions were not usually given a choice as to where they were sent, for this posting the commanders were of a more flexible mind. Many Romans found the Jews difficult to deal with, and as this assignment would mean duties that would take them often into Jerusalem, a centurion with an understanding of Jewish customs would fit, since the locals were known to be rebellious. The commander in Bithynia, knowing that Julian shared his living arrangements with a Jewish woman, summoned him to appear before him.

'Centurion Julian, it has come to my notice that you cohabit with a Jewish woman.'

Julian was about to try to explain how this arrangement was worked, but the commander raised his hand. 'Let me finish, before you speak! Whatever your relationship is with this woman, I care not. What I do care about, however, is that there is a posting for a centurion coming up in Caesarea, and I know many would not be happy to go because they do not understand the Jewish customs, or their invisible god. This would be a long-term posting. For one who could adapt to their customs, it could be a very pleasant position, as well as being of great value to the peace of our Empire. What do you think, Julian, would you be interested?' He added, as an afterthought, 'I could order you to go, anyway.'

Julian stood to attention. 'Sir, the woman who shares my quarters is under my protection, because of the nature of her circumstances. However, it is true – I have learned a great deal from her about the Jewish way of life. I have found it most fascinating, and I do hold a regard for their customs and way of life. I would count it a privilege to serve the Empire in Caesarea and the surrounding territories. If it would meet with your approval, I could travel with my men to Tarsus, which is the home of the Jewish woman, and return her to the family she was abducted from many years ago, then sail over to Caesarea from there.'

The commander rose to his feet and extended his hand. 'You have my authority to do so. Make the necessary arrangements. Your entire *Centuria* will travel with you. Make preparations to travel as soon as possible. And yes, go through Galatia, Cappadocia to Tarsus. You will probably have to winter there before you can sail to Caesarea. Dismissed!'

Julian saluted and marched from the garrison headquarters, trying hard not to let a smile escape from his mouth. This was his dream posting!

Back in his own quarters, he quickly called his men together and gave out his orders. Like a well-oiled battering ram, they set to work and prepared for the long journey. The auxiliaries sorted out provisions, while the soldiers packed up their own equipment. Messengers were sent ahead to the required places, with instructions that were to be carried out post haste.

Having set all things in motion, Julian called Gallus and ordered him to follow him into his living area. He sat Hannah and Leon down and, in front of Gallus, explained what was afoot. 'This means that in a few weeks' time you could be back with your own family once more,' explained Julian.

It took some time before this news could properly register with mother and son. She would see her father and mother again, after almost fourteen years, and Leon would meet his grandparents for the first time.

Travelling with a Roman *Centuria* of soldiers and auxiliaries was hard graft, and sapped the strength of those who were not fully fit. Hannah had been used to hiding and moving about with her 'husband', but the discipline and relentless marching of the army was much harder. Julian made provision for her to ride on a pack mule, but it was still hard going. Winter was getting close, so it was a great relief when, five weeks later, they arrived in Tarsus.

On the journey, over a few evenings when Hannah wasn't too weary, at Julian's request she told him as much about the Law of Moses as she could remember, and explained some of their customs and feast days. Julian drank it in and had a thirst for more.

It was good for Julian to be reunited with Cornelius, and housing had been made ready for them. Hannah and Leon had rooms to themselves, close to Julian and Gallus.

After two days of rest, Julian took Hannah and Leon to the market in Tarsus. He had been in enough Roman houses to know what was recognised as quality clothing, and pointed garments out to Hannah.

'You need new clothes to meet your parents. The ones you have, after our long journey, are little more than rags.'

She had never been taken to a market before to buy new clothes for herself or her son. Mostly she had worn clothes stolen by others, or taken from dead bodies, and she was overwhelmed, not knowing where to start. She looked down at herself and knew that Julian was right. Standing beside a Roman centurion whose uniform was clean and well kept with a red cloak draped from his broad shoulders made her feel it even more.

He took a long gown from a rack and held it up against her. 'I think you will look fit for an Emperor in this. Go behind those curtains and try it on.'

She did as she was told, hardly able to breathe. The trader's wife, having received a nod from Julian, followed her with undergarments and more gowns. Julian picked up a tunic for Leon, and the boy quickly pushed his head through the opening of an undershirt and then donned the tunic. By the time Hannah appeared, dressed in the new clothes, Leon was standing like a man with his head held up high and his arms folded across his chest. She laughed at her son, who seemed the most handsome boy in the marketplace. Self-consciously, she moved towards Julian and stood in front of him. The wife of the stallholder had an eye for business, and knew it was in their best interests to make the most of Hannah. She had brushed Hannah's hair and arranged the clothes to make the most of her figure, and the transformation was amazing.

Julian could not believe his eyes, and stared at her. 'Venus has indeed blessed you with outstanding beauty!' The trader was quick to see the attention she was drawing, and his wife whispered in Hannah's ear, 'Do a twirl, dear; that always gets them going,' and she placed her hands on Hannah's shoulders and moved her around.

Hannah could see the approval on Julian's face, and she coloured. 'Stand beside your mother, Leon,' Julian said, as he gave the boy a gentle push. Hannah reached out her hand, and Leon took it. Clapping his hands, the trader voiced his own approval, and the small crowd that had gathered joined in.

'We will take them all,' Julian said, 'plus an extra tunic for Leon and that garment over there for Hannah.'

Hannah was about to go back behind the curtain and change into her old clothes, but Julian stopped her. 'Keep on what you have. Our friend here will no doubt be happy to dispose of those rags you have left.' A request he was only too willing to carry out.

Julian paid the man, then they moved on to purchase new footwear. People's heads turned as they saw a Roman centurion approaching, clad in his red cloak, with an elegant and slender, tall, dark-haired woman and a well-dressed young man. Julian felt more like Caesar than a centurion!

'I think it's time we found your parents, Hannah. Come, Cornelius said he believes they live this way.'

Hannah's emotions were all over the place. She had never been the centre of attention before, never been looked at by a man without lust in his eyes, and this man she had come to respect like no other. And she was about to meet her parents, who would have given her up for dead many years ago. Her stomach turned as they went round a corner into a street that Cornelius said they lived in.

They stopped in front of a modest, single-storey house. It was clean, and she noticed the door was new. Julian could see she was trembling. 'Hannah, I'm sorry if I've rushed things. Is it too much for you to take in?'

'No. Whichever way we do it, it will be emotional. Will you go first and explain?'

Before he could knock, the door cracked open and a small voice enquired, 'Sir, have we not obeyed some edict that we should have? We try and keep up with all that is required of us.'

The old woman inside had seen the centurion standing by their door and was fearful that they were in trouble. She opened the door wider, and could see a well-dressed woman and a boy standing behind him.

Smiling, Julian assured her that she was not in any trouble with the authorities. 'All is well, good lady, have no fear. Is your husband at home, for I have news for you that I think you will both want to hear?'

'If you will come through, Sir, he is sitting out the back making the most of the early winter sun.'

They followed her through the two-roomed house, Julian ducking his head as he entered. In a small yard at the back sat a man who, for his years, looked fit and healthy. On seeing the centurion, he quickly rose to his feet, and some of the negative fears that his wife had experienced stirred in his stomach.

Julian was used to this reaction and quickly did his best to counteract it. 'We come in peace, Sir, and have only what I believe is good news for you.'

He needed to say no more, for the old man had seen the woman standing slightly behind Julian. He rubbed his eyes and looked again at the woman, and then up at the centurion. 'Hannah?' was all he could say, in a raspy voice.

The centurion nodded, and stood to one side to allow Hannah to move towards her parents. The old woman put her hand over her mouth and shook her head in disbelief. 'But it can't be, she...'

'Yes, Mother, I am Hannah.' And all three fell into a heap around each other's necks.

Julian stood back with his hands on Leon's shoulders, and whispered in his ear, 'Give them a few minutes, then we'll introduce you to your grandparents.'

Old Joel, through his hazy vision, caught sight of the red cloak on the centurion standing in his backyard and remembered the protocol. 'Sir! Forgive an old man. My hospitality is lacking. Welcome to our humble home. I find this meeting overwhelming, and am not sure how to respond to a centurion of the Roman Imperial Army.'

Julian held up his hand. 'You are responding in the only way I wish to see. But there is more. See! This fine young man is your grandson.' He moved Leon forward, and Joel held the boy's face between his hands.

'My grandson? Are you then, Sir, my son-in-law?'

For a moment, Julian was caught unawares, as he had not thought of Hannah's parents presuming him to be so.

Hannah walked over to Julian. 'This, my father, my mother, is Julian, the man who saved our lives and treated us with the greatest care and respect. His idea of Roman justice is to restore abducted daughters to their long-lost parents. Today, he has fully fulfilled his word to Leon and to me.'

Hannah's mother could take in no more, and sank down on the stool by her husband. 'My daughter, after all these years – and a grandson! I can't begin to take it in. How? A Roman centurion in my home as protector to my daughter?'

Hannah brought Leon over to his grandmother, and hugs and weeping followed.

Joel took Julian by the elbow and guided him back into the house. He fussed about and found an old leather wineskin containing a vintage wine he had been saving for special occasions. He knew there would be no occasion more special than this one. Finding some cups, he handed them to the centurion, and they went back outside to join the others.

They drank a toast all round and, at a time Julian judged to be the most fitting, he excused himself and left the family. The rest of the day and well into the night they spent telling their stories, laughing and weeping together.

Back at the barracks, Julian sat by the fire Gallus had lit in the courtyard and warmed himself against the cooler air of the evening. He had fulfilled his word. What now? In a few short weeks, he and his men would sail to Caesarea and the 'Venus-blessed' woman would be with him no more. Did he regret not taking advantage of her while he had had the chance? No, he was content that he had done what a true Roman centurion should do. Would he miss her? Yes, he would miss her and he would miss her son.

He pictured Leon kneeling with him on the beach of the Black Sea. A bond had been forged that day, and Leon was to him like his own son.

He would miss him.

Shaking himself, he called to mind his oath: 'I swear that I shall faithfully execute all that the Emperor commands, I shall never desert the service, and I shall not seek to avoid death for the Roman state.'

Leaving them would be a lot like death. When he had taken that vow, he had been saying his life was now not his own, but was on loan to the Roman Empire. Standing up in front of the fire, his face lit by the flames, he saluted the Roman insignia that hung on the wall and made his declaration again, but this time he knew more of the cost involved.

'I shall never desert my service, nor seek to avoid death – even the death of losing Hannah and my boy – for the Roman state.'

His mind was clear; he was first and foremost an enlisted soldier in the Roman Imperial Army.

Chapter 7

Joel escorted his daughter and grandson back to the Roman barracks. Julian was not in his quarters when they arrived, but faithful Gallus was there to meet them, having been given orders to receive them and see to their needs. Seeing that Julian was not there, Hannah and Leon retired to bed, and Gallus escorted Joel safely back to his own home.

Life in the Roman army was run for the benefit of the state, not the individual soldier. The winter was proving to be later in coming and, owing to the calm weather, ships commandeered by the army were willing to sail to Caesarea within the week. Julian welcomed this news with relief. He had renewed his oath and his mind was as set as the day he had stood beside his father in the arena. Now he wanted to shorten the agony of seeing Hannah and Leon, and get on with the job at hand.

Hannah and Leon moved from the Roman barracks into the family home. It was a tight squeeze but it was more than compensated for by the love they could show to each other after all they had endured.

A few days later, Julian was walking down to the harbour to inspect the ships. He felt a hand on his arm and swung around, his right hand automatically on the hilt of his sword. He was surprised to find Joel standing beside him.

'Have you a few minutes to spare, Sir?'

Julian nodded and they entered an inn on the quayside and found seats in the corner.

'You, Sir, have been the most inspirational Roman I have ever met. Your integrity is beyond that of any man I have ever known in my own race, let alone among the Gentiles. You have given me back my daughter, whom I had thought had died many years ago. My wife and I will never cease to be thankful for all your kindness. I know, Sir, that you are planning to sail within the week. Sir, could you tell me your intentions concerning my daughter, and my grandson?'

'My intentions, Joel? They have not changed since I first met them. My intention then was to restore them to their rightful family, and that is what I have done.'

'You have no feeling for them of a more personal nature?'

Julian controlled his face, but his eyes were moist. 'I have the deepest feeling for your daughter and her son. He is to me like my own son, but I have an order to obey and must leave for Caesarea.'

'You would wish to take them with you?'

'You want me to do that, Joel? Would you really want to lose them again in such a short space of time?'

'No, I wish for her to be the one who would close my eyes in death, but that would be selfish of me.'

'And of me if I were to take them away, Joel. Perhaps, when she has closed your eyes when you die, if she still wanted to find me, I will be waiting.' He stood up. 'I need to view the ships, but, Joel, I promise I will see you all before I sail. I appreciate you talking to me like this.' He left the old man and boarded the first ship, as Joel walked home.

Joel entered the house, and Hannah questioned him as to where he had been. On telling of his conversation with Julian to her and Leon he said, 'He loves you, Hannah, of that I have no doubt. But he is first a soldier. You could go with him, but a Jew married to a Roman would not be an easy thing to live as in Caesarea and the surrounding area. Leon he sees as his own son, but he would not want to take you both away from us so soon.'

The ships were ready by the end of the week and, as promised, Julian made his way to the humble house in the street next to the harbour. Hannah's mother opened the door and almost suffocated him with a motherly embrace. Regaining his breath, he gave a manly hug to Joel and then went out into the yard at the back to find Hannah and Leon. Hannah stood on her own, dressed in the clothes he had bought her the week before. Her hair was flowing in the breeze, and the same breeze moulded the gown to her body.

He saw Venus!

She looked at him, not knowing what to say, and slowly they narrowed the gap between them, then she held on to him with every ounce of strength in her body, 'You have to go?' she whispered.

'I have to go.'

'Let me come with you.'

'If, when you have closed your parents' eyes in death, you still want me, I will keep myself for you. But your place now is to stay here with them.' He kissed her on the lips then stepped back. 'Where's Leon?' he asked.

'He was here just now. I guess he left us to be on our own,' she said quietly, as tears cascaded down her face. They entered the house, and suddenly Leon stood in the doorway with a bundle under his arm.

'Please, Mother, let me go with Julian. He is my father now. Grandfather and Grandmother, it is good to be with you, but my leaving will not be much of a wrench for you, as you never knew I existed. I will miss you, Mother, but I want to serve with Julian in Caesarea.'

Her heart was torn, but she made no protest. 'If you're sure that's what you want, go in peace, my son, and may the Lord God Almighty be with you.'

Hannah hugged them one last time. Somehow, Leon going with Julian helped. It was the feeling that a real part of her was going with Julian, and she felt it to be a comfort. She knew he couldn't be in better hands, and Julian was the father she would have wished for Leon from birth.

'I will come to you when the time is right, my darling,' Hannah said in his ear, as he passed her on his way through the door.

Father, mother and daughter stood by the harbour wall, as a Roman centurion stood in the bow of the ship with his arms around the shoulders of his new servant, his adopted son. The wind filled the sails, and the part of being a soldier Julian dreaded the most was emphasised by the tossing in his heart.

He hated sailing!

Leon found he was a natural sailor, and loved every minute. He was up helping the sailors in any way he could. It boosted his confidence, as he was able to revel in the swelling of the sea while his centurion-father-master spent most of the journey leaning over the side of the ship.

Two weeks at sea was more than enough for Julian, and never was he more glad than to step on ground that didn't move up and down. He'd lost almost a stone in weight as he had eaten so little food. A contingent from the garrison was there to greet them, and the state of Julian did little to impress the centurion who met them.

Saluting, Julian said, 'I am a soldier before I am a sailor.'

'That, Julian, is very evident! However, we have received glowing reports about you and are glad to have you aboard!'

'By "aboard", I take it you mean ashore,' Julian answered dryly.

Slapping him on the back, the centurion laughed. 'The ground will become still after a while, I assure you. Come, I will take you to your quarters. I take it your men know what is required of them?'

Julian nodded, but to avoid any confusion he mustered enough strength to raise his voice and shout from the harbour wall, 'My men! You know your duties. Gather up your equipment and follow us in a military manner to the garrison.'

Turning to Gallus, he said, 'Take care of my horse, and keep an eye on Leon. I need to walk to find my legs again.' Gallus gave a slight bow of his head and, rounding up Leon, walked the horse off the ship, and they made their way inland.

Fully recovered from his seasickness, Julian ate a hearty breakfast and felt ready to take up his new posting. In the parade area, his men sprang to their positions before he gave the order. 'Tomorrow we get back into training. Twenty miles, full kit, starting at sunrise!'

None would protest openly, and few inwardly, as they too were ready for action and keen to find their land legs after the time at sea.

At sunrise, Julian rode out on his horse as eighty fully equipped soldiers plus five auxiliaries with mules stood in marching lines, ready to move off. They set out along the coast southwards, towards Joppa. There was a slight sea breeze; the road was straight for most of the way, and fairly flat. At ten miles they stopped for a break and refreshment. Some of the men were beginning to feel the stress of the march, and the auxiliaries were ordered to attend to them. Half an hour later they headed back to Caesarea and arrived at the garrison by early afternoon. Julian gave them the rest of the day off, and sent any who were unfit to the medical wing. He returned to his quarters to find that Leon had worked hard as his valet, and all his personal belongings were placed where Julian would have put them.

'You've done well, Leon, and must have remembered how my room was set out at Tarsus. You will make a good valet!'

Leon bowed with a smile. 'At your service, Sir!'

'Leon, I think it would be in your best interests if you were known to be my personal servant. That way you come under no military control other than mine, and it will save any confusion over who can tell you what to do. In my heart, I see you as my adopted son, and I will personally care for all your needs from my salary.'

Leon was only too glad to fit in. He was missing his mother, but, before they had been captured by Julian's men, their relationship had been subject to change without prior notice. He was fairly hardened to change in his family life.

Chapter 8

Two weeks after arriving in Caesarea, Julian was ordered to appear before Pilate, the Procurator in full control of the province of Judaea. The military presence was large, with more than 120 cavalry and almost 5,000 infantry, plus a detachment on garrison duty at Jerusalem. Pilate appointed the High Priests in Jerusalem, and controlled the Temple and its funding. The Priests' vestments were in his custody, and were released only for festivals when he took up residence in Jerusalem and brought in additional troops to patrol the city.

Julian and his men were appointed to escort Pilate and his wife to Jerusalem. They were then to travel along the Jordan to Capernaum so that Pilate could make a report as to how he found the outpost there. Then he was to travel back directly to Caesarea. Leon would be travelling with them, under the watchful eye of Gallus. Mules were loaded with extra supplies, and each man shouldered his full kit.

Travelling to escort officials was not as arduous as a training march, as the pace was slower, but it meant more days on the move. To travel the seventy miles from Caesarea to Jerusalem took five days, and they arrived in Jerusalem in the middle of the afternoon on the sixth day. He instructed his men to find their own sleeping arrangements in the barracks by the Governor's headquarters. It was his responsibility to personally escort Pilate and his wife to their quarters.

On his first meeting with the Governor, Julian was unimpressed. Pilate had considerable standing with the Senate in Rome because of his marriage to the daughter of one of the most influential senators. His bearing and manner appeared to Julian to be arrogant and, at the same time, that of someone who was insecure.

Once his duties had been fully carried out, he was glad to get back to the barracks. Julian found that Leon had again anticipated his needs, and everything was ready for him to rest. The bond between them strengthened daily.

Pilate ordered that they stay in Jerusalem for a few days, so their journey to Capernaum could be used to convey a letter to the outpost. This gave Julian time to explore the city.

Taking Gallus and Leon with him, he wandered the labyrinth of narrow back streets and then walked into the Temple area. The building was not as he had imagined it would be in comparison to the many temples he had seen in Rome. It was impressive, but lacked the statues and effigies that adorned those in Rome. The Temple area itself was large, and he, being a Gentile, was unable to go beyond the Court of the Gentiles, unless Pilate ordered it. Taking the weight off his legs, he sat on a low wall and watched Jewish worshippers entering and then leaving the Temple. His army training and survival tactics of his early home life gave him a sharp focus as he observed the movements of the people.

The humble poor silently shuffled by with as little fuss as possible, and brought pigeons for their offerings.

Those seeing themselves as important and well-to-do made a show of the animals they were bringing.

The Pharisees and the priests strutted with an air of superiority as they went about their duties. Some genuinely cared about what they were doing, alongside those who were observably in it for the position and the money.

He watched them pray, and wondered what they understood of their God. Despite the hypocrisy of some, he gained an overall sense of something greater than the worship he had been accustomed to at Rome. Who was this 'invisible God' whom they worshipped? He had seen Jews in other provinces as they attended their synagogues, and now, here at the Temple in Jerusalem, he could see something of how their worship gave them a sense of national identity and purpose.

As he left the Temple area, people moved aside to let him pass, out of fear or respect for a centurion of the occupying army. He sensed it was more out of fear.

Standing in the shadows of a doorway, Julian watched a small group of men pass without seeing him, as Gallus and Leon were standing in front. They were talking in low voices, and ducked down a narrow alleyway, giving the impression that they were plotting something.

'Leon, are you willing to risk following them to see if you can find out what they're saying?'

With a nod, Leon stepped into the semi-darkness of the alley, while Gallus quickly and silently disappeared down a parallel alley with the hope of joining Leon further down. Drawing his sword, and removing his helmet to lessen his height, Julian ducked into the alley a little way behind Leon.

After a hundred or so paces, the alley opened on to a small square. A couple of rough tables with benches on each side were set up against the opposite wall, beside an open door that led into an inn. The group of men were huddled at one table, each with a mug of beer that the landlord had just served them. Leon sat with his back towards them at the other table, and the landlord approached him. 'Want a drink?' he demanded roughly. 'If you sit at my table, boy, you pay for a drink.'

'Some water and wine, please,' Leon said, without making eye contact, and the landlord entered the inn to fetch it.

Julian kept back in the shadows of the alley, and he could see Gallus hiding in another alley to Leon's left.

The wine was brought and banged down on the table. 'Two denarii,' said the landlord, holding his hand out.

Leon paid him and added some water to the wine, trying to look as if he was half-asleep. A couple of men wandered through the square, one of whom joined the group of men and handed them a piece of parchment, then walked off. Julian caught Gallus' eye and motioned for him to walk out and collect Leon from the table. As Gallus was not in military uniform he didn't look out of place, so he causally strolled past Leon and beckoned for him to follow. Leon got the message and emptied his cup, then stood up and walked off. As he passed the group of men, one stuck his foot out and tripped him up, sending him sprawling on the ground. Another was on his back before he had time to move, then a third stood on his arm and thrust a dagger in front of his face.

Julian held his nerve but tightened his grip on his sword, ready to spring out if things got worse. Gallus had disappeared down another alley but, understanding his master, paused after a couple of paces.

With the knife-point touching Leon's neck, the man on his back stood up and grabbed both of the boy's shoulders, pulling Leon to his feet. The one who had tripped him up ran his hands quickly over Leon's body, checking for weapons. Finding none, he stood back, and they pushed Leon's face down onto the table and held him there. Holding his nerve, Leon said nothing, but his mind went back to the many times he had been roughed up by those who had moved around with his father, if they hadn't recognised him.

'Where you from, boy?' one of the men demanded. 'You don't look like you belong around here. Too smart a tunic for the likes of us.'

'Tarsus,' Leon said, thinking it would be better to be truthful, as he knew his accent would give him away.

'Tarsus?' said the one who hadn't moved from the table in all the commotion. 'Let me get a better look at him.'

The one forcing Leon's face onto the table held his arms in a vice-like grip and yanked him upright, so he could be scrutinised. 'I lived in Tarsus, and you sound like you come from there. What're you doing so far from home, lad?'

Thinking on his feet, Leon answered, 'Been a cabin boy on a merchant ship, and landed in Caesarea three weeks ago. We had merchandise that was bound for Jerusalem, and they let me come to see the city. I'd heard so much about the Temple.' His answers were, for the most part, truthful, and it seemed to satisfy his captors. The grip on his arms was less, but he was still held with little chance of breaking free – the dagger still only a few inches from his face.

The one who had lived in Tarsus was looking intently at Leon's face. 'What's your name, boy?'

Leon looked at him before he answered, and his heart almost stopped. He was looking into the eyes of a man who had joined with his father in the uprising at Pontus and the surrounding area.

'Leon,' he answered simply.

'Leon the Lion, whelp of my old partner in rebellion, Celsus. I don't believe it! I was told you were all wiped out by the Romans. How did you get away?'

'Azor!' Leon exclaimed, as if he were being reunited with a long-lost family friend. 'I thought I knew your face. They crucified my father, and I escaped with my mother. We went into hiding, and then worked our way back to Tarsus. My mother found her parents and she's staying with them, as they're almost too old to care for themselves.'

Azor nodded to the man holding him. The hands on his arms released their hold, and the dagger at his throat was put away. 'Landlord, bring some more of your wine for our young friend here.'

He turned to the rest of the gang. 'This, my friends, is the lion cub of a true saboteur and fighter for our cause. His father struck down more Roman scum than any other man I had the privilege to fight with.'

The landlord brought out the wine, and Azor offered a toast to Leon's dead father: 'To Celsus, the Roman-killer – may he rest in peace.' They drank and banged their cups down on the table.

Mark, the one who had tripped him up, was not totally satisfied with having Leon at their table. 'Why were you wandering about here on your own? This side of the city is not the usual path for Temple visitors.'

'I was given too much to drink last night, and my head was none too clear this morning. I wandered off and got a bit mixed up with all these alleys. This was the first place I'd seen where I could have a sit-down and, as you know, the landlord here won't let you sit unless you drink.'

Satisfied, Mark landed a punch on Leon's arm. 'Sorry I tripped you, son; just you can't be too careful when you find a stranger in the back streets.'

'You intend to follow in your father's footsteps, Leon?' Azor asked. 'You must hate them for killing your father in the way they did.'

'The mention of crucifixion makes my blood run cold. Sometimes I wake up in the middle of the night covered in sweat. But with all the effort my father put in, did it do any good? What did it achieve apart from getting him crucified?'

The group of men glanced at each other before Azor said, 'Leon, your father was a fighter first, and family came second. I can understand how you feel. But if we don't become a thorn in the side of Rome, we'll never know freedom. We're fighting to avenge the death of people like your father, and to bring freedom to our nation. In memory of your father, think seriously about joining us as you get older. Now get yourself back to your fellow seamen before they wonder where you are and bring attention to us.'

Leon left the table and walked back along the alley he'd come out of. Julian, who'd watched it all but was too far away to hear, quickly stepped back and walked ahead of Leon. Gallus was well on his way down a different path, circling around so that he came up behind Leon to check if he was being followed. He kept his distance, and saw that no one was behind.

Julian walked back to the barracks, with Leon keeping him in sight as he walked slowly behind him.

Chapter 9

In the security of the Roman garrison, Leon leaned against the wall of the building that was assigned to Julian and his servants. He felt his knees sag and he sank slowly to the floor with his back against the wall. Julian hurried over to him, shouting orders to Gallus, 'Get some cold water, and bring it over here.'

Gallus had already anticipated this and was on his way. Julian, crouching down beside his servant, placed a hand on his shoulder. 'Take it easy, Leon, deep breaths. You kept your nerve and somehow convinced them you were not a threat. I'm sorry I put you through that; I should never have asked you to do it.'

Taking a long drink of the water Gallus offered, Leon looked at Julian as a wry smile spread over his face, 'All in the line of duty, Sir! But I didn't do too bad, did I? I knew you were there if I needed help.'

'You did better than "not bad"! You handled yourself like a professional,' was Julian's reply. 'But I could have got you killed. Even if both Gallus and I had come to your rescue they could have killed you before we closed the gap. I was wrong to have sent you to spy on your own people. Do you want to tell us what they're planning? I'll respect your decision if you'd rather not.'

Leon told them everything that had been said, finishing up with, 'If I went back, I could pretend to want to join them, and find out more.'

'No! You're too young, and it wouldn't be long before they found out you travelled here under Roman protection. We would gain nothing – only your death. I may send others to see if they can gain the confidence of the landlord, but you will be serving me here, you understand?' Julian spoke with authority, and Leon understood his words were not to be questioned.

'It does bring up another question, Leon, one you'll need to think about. Rome is in control of the Jewish homeland. Your people are under our rule, and what is decided in Rome is what will happen here. I am a Roman centurion with orders to enforce the will of Rome, by whatever means considered necessary. For you to serve Rome in any way as you get older may be seen by your fellow countrymen as the act of a traitor.'

Was the question he asked just for Leon? In his mind, he had his own questions as to the rights and wrongs of all that was done in the name of Rome. He knew the old adage, 'Ours is not to reason why, ours is but to do and die,' and for all its faults, he would honour the oath he had sworn when he enlisted. The army had given him a good life, and he was not about to change his overall loyalty. But he questioned some of the practices, especially crucifixion. For that reason he wanted Leon to know his own mind in what he felt was right for him to do.

'I'm half-Jew, half-Greek. My father used my mother and, although at times he showed her a little kindness, his life did nothing to endear me to the cause of the Jewish nation. My whole life, until we were captured by you, had been one of hiding, killing and running. You've been the only man who has shown me something I want to be. Rome killed my father, but my father wanted to kill Rome, even if Rome to him was a soldier, a man, a woman or a child. Is that the way God wants us to be? If our God is all that I've been told He is, then my father's way was no more right than the Roman way. Do I have to choose between killing for Rome or killing for Jerusalem?'

Leon's eyes were searching the face of the man who sat beside him, the one who had saved his mother and did not abuse her, the one whose allegiance was with the army that had crucified his father. 'What is the truth, Julian?'

The strong, experienced Roman centurion watched the face of the boy he loved as his own, and whispered, 'I wish I knew, Leon, I wish I knew.'

Orders came for them to move on to Capernaum, so Julian passed on to his superiors all the information that Leon had gleaned from his time at the inn. The matter was no longer in their hands, and would be followed up as was seen fit. Julian and his men made ready and set out on the ninety-mile trek to Capernaum.

In the Jordan valley, the road was good, as the terrain was reasonably flat and the Roman road made the surface level and easy for marching. Gallus and Leon herded the pack mules and Julian rode his horse, surveying the countryside from his vantage point. The incident with the plotters at the inn had galvanised his mind, and he was under no illusion about the fact they were not loved by the indigenous populace of the country.

When setting up camp, he doubled the guard and slept with his sword close by his side. On the fourth day, late in the afternoon, they approached a narrowing in the road as it passed over some rocky terrain, and to Julian it looked like a perfect place for an ambush. He alerted the leaders of his *Centuria* and they changed formation, ready for action. The men fell silent as they marched, and the leading

Contubernium entered the narrow part of the road overshadowed by rocks and scrub. Julian sat upright in his saddle and scanned each side. To his right, the side of the river Jordan, he caught a flash of light reflected off a weapon.

'Split to the sides, and attack!' he ordered, before the waiting ambush had time to mount their offensive.

'Units, advance!' he shouted, as he rode with his spear lowered.

Clearing a few low boulders, his mount landed on top of a band of armed men, confused by the sudden arrival of a warhorse and rider. Julian's spear found its mark, and he wheeled round to strike with his sword, as two tried to escape back into the rocks away from the road. His men were quick to seize the advantage and, with shields held high and spears and swords ready, they pushed forward in a V formation, then fanned out on each side of the road.

Those in the ambush were outnumbered and totally overpowered by the military superiority of the Roman fighting machine. Within the space of half an hour a stillness hung over the area. Julian marshalled his troops and asked for an account of the fighting. None of his men had been lost; about twenty were wounded, but only two seriously. Twelve prisoners had been taken and twenty-two lay dead. A number had retreated and run off, or hid in the surrounding area, licking their wounds.

Gallus attended to Julian's horse, as its front leg had received a deep cut, and the pack mules were tethered together to prevent them running off. The dead were laid out, and any identification taken. Leon walked over and stood by one. It was the body of the man who had tripped him up at the inn – Mark. 'They meant what they said. Gallus, they wanted to be a thorn in the side of Rome.'

Gallus looked and nodded. 'A lethal game to play, Leon, and I prefer to be on the side of Rome.'

With the identification taken from the bodies, the dead were stripped and then buried in a clearing not far from the road. They marched on, so as to be in more open country before setting up camp for the night.

Julian didn't push then too far or too fast, and at the earliest suitable spot they set up camp. It was on the banks of the Jordan, and several of the soldiers took the opportunity to swim in the river. Julian inspected the wounded and offered them extra wine and rations from the supply carried by the mules. Again, the guard was doubled for the night, and the fires were kept well lit around the edges of the encampment.

At daybreak, Julian assessed the condition of the wounded, and made the decision to rest the men for another day. He allowed them to swim in the Jordan, but only ten at a time, so that they would not be caught should a counter-attack be mounted against them. Sitting by the water's edge, Julian took in the surrounding countryside and liked what he saw. The Jordan was flowing, but not in flood, and the bank was lush and green.

Leon joined him. 'You're a good centurion to be with, Julian. How did you spot the ambush?'

'Training and past experience, Leon. You learn to read the countryside and weigh up the risks. I know some of the men can be envious of me riding while they walk, but it serves not only for my benefit, but for theirs as well. Being that much higher gives a better vantage point for spotting trouble ahead. When I saw the narrowing of the road and the terrain we were going to pass through, I knew it was a good place to man an ambush. The sunlight caught the blade of a sword or some other weapon, and I acted quickly to prevent them from taking the first move. Glad I didn't let you go back to the inn?'

'I trust you, Sir,' Leon said. 'Something I never did with my father. For all his talk about the Jewish cause, he was on the lookout for himself first. You have your men in mind, like letting them rest today rather than pushing on.'

'Be straight with the men, and they will be loyal to you. That's how I've tried to operate right from the start, and it's served me well.'

The next morning, they broke camp early and made good progress towards Capernaum, and arrived at the Sea of Galilee before dusk. Five miles short of Tiberias, they stopped for the night, leaving them only half a day's march to reach Capernaum the next day. The prisoners had been submissive, giving no trouble to their captors. In the fading light, Julian walked over to them to see how they would react to a figure of authority. Till now, he had kept his distance.

It was observed who the spokesman of the twelve was, and as Julian approached, one called Simeon spoke out, 'What are you going to do with us?'

Julian chose to ignore the question for the time being, and asked, 'Have my men given you enough to eat?'

Another answered, 'We're not complaining.'

'Good. Glad to hear it. Feeding prisoners means less food for ourselves.'

They didn't respond, feeling the less said, the less likely they were to rankle their captors. Julian studied them for a while, before speaking again. 'Did you really think that with fifty men you could overpower a Roman *Centuria*?'

Without thinking, a third spoke, 'A hundred of us, and the benefit of surprise made it look possible.'

'Shut it, fool!' hissed Simeon. 'So what happens now?'

'I deliver you to the outpost at Capernaum in the morning, and they decide your fate. Ambush with the intent to kill more than a hundred Romans is not the most endearing to our authorities.' This was met with silence from the prisoners.

One broke down. 'They'll crucify us. Oh God, what will happen to my wife and kids? I only came along because Azor said we were only getting back what's been taken from us and we'd be home by nightfall. I didn't even get my sword out before I was cut down.'

He received a kick from Simeon. 'No one forced you, fool! Get a grip!' He looked at Julian. 'That's the answer to your question. If we'd had fifty who were focused, we would have won. But with half-hearted farmers like him, you're right, we had little chance.'

'None of your men got killed, did they?' asked another. 'Surely that means we won't be treated as murderers, will it? You wouldn't crucify twelve men seeing you already killed more than twenty of us, and none of your lot got killed.'

'Twenty-two, actually. But your intention was to kill all of us, was it not?'

Silence again, as they thought of the possibility of being crucified. Some whimpered, some were rigid with fear, and one or two put on an act of bravado.

Simeon spoke again, 'If it were up to you, what would you do with us?'

'It's not up to me. If it were, I'd exile you to a remote island and let you serve out your time labouring for Rome. But I have nothing to present in your defence. You were at the point of attack and, if I hadn't spotted you, I have no doubt you would have butchered us all.'

He walked away, wondering about the shattered homes that would be left in the region, and the hatred it would fuel. *There's always a bit of gall in every victory that takes the edge off the celebration of winning*, he thought.

At daybreak, they broke camp and marched the last ten miles into Capernaum. The locals watched, and word spread quickly that a new military detachment had arrived from Jerusalem, and with prisoners.

The prisoners were handed over, and Julian gave details of the skirmish to the commanding officer. A centurion stationed at the outpost took Julian round the compound, then out into the marketplace of the town, and down to the water's edge.

'I like the look of the place, Cato. How long have you been assigned here?'

'Five years, and I'm to be moved within the next six months. You'd be a good replacement, Julian. From the little I've noticed, you seem to understand something of the local people. The authorities in Rome intend to reduce the scale of the operations here and will most likely place a centurion in charge who has served over fifteen years. If you can put up with the Jewish way of life, you'd fit in well. Good place to retire to.'

Walking back to the town, Julian thought over what Cato had said. If, when Hannah had fulfilled her responsibilities to her parents, she was willing to join him, this would be a good place to bring her. She would be among her own people, and he could see himself settling down in his semi-retirement from the army, after his twenty years of service.

Chapter 10

The men had been rested and the wounded attended to. Julian was given a new horse so that his could recover from its leg wound. He was about to move off back to Caesarea without going back to Jerusalem, when a summons from Pilate came by a dispatch rider and his armed escort. He was ordered to ride to Jerusalem as quickly as possible and present himself to the Governor. He chose ten of his best men, and they rode hard to Jerusalem and covered the distance in two days.

Freshening himself, he entered Pilate's quarters.

'Centurion Julian, I understand that before you left Jerusalem you found evidence of conspirators within the city?' Pilate asked him.

'We did, Sir.'

'You were then attacked on the way to Capernaum?'

'Yes, Sir.'

'Linked?'

'Only in so far as this was probably part of an ongoing plan, Sir. I don't believe we were picked out because we had overheard their plot.'

'What makes you so sure?'

'Sir, it was only a few days after we had left Jerusalem. They wouldn't have had time to arrange that size of ambush for us in particular, so it would seem to me that they had planned the attack as part of their ongoing disruption of Roman occupation here.'

'I feared that's what you'd say. So this means that we can expect more insurrection at any time and in any place?'

'That would be my understanding, Sir.'

Pilate stood up, and paced back and forth across the room. 'You're sharp, Julian. Your alertness prevented your contingent from being wiped out. I want you to take as many men as you see fit, raid the inn, bring back the landlord and any others alive, and do whatever is necessary to get information out of them. Find out who the ringleaders are and arrest them. I want this insurrection and rebellion stopped! You understand?'

Pilate's voice rose as his rant went on. It was observed that pressure was on him from Rome to bring the province under control.

'Do I have another centurion to assist me, Sir?' Julian asked, trying to find out just how much Pilate had thought it through.

'You can have who or whatever you want! Just get the job done. If a few crucifixions will help put the fear of Rome in them, do it. You have my full permission and won't need to ask me first. Get back to me as soon as you have any good information. Dismissed!'

'Sir,' Julian said as he clicked his heels, turned around and marched out to the barracks. Most of his own men were still in Capernaum, so he gathered the ten who had escorted him and picked out another *Contubernium* that he was familiar with, and three auxiliaries. He explained the mission to them, and they split up into four groups of five.

Julian took the auxiliaries with him, and they headed into the city. Directing the groups to different alleyways, Julian and the auxiliaries walked into the small square where Leon had sat at the tables by the inn. He sent the auxiliaries, who were dressed in the clothes of the common man, into the inn while he sat down at one of the tables.

After a few minutes, they came out with the landlord carrying a tray with a flagon of beer and earthenware cups. He was taken aback to see a Roman centurion dressed in full military uniform seated at his tables, but moved over to the empty one and set the tray down. The auxiliaries sat down and poured themselves a drink, as the landlord turned to the centurion. 'We don't get many Roman soldiers here, and never a centurion. What can I get you, Sir?'

'Sit down and I'll tell you, landlord. If you can serve me with what I want, you may find yourself well rewarded.'

Tentatively, he did as he was told, but felt uncomfortable sitting down with a centurion, 'And what would your poison be, Sir? I have good beer, and a wide selection of fine wines, some even from Rome.'

He placed the tray on the table. Before he could lift his hand away, Julian pinned it to the table with his left hand, while taking a small leather pouch from the folds in his uniform. He let three or four silver shekels drop into the tray and leaned forward. 'No "poison", as you aptly put it. Just information on a poison that I understand is seeping out of your inn and into the hearts of the local troublemakers. Now, I'm sure it's nothing to do with you personally, but more like one of your unsavoury customers who drops off this "poison" to other ill-informed louts. You get my meaning?'

The landlord was a big man, slightly taller than Julian, and carrying more weight. He wasn't fat and unfit but well built, used to carrying heavy barrels. His full beard covered most of his face; his eyes were shaded by black bushy eyebrows, setting them back each side of a broken nose.

Being streetwise, he didn't let the racing of his heart show, but leaned into Julian and said, 'I'm not saying I know what you're talking about, but if I did hear anything, would these shekels stay on my tray?' So far he hadn't linked the three men on the other table to the Roman.

'If the information was good enough, these and more.'

'I did hear the other day a couple of men talking at this very table. They were talking low so I didn't hear much, but it was something about an ambush of Roman soldiers on the Capernaum road.'

'Interesting. When was this ambush to take place?'

'Last week sometime, I think. A whole lot of willing fighters were going to take part.'

'Did it happen?'

'So the word on the street says. But it wasn't successful from their point of view. They say more than twenty fighters were killed and another twenty taken prisoner, and crucified over the weekend.'

Sweat was running off the landlord's forehead as Julian kept his wrist pinned to the table. He was thinking that he could probably break free if he distracted the centurion, but wasn't sure if he could reach his dagger from his belt quickly enough if he did. And he knew that to kill a centurion would bring the full force of Rome around his ears.

'All you've told me so far is history. That's free information on any street in Jerusalem. I need names, places, plans – real information. Your establishment is known to entertain rebels. Give me names, and I will see

195

you protected. Give me nothing, and I will have your inn turned upside down and inside out until I find what I need to know. By your own mouth, you have insurgents at your tables. Names! Now!'

Julian gave a slight nod, and the three auxiliaries stood round the landlord with weapons in their hands. The colour drained from what could be seen of the landlord's face, as he desperately tried to think of a way to get rid of the Roman and his henchmen.

Julian released his grip on the landlord's wrist, and scooped up the money from the tray. 'Good money, or a bad night or two in a Roman prison with feet slammed in the stocks ten feet underground. Your choice.'

'My choice! What choice? Give you names, if I had any, and get killed by my own race, or not give you names and get killed by you! That's no choice!'

'You made your choice when you supported those who plotted to kill me and my men.'

'Your men!' He groaned at this piece of information and realised he was in up to his neck. And he wanted to save his neck!

'Never mind the money, can you protect me if I give you names?' He swallowed hard, and his hands trembled as he looked in the face of the one who held authority to kill or let him live. He felt the pressure of the three men round him.

Julian stood and clapped his hands once. From four alleyways, twenty fully armed soldiers marched over and stood in a semicircle round them, facing outwards, with shields locked together, spears and swords at the ready.

'Is that enough protection for you?' Julian asked coldly. 'And if you want, we can transport you from Jerusalem to any place you would like to go in all the Roman Empire, and set you up with a new inn.'

'You would do that?'

'If we have names that prove to be true, you have my word. We can move you and your family right now and house you at the garrison. Then, when your information proves right, move you on.'

'How can I trust you? I could give you names and you could leave me here.'

'As you said, what choice do you have? But know this, and know it well. I am a Roman centurion, and I am a man of my word. I have the authority of Pilate to do whatever it takes to get this insurgency under control.'

'Matthan, Jeconiah, Barabbas and Abner are the main ones. They are ruthless, and I've just signed my death warrant if you leave me here. I can tell you where they were the last time I knew, but they could have moved on by now. It's the God's honest truth, Sir. You need to move quickly or they'll be gone. They have contacts with more than two hundred men in Judaea.'

Julian was ahead of him and had passed the names on to five soldiers with orders to inform Pilate and tell his fellow centurion to find the places, and round up as many rebels as they could. He ordered the fifteen soldiers to protect the landlord and his family as they gathered up whatever they wanted, and escort them to the garrison, leaving four to guard the property from any raiders. He himself hurried off with the auxiliaries, and quickly got back to the garrison to supervise operations.

Chapter 11

Contingents of soldiers were dispatched to various places in Judaea. Within two weeks, Matthan and Abner were captured, along with several of their rebel fighters. Barabbas and Jeconiah went underground and avoided capture. Pilate was flushed by the successes, but enraged that two ringleaders had escaped.

It was known that some of their followers were Galileans, so, in his anger and determination, Pilate looked for ways to send shock waves of fear through the populace. An unconfirmed report was given to Pilate by a centurion who wanted to prove himself, because of Julian's success. It was rumoured that some of the Galilean rebels were in Jerusalem for the feast, and were worshipping at the Temple. Pilate sought no confirmation and seized upon the opportunity to send his 'shock wave of fear'.

Instantly, he dispatched fifty soldiers to the Temple. They burst through the Court of the Gentiles and the women's court and entered the main Temple area. Some innocent Galileans were offering their sacrifices at the altar. Following orders from their centurion, the soldiers set upon them and butchered them in front of the altar. Some of their blood splashed onto their sacrifices. People screamed and ran in fear, the priests fled into their preparation rooms, and utter chaos was mixed with the carnage.

Pilate sent his shock wave.

Julian was out in the countryside with a small contingent of soldiers, looking for more conspirators. The sun was setting, so he made his way back into Jerusalem. The atmosphere held a feeling of foreboding and he hurried his men into the garrison. Checking to see if the landlord and his wife were still safe, having given his word to protect them, he found them safe in the rooms assigned to them.

The landlord was sitting silently hunched over the table, with his wife trembling beside him. 'What have I done?' he asked Julian. 'You gave me no idea about the lengths you would go to, to prove you are in power. May God forgive me, for I can't forgive myself. And you! A man of your word, you said! You might as well kill me now, for they'll get me sooner or later, after what you've done today.' He spoke as one who was totally broken, and in shock.

'What in the name of the gods are you talking about? I've been out in the surrounding area for the last three days, and have come straight here to check on you to see that you are safe.'

The landlord looked up and could see that Julian knew nothing of the butchering of the Galileans in the Temple. 'You haven't heard?'

'Heard what? I sensed a heaviness over the city and thought something must have happened; that's why I came straight to see if you were safe.'

'Pilate sent soldiers into the Temple and killed some Galileans in front of the altar as they were worshipping. Have you any idea what that will do for the conspirators you're trying to quash? It will only strengthen their resolve to rid Judaea of Rome. I'm finished. I don't want to stay cooped up in your fortress for the rest of my life. Your Governor's a fool and knows nothing of how to curb an uprising. And if my calling him a fool means you will kill me, so much the better.' He spat on the floor in utter contempt of Julian and all he stood for.

Julian shouted for a servant. One ran in instantly. 'Sir?'

'Is it true what I have just been told? Did Pilate order soldiers to kill Galilean worshippers in the Temple?'

The servant was half-afraid to answer.

'Speak up, man. Is it true?'

'It's true, Sir. This afternoon fifty soldiers under the command of Centurion Barca entered the Temple, and killed the worshippers, on the Governor's orders. He had heard rumours that they were part of the rebel group who ambushed you, Sir.'

'Rumours? Rumours? Did he try to find out if they were true?'

'I don't think so, Sir, but I'm only a servant, Sir. I was told that he was looking for a way to show everyone that he was determined to stamp out rebellion at any cost.'

'I can't believe it!' Julian sat down at the table with the landlord, 'Bring some wine out here for me and my friend.'

The servant bowed, and did as he was told.

Receiving the wine, Julian poured a goblet for the landlord and himself. They drank in silence, both staring at the floor, until the landlord spoke, 'You really didn't know, did you? And you think the same as I do about it?'

Julian drained his goblet, refilled it, and topped up the landlord's. 'I'd been told nothing, and all I'm prepared to say is that I don't think it was the wisest move to make.' He sighed deeply, and banged his empty goblet down on the table.

The landlord watched this centurion who had both threatened him and protected him. He had given him his word and kept it, and was as disturbed by what his commander had done as he himself was. Somehow, he felt a strange bond with this man who was both his enemy and his protector. A Roman he could trust?

'I will do all I can to see that you're not, as you put it, cooped up here for any longer that you need to be. I will arrange for you to be moved from here at the earliest opportunity. I can say no more than that.'

'Where can we go?'

'Away from here would be a good start, and maybe no one knows that it was you who gave me the names. The street is not always as informed as you may think.'

The landlord was somewhat comforted by what Julian said, and with a grunt went over to his wife and took her off to bed. Julian sat for a long while, staring at the floor, finding it incredulous that Pilate could be so brutish and stupid to have done what he did.

His thoughts were interrupted by a messenger informing him that Pilate wanted to see him right away. He sighed again, got to his feet and followed the messenger into Pilate's private apartment.

The Procurator of the province of Judaea sat on a couch overlooking a balcony. He looked dishevelled, with two days' growth of stubble on his face, his hair tangled and bags under his eyes. It was obvious he had been drinking heavily, and when he spoke, his speech was slurred.

'Julian! The information you got, and operations executed, have been very productive I believe… good man. Just you… You have just got back from further operat… further operations, I'm understanding. You have a flair for this type of… of work, yes?'

Julian was looking for a good answer to give, without saying something he might regret later. And while Pilate was the worse for drink, Julian felt he was still capable of arriving at conclusions – the wrong ones!

(It was only later he realised what he did in that split second – he sent up a silent prayer to the God of the Jews for wisdom, not to the gods of Rome.)

'Sir, yes, the information proved to be correct, and two of the ringleaders together with several of their followers have been captured. Anything that brings justice and peace to the Empire, I find rewarding. I serve to further the good name of Rome.'

Pilate sprang to his feet, tottered forward, and stopped himself from falling as he grabbed the balcony balustrade. A cool evening breeze blew in and cleared his head a little. 'You have heard we have killed some Galileans at the Temple? They were believed to be collaborators with Barabbas, one of the leaders we have yet to catch. Put the fear of the Roman gods into the locals, I believe. You would agree, Julian?'

'They will certainly be afraid, Sir. If their Temple is not off-limits in your eyes, then they have nothing left. No doubt you will have the Chief Priests knocking at your door.'

'You think they will not take kindly to my intervention? Roman security comes first in my book, and they'd better get used to it. I don't think they'll forget this in a hurry!' He smiled as he spoke, but gave Julian the impression he was fishing for compliments to support a move, the wisdom of which he was himself beginning to doubt.

'They will surely remember it, Sir. But it could strengthen their resolve to rebel more than prevent it.'

Pilate walked slowly over to Julian and stopped with his face in front of his, 'Are you questioning my leadership, centurion? You feel I should have let them walk away?'

'I do not have the information you were given, Sir, so I'm not in the position to make an informed judgement. My only query would have been as to whether the inner Temple area was the best choice.' (Again, as he looked back, he remembered he had shot up another prayer to the God of the Jews.)

Pilate backed off and sat down. 'I value your judgement, Julian. Time will tell which of us is right. If the Chief Priests come calling, I will send them to you. You seem to understand them better than I do.' He laughed. 'I'll let you handle their tongue-lashing! But if they get out of line, I'll give them a Roman lashing!' He laughed at his own joke, and picked up a goblet to drain the last drop of wine in it.

Inwardly, Julian groaned. Has this man no sense?

'You left the majority of your men in Capernaum, I believe. I want you to go back there with the men you brought down here with you. With the current unrest, I feel they may need more manpower. You will stay there for at least the next six months until I have opportunity to reassess the situation. Any questions?'

It was hard for Julian to hide his relief. He had, at the back of his mind, been worrying about Leon, and was keen to get back to check on his welfare. 'No questions, Sir. But I will be sorry to miss the tongue-lashing of the priests.' He dared to smile at Pilate, as he answered.

'I think I can handle it, Julian. The reason I want you back there is because I can see you have the bearing of a diplomat, and that could be useful in a small outpost for keeping law and order. Get ready to leave in the morning.'

Julian was about to leave, when he remembered the landlord. 'Sir, if I may be so bold as to ask a favour of you? The landlord who gave me the first information is in danger of losing his life if he stays here. Would you grant permission for me to take him and his wife with us?'

'Permission granted. One less thing for me to worry about before I return to Caesarea.'

Bowing, Julian left Pilate with a spring in his step, and returned to his quarters. He disturbed the landlord and his wife, although they were far from sleep. 'First thing in the morning, pack anything you want to take with you. I have permission to take you with me to Capernaum.'

'We'll pack now, Sir. Sleep eludes us and we'll be only too glad to leave Jerusalem as quickly as possible.'

Julian nodded, and sent a messenger to tell his men to be ready, and he gathered his few things together for himself.

Chapter 12

Few people were up when a small band of soldiers and two of the local populace left Jerusalem on the Jordan road to Capernaum. All were on horseback, apart from the landlord and his wife. He was driving a pair of horses, pulling a small cart that contained their few belongings and the rest of the soldiers' equipment and rations. Julian set a pace that would be the quickest the cart and horses could safely manage, and by mid-morning Jerusalem was far behind them.

Stopping by the edge of the river so the horses could drink, Julian gave them time to stretch their legs while he stood by the water's edge. The landlord came up beside him. 'Sir, you are a man of your word. I dare to think it might be possible to start a new life somewhere else after all.'

'As we are travelling together, I think it's time I knew your proper names, landlord,' Julian smiled.

'Ben-Abel, Sir, and my wife is Hannah.'

'Your wife's called Hannah?'

'Yes, Sir.'

'There is a lady whom we had to leave in Tarsus. Her name is Hannah, and one day I dream of her becoming my wife.'

Ben-Abel understood that Julian was opening the boundaries of their relationship by the disclosure of his personal life. 'I hope your dreams come true, Sir.'

Their eyes met. 'And yours, Ben-Abel. You could do worse than settle for a while in Capernaum. If you were to change the cut of your beard, and to dress in a different style, you wouldn't be known. A different occupation, and you would blend in.'

A wry smile came to Ben-Abel's face. 'With a nose like mine, I'll always stick out in a crowd. But I'm willing to give it a try. I suppose not many people come from Jerusalem to Capernaum; more go the other way for the festivals. And not being a very religious man myself, I won't miss going.'

Julian called his men together. 'Time we moved on. The nearer we get to Capernaum, the better.'

Mounting up, they continued their journey, and by nightfall they had covered thirty miles. The soldiers arranged guard duty among themselves, and everyone settled down for the night. Julian was ill at ease: they were a small group and vulnerable. He took small comfort that Pilate's 'fear' policy would make so-called freedom fighters cautious to try anything so soon.

After a restless night, he was glad to get started at first light.

Their second day passed uneventfully, and they covered more miles than the first, which brought them to a more populated area for their next camp. The guard duty was set up, and Julian insisted on taking his turn. He found guard duty better than trying to lie down to sleep.

Another early start, and they arrived in Capernaum by early afternoon.

Leon was overjoyed to see Julian, and they embraced like long-posted soldiers when returning to their garrison. Gallus was equally pleased, and they shared news over supper. The story of the Galilean killings hadn't yet reached Capernaum. It was likely that some of those murdered in the Temple came from Capernaum, and Julian knew it wouldn't be long before rumours started.

Ben-Abel and Hannah were assigned a room near Julian's and, for the first time since leaving the inn, they slept peacefully all night.

Julian and Leon walked down to the lakeside and sat together, talking late into the night.

'You miss your mother, Leon?'

'Yes, but I know she's safe, which is more than I did when we were with my father. It was my choice to come with you, and I don't regret it.' He looked at the man he admired. 'Do you miss her, Julian?'

A strong arm pulled the fourteen-year-old boy tightly to his side. 'Yes, I miss her. If we had the chance, would you be willing to go with Gallus and bring her back here to be with us?'

'And get to sail again! You bet! You wouldn't be coming?'

'Duty calls, I'm afraid, Leon.'

'And sailing's not your thing!' laughed Leon. 'You really think we could?'

'I'm stationed here for at least six months. After that, we may be sent back to Caesarea. If we do, I think I could arrange a passage for you and Gallus to go back to Tarsus. But I 'll be sending letters to her as soon as I can, to find out how your grandparents are. I'm certainly not wishing them dead, but I would love to see your mother again.'

Leon squeezed Julian's arm.

News of the Temple killings reached Capernaum about a week later. The rumours flying about were a long way from the truth of what really happened, although that was bad enough. Two of those killed did come from Capernaum, and they were honest, innocent people. The story that was attracting the most attention was that it was someone from the synagogue in Capernaum who had informed Pilate of false worshippers at the Temple. (This had been spread by Pilate as a smokescreen to deflect blame from himself, and accounted for the fact that he wanted Julian and his *Centuria* of soldiers to stay in Capernaum, knowing that there would be trouble.)

On hearing the rumours, the leaders of the synagogue were shocked and afraid of what repercussions would follow. Jairus, one of the rulers, along with four others, went to the barracks to meet with the commander. The commander, having been informed by a messenger direct from Pilate, assigned Julian to deal with it.

Anger was deflected from Rome, but most of the local people who attended the synagogue gave little credence to it. But those who had no time for the Temple worship and had lost others fighting against Rome were inflamed by the stories and ready to believe them.

'How many rulers do you have at your synagogue?' Julian asked.

Jairus answered on behalf of the group. 'Ten, Sir, and we all live within the boundaries of Capernaum with our families.' He looked at the rest of the group and continued, 'It was under Pilate's orders that these men were killed. They were honest, peace-loving men who had no history of causing trouble for Rome. The fact that Pilate sent his soldiers into the very Temple to carry out their despicable deeds is beyond our comprehension. And now we've been set up to take the blame!'

Julian held up his hand and said in a soft, measured tone, 'Sirs, please listen to what I have to say. I share with you the repulsion over what has happened, and deeply regret what took place at the Temple in Jerusalem. Bad information was given, and decisions made without a full picture of what was involved. I humbly, on behalf of Rome, offer you my sincere apologies for the desecration of your holy place and the offence it has given to your God.'

He made a deliberate act of removing his helmet, and paused quietly before proceeding with his speech. 'I personally will see to it that you have all the protection your families need over the next few weeks, until this blows over and the falseness of these stories is exposed. If you could furnish me with the names of the unfortunate men who were innocently caught up in this dreadful miscarriage of justice, I will see that at least some measure of compensation will be given.'

He scanned their faces as he concluded, 'It is my duty to add, that because of the recent uprising within the province of Judaea, Governor Pilate has been under extreme pressure to bring it under control. Under pressure, mistakes are sometimes made. This, I understand, is of little comfort to the families involved.'

Jairus and his friends were subdued by what Julian had said, and the meeting continued in a more conciliatory mood. They accepted his offer of protection for their families, but chose not to have it personally, as they felt it would distance them from the general public, and hinder any bridge-building.

Jairus was willing to take Julian's sympathy and offer of help to the families, and to come back with their response.

Having obtained the location of their homes, so that Julian could provide protection, the meeting ended and Julian issued the necessary orders to his men.

There was a lull for a couple of days, and Jairus and his fellow synagogue rulers began to feel that they had over-reacted to the supposed threat.

Chapter 13

Julian awoke to the sound of a disturbance in the street. Dawn had not yet broken, and there was a reddish glow in the sky. Jumping from his bed, he quickly dressed in his uniform and, grabbing his sword, ran into the courtyard, shouting for his men to make themselves ready. The smell of smoke filled the cold dark air, as a red glow lit up the sky over to the side of the market area.

'Fire! Fire!' shouted someone in the confusion. 'Round by the market! Fire! Fire!'

Julian knew the layout of the town, and guessed what was burning. 'Gallus, send twenty men over to the synagogue with anything that might help beat out the flames. If there are buckets, bring them: we may be able to get water from the horse-pond.' He ran down the street, while soldiers spilled out of the barracks equipped with buckets, flails and spears.

His assumption was right. As he turned the corner, the flames were licking furiously through the roof of the synagogue. Walls cracked under the heat, and the bucket chain the men set up from the horse-pond was more for a demonstration of cooperation than a serious attempt to douse the flames. A bucketful of water every half-minute was futile in the face of the inferno.

With a loud roar, the roof collapsed, sending sparks high into the air.

'Nothing we can do for the synagogue. Fan out and watch for sparks spreading to other buildings,' Julian ordered.

His men changed direction, encircled the burning building and watched the surrounding area.

The synagogue had stood in its own grounds, with a burial plot to the left and a grassy area on the other three sides, so nothing was built too close. A crowd quickly gathered, some only half-dressed, as they ran from their homes to see what was happening.

The sight of the burning synagogue was a jolt to their senses, but the presence of Roman soldiers with buckets in their hands instead of weapons, and a centurion with his face blackened with soot and ash, surprised them even more. Jairus arrived, and the crowd watched as the centurion went straight over to him, and by his gestures, was observably sorry about the destruction of the building.

The first rays of the sun dulled the brightness of the flames as they finished devouring all the perishable structures of the synagogue. The Ruling Council wandered around the smouldering heap in disbelief. What had been their meeting place for many years was no more.

Jairus, with Julian beside him, moved closer to the rubble. Following Jairus' instructions, Julian took a spear and prodded a charred shape at one end of the rubble. Shaking his head, and with tears in his eyes, Jairus said, 'The scrolls... all gone, nothing left at all. Not even a fragment.'

Out of respect, Julian removed his helmet and stood with his head bowed beside the weeping ruler and the rabbi who had joined them.

With the fire over, the crowd dispersed, leaving the rabbi, the synagogue rulers, Julian and his soldiers standing together in front of the mess.

'I deeply regret we didn't anticipate the destruction of your synagogue,' Julian said, as he placed a hand on the shoulder of the rabbi. 'It's too late to save it now, but I'll post a guard to prevent trophy-hunters desecrating it even more.'

The rabbi was surprised at the sensitive concern of a Roman centurion. 'I appreciate your willingness to help, and everything you and your men have tried to do. We accept your offer of guards.'

'The scrolls were very valuable?'

'Both in what they teach us and in the time and cost it takes to have them copied by the best scribes. They are the Word of God Almighty given by Moses and the prophets to God's chosen people,' sighed the rabbi.

'And our beautiful synagogue!' Jairus added. 'My father brought me here in his arms, and his father before him. So much gone in so little time, and now no local place where we can gather together to worship Jehovah.'

With no boast or hint of a declaration to impress, Julian addressed Jairus and his friends. 'I will personally see to it that it is rebuilt for you. Pilate may have desecrated the Temple in Jerusalem, but we can do something here to consecrate a place for you to worship your God.'

Without thinking how it might look, Jairus embraced the ash-covered centurion – the enemy of the Jews – and openly cried on his shoulder. As he broke away, he whispered in Julian's ear, 'May the blessing of Abraham, Isaac and Jacob rest upon you.'

Over the next three months, mainly at Julian's expense and with the voluntary help of some of his soldiers, and the use of local craftsmen, the Capernaum synagogue was rebuilt. Those who had razed it to the ground were never caught, but if they had been around to watch, they would have seen that their act of destruction with the intent to stir division and hatred between the Jews and Rome failed miserably.

Through the wisdom of Julian's administration, at best deep friendships were formed, and at worst mutual respect was established, at least on a local level.

With the completion of the rebuilding, Julian was known and respected as one who loved the Jewish people.

Chapter 14

After six months in Capernaum, Julian was summoned to meet with Pilate at Caesarea. Taking Leon and Gallus with him, they rode to the coast, leaving his men under the authority of Centurion Cato. Two days of hard riding saw them arrive in Caesarea and, after a quick refreshing, Julian presented himself before Pilate.

He received a warm reception. 'Centurion Julian, I have received nothing but good reports of your handling of the situation at Capernaum. You will be pleased to hear that another of the ringleaders has been captured, and suitably dispatched by way of crucifixion, leaving only Barabbas.' Pilate waved him in the direction of a seat. 'Sit down, Julian, but pour yourself a drink before you do.'

Julian obeyed, wondering what was coming next.

'I believe when we last spoke at Jerusalem we talked about the possible changes in the outpost at Capernaum. Decisions have been made and we will be withdrawing the commander-in-charge and also redeploying Centurion Cato. You have now served more than seventeen years, so will be coming up for retirement in two. Rome has decreed that all fit and able centurions will now stay at their last posting and continue to serve in a semi-retired capacity, thus cutting expenses. I am offering you the position. I could, of course, order you to take it, but, owing to your outstanding service and diplomacy over there, I give you a choice. You can leave the army completely and be returned to Rome, or you can take the post in Capernaum until you are deemed unfit to handle it. I am at liberty to grant you one or two personal requests concerning your living arrangements, should you have any.'

Julian was short and to the point in his reply. 'I would be happy to serve the Empire in such a way as you have described, Sir. The living quarters that I have had up until now are more than adequate, so my only request would be for Leon, a young man who has been my personal servant for this last year. His mother is in Tarsus, and when her ageing parents have died, I would like her to be granted passage so that she could join me at Capernaum.'

Pilate waved his hand in the air. 'A trivial matter! Make whatever arrangements are necessary, and have her transported over. In your semi-retirement you will need something to keep you occupied.'

Pilate even smiled as his attempt at humour. 'Good! The matter is settled. You can take your time in the arrangements for your woman, but I would like you back in Capernaum within eight weeks, as that is when Cato will be transferred and the commander removed.'

The ship sailed out of Caesarea with one very excited Leon on board. He was escorted by Gallus, and they were expected to arrive in Tarsus within two weeks, if the weather was favourable.

Chapter 15

Hannah had closed the eyes of her mother, and they laid her to rest in the burial ground by the local synagogue. Joel was deeply sad and his strength was fading, but he tried to keep himself motivated for Hannah's sake. How he blessed the day the centurion had knocked on their door with his long-lost daughter and his grandson.

A week after the funeral, Hannah went to answer the door. She clapped her hand over her mouth to stifle a shriek of delight as her son fell into her arms. Joel, hearing the commotion, slowly made his way to the door, and his face lit up with elation. His grandson was back! In the ecstasy of the moment, Gallus was left standing on the doorstep, and it was only when he dropped their travelling bag on the floor that Leon remembered his faithful protector and guide.

'Gallus!' Hannah shouted. 'What a wonderful gift you have brought us. Please, come in – we will celebrate!'

Gallus bowed and entered the house as Leon and his grandfather walked arm in arm into the yard at the back. Leon sat down and began to tell of all his adventures, while Hannah hastily found them something to eat and drink. Gallus hovered near her, so she could talk to him.

'Gallus, how is Julian? I did receive a letter from him a while ago but have not been able to find a messenger to take a reply back for me. Is he well? Is he still in Capernaum? Has he been posted there now, or is it still temporary? Why are you here? Has he missed me?'

Gallus laughed, and started with the last question first. 'He has missed you very much, Hannah. He's kept himself faithful to you, and his integrity and diplomacy have won him a permanent appointment at Capernaum.'

He helped her carry the food and drink out to Leon and her father. 'He is well – ask Leon! ' he added.

'You talking about love-sick Julian?' laughed Leon. 'He's fit and well, but wants my mother to come and join him as soon as possible – as do I!'

'And you should go as soon as the ship sails back to Caesarea, my darling,' broke in Joel.

'I can't leave you now, Father, so soon after the death of my mother,' Hannah protested.

'Who said anything about leaving me here? I'm coming with you!'

'But, Father, you're not strong enough to make a voyage; the sea can get rough, you...'

'I might die! True, Hannah, but then you can bury me at sea! I have nothing to stay here for, and I want you to be happy after all you have done for your mother and me in this last year. How soon does a ship sail, Gallus?'

Gallus was enjoying the enthusiasm of this old man, even if he himself could have done with a few days to get his land legs back. 'I think there is one we can sail on that leaves in three days. I have the paperwork signed by none other than Pilate to gain passage for up to five persons.'

'We'll go!' shouted Joel, with the little breath he could muster.

Hannah stood with her mouth open, but no words came out. Her mind was in a whirl. A few days ago she had laid her mother to rest; now here was her father ready to go globetrotting! She shut her eyes, and in her mind remembered the kiss and long embrace she'd had with the man who had saved her, the man she loved. Was it possible that in a little over two weeks she could be in his arms again? Opening her eyes, she looked around the house. What of all this? But her father was already a jump ahead of her.

'There's little of value for us to worry about here, Hannah, other than a few keepsakes of your mother's. The rest of the furniture has served us well, but is way beyond any value apart from firewood. Benjamin next door offered to buy this house before you came back, so he could extend his own. He has money, and could settle with me well within time to leave.'

She sat down beside the old man. 'You really want to go, Father?'

'My love, I don't want to stay! Let's have one more adventure before I die!'

She kissed him on the cheek. 'I love you! It has been so good being with you this last year. You're right – let's have one more adventure!'

A cheer went up from Leon and Gallus and, after eating a simple meal, they all set to preparing for this last adventure.

Benjamin was still willing to buy, and stuck with the price he had offered. He was able to hand over the money before they sailed. Hannah packed the few clothes she had, and her father's. Another chest held all the keepsakes she wanted of her mother's and they were ready, well within time to catch the ship before she sailed.

The last day in Tarsus was spent seeing old friends, and a last visit to the grave. Gallus helped the frail Joel down to the docks, and two dockers loaded their possessions. Leon stood beside his mother as the ship pulled out to sea. The wind was in her hair, and a deep smile covered her face. The wind sculpted her figure in the folds of her dress, and he understood why Julian was looking forward to seeing his mother again.

A week out at sea and Leon the sailor began to feel that he wasn't so sure of his sea legs. His mother and grandfather stayed below deck as the winds increased, and the sea swell became deeper. Gallus was worried for the sake of the old man, as they were flung about. Going below deck, Leon could see his grandfather was struggling to breathe, and his mother looked sick and anxious.

Joel reached out a trembling hand and held on to his beloved daughter. 'Fear not, child, I said this would be...' he struggled for breath, '... this would be my last adventure. It's not so much the ride as... whom you ride with! And I am riding with those closest to my heart. What a way to go!' A smile spread across his face, he sank back, rocked by the tossing of the sea, and his eyes closed.

Hannah fell over him and pushed her face against his as the heat left his body and his hands went limp. She kissed him over and over again, as Leon knelt beside them and held on to his mother.

For a moment it was as if the sea stopped tossing the ship, and they were suspended in mid-air. Then there was a sickening crash as a huge wave dropped them into a deep hollow and then lifted them up to do the same all over again. They were all thrown over the lower deck. Leon reached out to hold his mother, while Gallus tried desperately to grab them both. The lifeless body of Joel was thrown across the ship like a sack of grain. Gallus got hold of Leon, and Leon hung on to his mother.

Above the noise of the storm, the ship's captain bellowed, 'Man the lifeboats! Man the lifeboats!'

Fighting desperately to stay on their feet by hanging on to anything that wasn't moving, they inched their way to the ladder that led to the upper deck. Gallus got to the ladder and, when Leon and Hannah were able to hold on to it, climbed to the upper deck to see where the lifeboat was.

The captain saw him, and shouted above the storm, 'Over this way, get them to the lifeboat!'

Hannah climbed the ladder, with Leon helping her from below as Gallus held on to her from above. She made it to the deck, and Leon was close behind. The captain threw them a rope to hold on to, and Hannah crawled over the tossing deck that changed direction with every crashing wave. Gallus held on to Leon, and Hannah reached the lifeboat with the captain's help. A sudden shudder went through the ship as she struck rocks. The captain was catapulted over the side, and Hannah was thrown into a wave as it broke over the side, and she was seen no more.

Leon's cry was heard over the scream of the wind and the crashing of the waves. Gallus held on to him with every ounce of strength he had. He looked through the spray, but the lifeboat was nowhere to be seen, so he looked for an alternative. The large wooden grating that ventilated the lower deck was being tossed across the deck, ropes tangled round it.

'Hang on here, Leon!' shouted Gallus. 'I'm going to grab that grating.'

As the ship rolled, he let go of the ladder rail and made a grab for the grating. He reached it and wrapped a dangling rope round his arm, then waited for the next roll of the breaking ship to pitch him towards Leon. On the second wave, he launched himself across the deck, and crashed into the hand rail of the ladder. Leon saw what he was trying to do, and reached out and caught hold of another rope attached to the grating. Together, in time with the waves, they manoeuvred the grating so that Leon could pull himself onto it. Gallus did the best he could to lash Leon to it and then, on the roll of the next wave, he heaved with all his might, and together they cast themselves into the churning, boiling sea.

Holding on, Gallus managed to get a rope around himself, then threw his body over the boy and held on for dear life. Leon blacked out, and Gallus prayed to every god he could think of, ending up by offering a prayer to the God of the Jews. Fighting to keep control, he felt his strength ebbing away. As they tossed and turned in the swelling sea, Gallus became totally disorientated.

His mind became fuzzy and, after what felt like an eternity, he cried out, 'Julian, I did all I could to save the boy. I'm sorry I failed you.'

Chapter 16

'You didn't fail, Gallus. You saved him.'

Gallus forced open one eye and tried to focus. His brain couldn't process his surroundings. The light was bright, and he could see dark shapes bending over him.

Someone kissed his forehead. 'Good, faithful Gallus, you got us both to land.'

Some of the fog lifted; he knew that voice. His lips parted and he whispered, 'Leon?'

'Yes, Gallus, Leon and Julian.'

More fog cleared from his brain, and he suddenly tried to sit up. 'Hannah? Where's Hannah?'

Gently but firmly, Julian held him down. 'You must rest, Gallus. Sadly, Hannah is not with us. The sea took her.'

'Where are we?'

'Halfway between Antioch and Caesarea. You and Leon, along with about fifty others, were washed ashore along the coast. Word was sent to Caesarea and I rode here as fast as I could to find you. You have been out of it for two days. Leon is safe, my friend. You didn't fail in your duty to protect him for me.' Julian bent down and kissed the face of his trusted servant.

Closing his eyes, Gallus sighed and settled back, his mind at rest. Somehow they had made it. After a few minutes, Gallus spoke again, 'Which god helped me, Julian? I prayed to them all, even the God of the Jews.'

'Rest, my friend, we can talk about that later. Save your strength for now.'

Leon had been delirious when he had been found, still tied to the wooden grille, with Gallus lying beside him. As drink and food refreshed him, his memory of the voyage came back to haunt him. He was standing, looking out to the sea that had both washed him to safety and drowned his mother. He recalled the last words of his grandfather, and tears streamed down his face. Julian came over to him and placed a hand on his shoulder. Leon had said nothing of the storm, or their departure from Tarsus. Julian knew nothing of the death of Hannah's mother or father.

'Want to talk about it?'

'He wanted to come with us. He was so excited about having one last adventure. He got his wish, didn't he?'

'Who, Leon, who wanted a last adventure?'

'My grandfather. He sailed with us and died just before the storm destroyed our ship.'

'Old Joel was with you?!' Julian said in amazement. Then he softly voiced the question he hardly dared to ask: 'Did you see what happened to your mother?'

Leon leaned back on Julian. 'She was washed overboard with the ship's captain as they tried to get her into the lifeboat. I'm so sorry, Julian, she was looking forward to being with you.' He turned to look at his unofficial adoptive father. 'When we left Tarsus, she stood at the bow of the ship. The wind was blowing her hair, and she was wearing the dress you bought her. A big smile was on her face, as she was thinking of seeing you again. She loved you, Julian, and I told her you loved her. She knew it was true.'

'Thank you for that, Leon. I'll never forget your mother and I will never let anything bad happen to you, if it is within my power to prevent it.'

They both stood looking out to sea for a long time, saying nothing.

'Will you go to Capernaum?' Leon asked.

'You want to?'

'Yes. I told Mum about it, and she wanted to go with us.'

'Then we will. When Gallus is fit enough to travel, we'll head back to Caesarea, rest a few days, then go straight to Capernaum.'

Six weeks after they had left Capernaum on Pilate's orders, they returned. On the way to the Roman army quarters, they passed by the new synagogue. It was the end of the Sabbath, and Jairus and the rabbi were walking away from the building. Seeing Julian riding by with Leon and Gallus, they went over to greet them.

'Julian! Good to see you back. And Leon and Gallus. I trust it has been a successful time for you all.'

Julian couldn't trust himself to answer, and Gallus, sensing the distress of his master, led Leon's horse on, leaving Julian alone with the Jews.

Julian dismounted, tethered his horse to a post by the road and walked over to the two men. Standing in front of them with the synagogue in the background, he spoke softly, 'Successful in the fact that I am posted here for now and into my retirement, and will be in charge of this outpost for Rome. Beyond that, success is not a word that I would use to describe the emptiness in my heart.'

His face was straight as he spoke, and Jairus and the rabbi could see he was a man in deep distress, fighting to hold back his tears.

'Shall we take a walk by the lake?' Jairus offered.

Julian nodded and walked towards the water through the marketplace, and down to the lake. Jairus waited until he was ready to speak.

'Over the past few weeks, I have found myself praying to your God without realising it. It became almost a natural reaction. Instead of calling on the gods of Rome, I cried to your God. Rabbi, Jairus, since helping you rebuild the synagogue and having watched you, I have come to believe in your God.'

He looked across the lake as if trying to find a word that might be floating on the water. 'I went to Caesarea on the orders of Pilate, and then I waited there while Gallus and Leon sailed to Tarsus. They were going to fetch Leon's mother, the woman I was going to marry, and bring here to be with me. She trusted in your God, being half-Jew herself.' A tear became too large to stay in his eye, and ran down his face. 'A storm smashed the ship they were sailing on and took her…' He dropped down onto the shingle of the shore and let all his pent-up grief pour out. Huge sobs rose from his belly and shook his entire body as he sat on the ground, a Roman centurion between a Jewish rabbi and a Jewish synagogue ruler.

They wept with him.

Turning to the rabbi and then to Jairus, Julian said, 'Teach me the ways of your God, for I understand so little.'

Together, they slowly made their way back to his horse. He mounted, and said, 'Let it go no further, but Leon and I have only you and your people as our family now.'

They bowed their heads in acceptance as he rode off to a different future than the one he had visualised.

Chapter 17

Duty and his oath to Rome enabled Julian to pull his life back together. The first few weeks back in Capernaum were extremely busy for him, overseeing all the changes that were taking place at the outpost. The Commander departed, as did Cato and his *Centuria*, leaving him in total command. Because of the pressure of the administration, he had little time to spend with the people in the synagogue, and not enough time with Leon.

The boy was becoming a man; he was now almost fifteen. Sensing his quietness, Julian took time to walk out with him. 'Leon, life has been too hectic of late. Now things are more in place, I'll get to spend more time with you. It's been a long, hard journey over these last few months.'

'You are all I have, Julian. What if anything happens to you? I'm not a soldier – what would I do?'

'The first thing I want to do, Leon – and that's why I want to talk to you now – is to adopt you by Roman law. That way, should anything happen to me, all that belongs to me becomes yours, and it will give you some measure of security. What do you think – son!'

'Sounds good to me, Abba!' Leon punched Julian's arm as hard as he could. Julian shot out a hand and grabbed Leon's shoulder and knocked him to the ground. They rolled over in the grass, and playfully, Julian let Leon pin him down and sit on his chest.

'Some soldier you are, Abba! Letting a weakling like me overpower you!' he laughed.

With that, Julian arched his back and threw the boy like a feather pillow off his body, rolled over and held Leon flat on his back, with one hand.

'Maybe there is still strength in the old man!' He got to his feet and pulled Leon up with him.

With an arm round his shoulder, they walked beside the lake, cementing their relationship together as father and son.

After six months in his new position, the respect for Julian grew in the town. And the majority of the people, even the non-religious ones, had regard for their Roman commander. Julian and Leon attended the synagogue when Julian's duties allowed, and the rabbi could often be seen at Julian's house, where he taught him the laws of Moses and the customs of the Jewish race.

After a session of teaching, Julian asked the rabbi, 'Rabbi, why, if our God is so powerful, do bad things happen? Why did Hannah have to drown?'

The rabbi watched Gallus across the yard, as he harnessed a pair of horses to a cart. 'If part of the harness on a pair of horses is broken or becomes tangled and twisted, would they work together, and pull the cart in a straight line? Or would they lurch from one side to the other? Could it cause the one driving the cart to fall off, or the cart to turn over?'

'It could. The pull on the reins wouldn't be able to direct both horses the same way, and they could try and turn in opposite directions. A broken harness could get tangled and one might break a leg.'

'Moses taught us that something is broken, Julian: our relationship with the Almighty. He gave us the laws to show us the brokenness and help us keep on track, but it's tangled up with our will to want to go our own way. He has promised that a Messiah will come, who will repair the brokenness and restore our relationship with Him. But in the meantime, bad things happen to good people. That's how I understand it, Julian, and I long for Him to come soon.'

Julian thought over what the rabbi said, 'I can see what you say makes sense, but it doesn't bring back the woman I loved. When will this Messiah come? What will he do?'

'I don't know. But many feel that the time is right now. Some say that He is already here. What will He do? Again, some believe He will rise up like a mighty warrior and restore the fortunes of Israel. But I feel it has to be something bigger than that to restore *shalom*, peace to the whole world. Something much bigger, much deeper.'

Julian had a wry smile on his face. 'Sounds like us Romans are in for a hard time! I know that some of our "justice" needs "re-ad-justing". A holy God would need to deal with that. But I have to tell you, Rabbi, I saw a lot of false justice and error among the priests and Pharisees at the Temple in Jerusalem.'

'That's why I see the Messiah will have to do more than just overthrow an outside power over us. We have unseen powers within that need dealing with. King David knew that God sees the heart, Julian, and he saw his own heart needed cleansing. It's bigger than national boundaries.'

Julian got to his feet, 'When He comes, the Messiah, say a prayer for me, Rabbi. This old Roman soldier has blood on his hands, and a hole in his heart.'

'You and me both!' answered the rabbi. 'I'll pray for you and you can pray for me!'

Chapter 18

A year into his posting at Capernaum, a year after the storm that took Hannah, Julian noticed that his faithful servant, Gallus, was not as quick as he once was. One morning, as Julian walked across the courtyard, he saw Gallus bending over the horse-trough, coughing so hard it racked his whole body.

'Gallus,' he called, 'you sound dreadful! How long has this been going on?'

Straightening up, Gallus answered, his face red with the exertion of the coughing fit, 'If I'm honest with you, Sir, it started soon after the shipwreck. I think it has to do with all the seawater we got down us, and straining to stay alive. But it's got worse over these last six or seven weeks.'

'Go and see our army doctor, Gallus, and take the rest of the week off. Leon can see to what you were doing. I've noticed he's good with horses.'

Gallus did as he was ordered, and saw the army doctor, then rested for the rest of the week. Julian and Leon watched him closely, and could see he wasn't getting any better. A maid was appointed to care for him daily, and Julian and Leon took turns themselves to stay with him overnight.

By the end of the second week, Julian was deeply concerned for his faithful servant. He called the army doctor and asked for his professional opinion.

'Sir, I don't know what else I can do for him. I think his lungs were damaged by the sea, and it's something that has been getting slowly worse over time.'

'Are you saying he will not recover?'

The doctor looked at the floor. 'I fear so, Sir.'

'Do what you can for him – the best, whatever it costs. Anything you feel can help him, let him have.'

'Yes, Sir,' answered the doctor, and he gave some instructions to the maid before he left Gallus' bedside.

Julian sat beside his servant and friend. 'Gallus, is there anything I can do for you? Anything you want? It pains me to see you like this. Without you I would not have Leon as my son. I owe you such a debt of love.'

Gallus smiled weakly. 'You have been the best master I could have had, Julian. I wish for no more…' He broke off with yet another bout of coughing.

A week later, Gallus was so weak he was paralysed, unable to move. Julian feared that Gallus' life would soon end. Leaving Leon to watch over him, he went out to try to come to terms with it. 'Oh, God, do we have to lose Gallus too? He has been so faithful. Can you not take him now?' Without looking where he was going, he walked into the marketplace. There was a stir in the market!

Jesus was on his way into Capernaum.

Some had heard the stories about this man – a new rabbi who told stories that could draw in crowds, and that he was able to heal people. Many people left the market and ran down to the coastal road by the lake. Julian walked into the market and was aware of the lack of people buying. Approaching a stallholder, he inquired, 'Why so few people in the market today? I've not seen it this quiet before.'

The stallholder was none too happy. 'Some travelling rabbi. He's supposed to have some magic power to heal people. Everybody has run off to see him. Trade is dead, and I'm going to be left with a lot of rotting vegetables if he hangs around.'

Hurrying over to another stall, Julian questioned, 'Have you heard where everyone is today?'

'Wish I didn't have to man this stall, Sir. Jesus is on his way here, and I'd love to hear him. Amazing bloke, I'm told. Loves kids, talks to the likes of us, not just the Pharisees or the powerful.'

'Jairus, I must go and see Jairus; he'll know what's going on.' Julian turned and strode briskly out of the market square towards the synagogue. As he turned the corner into the street leading to the synagogue, he was met by several of the synagogue officials.

'Jairus, tell me about this man, Jesus. Everyone in Capernaum has run off to see him. What do you know about him? I've heard he can heal people.'

'We have heard the same and many other things, Julian. Many believe he is even the Messiah! We are on our way to meet him. Come with us.'

'No Jairus, I'm a Gentile. Please, ask him to come and heal my servant Gallus. He'll die if he doesn't.'

They hurried off, and Julian ran back to see Gallus.

A large crowd was on the road, and as the small group of synagogue officials drew closer, the crowds parted to let them get to Jesus. They pleaded earnestly with Jesus that he would come and heal Julian's servant.

'Sir, this man deserves to have you do this; he loves our nation and has rebuilt our synagogue.'

Jesus followed them towards the home of the Roman centurion. As they approached his house, Julian came out and stopped them. 'Lord, I don't deserve to have you come under my roof. But just say the word and my servant will be healed. I myself am a man under authority, with soldiers under me. I tell this one, "Go," and he goes; and that one, "Come," and he comes. I say to my servant, "Do this," and he does it.'

When Jesus heard this, He was amazed and said to those following, 'I tell you the truth, I've not found anyone in Israel with such great faith. You know, many will come from the east and the west to take their places at the feast with Abraham, Isaac and Jacob in the kingdom of heaven, but they will miss out and be in great anguish.'

Jesus said to the centurion, 'Go. Let it be done, just as you believed it would.'

Julian bowed low, and then ran back into the house. He charged into the room where Gallus was lying, and stopped just inside the room. Across the room, not lying on the bed, but standing, and full of health and strength, was his beloved servant.

They ran towards each other, and it was Gallus who flung his arms round Julian and lifted him off his feet.

'Put me down, Gallus! Is this the way to treat your master?' said Julian, his face beaming.

'You'd better believe it, Julian! I think it's most appropriate!' was Gallus' joyful response!

Jesus said 'All authority in heaven and on earth has been given to me' (Matthew 28:18, NIV).

(Luke 7:1-10 gives the biblical account of Jesus healing the centurion's servant. Luke 13:1 gives the reference to Pilate mixing Galileans' blood with their sacrifice. And I have taken the licence to weave it into this story.)

Mud in Your Eye!
A Man Born Blind

A young man leading two pack mules has entered the market. He looks dusty and thirsty and it is easy to see he has been on the road for a while. He leads his animals over to a vendor who is selling bread and wine.

'A large, fresh loaf, my good man, and a cup of wine, please.' His face has a large smile on it, but it is his eyes that draw your attention. They are bright blue, and are darting all around the market, taking in everything.

'All my loaves are fresh, young man, if you don't mind!' the vendor quips in response to the request.

'I'd mind if they weren't!' our stranger replies, laughing. 'What a great day, isn't it? Look at the sky! Not a cloud in sight! And look at those bales of cloth he has on that stall over there – I love all the different bright colours.'

'Whatever. Here's your *fresh* loaf and wine.'

He pays the man, and leads his mules over to a merchant who sells olives and olive oil. 'Ishmael, good to see you! I've got you the best olives, all the way from the Mount of Olives at Jerusalem.'

Ishmael responds with a firm handshake. 'Glad you made it on time, Yoram, I was getting low on stock. You're looking well!'

'Looking – and feeling well!' Yoram replies. What's the secret of his exuberance?

Chapter 1

I sat with my back against an old olive tree, watching the dawn burst over the horizon. The whole valley was flooded with life-giving light. The rays of the early morning sun stroked the earth with the brushstrokes of a master artist. A dance of colourful sounds stirred, swirling round my feet and on to the distant hills. So bright was the melody it painted, the sound was deafening!

My eyes scanned the countryside before me. I drank it in like a thirsty man who had been without water for days. The joy of the moment of early dawn!

I rose to my feet in an involuntary response to the wonder before me. I staggered, not unlike a drunken man, intoxicated by the sheer delight of a new day's birth. Birds joined in with song, making it a melody of colour, warmth and sound that enveloped me like a large mantle.

I felt so alive!

Then – like a flash of black lightning – the tranquillity was shattered by the sight of a young woman, probably about sixteen or seventeen years of age, further along the path. She was standing out on the edge of an outcrop of rock looking down into the valley below, her movements suggesting that she was preparing to jump.

I stood stock still, unsure of what to do. If I ran towards her, would she jump before I could reach her? If I shouted, would she fall to her death? But doing nothing was not an option, so I began to walk towards her, slowly at first, then quickening my pace as I drew closer.

I called out as gently as I could, 'Please stay there until I can come up to you. Don't harm yourself.'

She took a step back from the edge and turned towards me with a startled expression. Dressed in expensive clothing, her hair in a mess and her eyes wide and wild, she answered me with a threat: 'Don't come near me. Stay away. If you come up here, I'll jump.' She moved back to the edge. Her feet were bare and her toes were now over the edge of the rock.

As she was speaking, I continued walking towards her and was now at the same level. Softly, I said, 'Please don't harm yourself. Let me help you. Life's too precious to throw away, and whatever's troubling you now may not be as bad as you think.'

She didn't turn to look at me, but kept her face turned towards the rocks below. But her feet did move back a little, so her toes were no longer beyond the edge. 'You know nothing about me. You know nothing about what my life is like.' Her voice dropped as she added, 'There's nothing left to live for.'

I took a couple of steps towards her and paused. 'You're right, I know nothing about you... but is this the best way out? There's always hope, always the chance to start again.'

She turned towards me, and with an expressionless tone, she said, 'What life? There's no point – life's empty. You don't know what it's like to have no future, apart from being told what to do, what to eat, where to go, whom to marry...' Her voice tailed off.

'I know something of what it's like to feel there's no future and nothing to live for. But no, it's not the same as your emptiness – just plenty of my own.' As I spoke, I moved a few more paces, leaving only about five steps between us. 'Want to talk about it? Sometimes it's easier to talk with a stranger than someone who's close.'

She took a step back from the edge, but still faced the drop, then, turning her head towards me, she said, 'Why did you have to come up here so early in the morning? I thought I'd be alone and wouldn't have to see anyone if I jumped.'

'I came to watch the sun giving birth to a new day. It speaks to me of new opportunities after all the ones that I missed because I couldn't see them,' I said.

'What do you mean, you couldn't see them? One dull day is much the same as another. What's there to see in this day that wasn't there yesterday?' She held me in her gaze as I took a step back – and she took a step back – away from the edge.

'Once I was blind, but now I can see,' I said quietly.

'You, blind? What do you mean you were blind? You mean once you didn't understand something and now you do?' She looked at me, turning her body so that she was facing me and not the edge.

I sat down on a boulder by the side of the path and pointed to another close by. 'If you sit down over here, I'll tell you about it. Then when I've finished, I'll just carry on walking up the path and leave you to make your own choice.'

Without taking her eyes off me, she walked over to the rock and sat down. The wild look had left her eyes and she seemed calmer. She looked as if she had been out all night as there were bits of grass and leaves on her clothes and in her hair. Her face was pale and drawn, but she had the bearing of one who had been brought up in a well-to-do home. Her accent was not one of the common people, and her hands were smooth and manicured.

'I was born blind,' I said slowly, 'and have only been able to see for the last year. That's why everything is so fresh to me, and the promise of a new day, and every day, is full of new shades to see and taste. I can't get enough of it. That's why I'm often up here to watch the dawn.'

'You really mean you couldn't see anything with your eyes? You were really blind? You lived in total darkness?'

'I didn't know it as darkness. I had no understanding of light or colour.' I had her full attention now, so softly I began to tell her my story...

'My parents had three children before me and they thought they would be unable to have any more. They I showed up, ten years after the younger of my sistera, Ora.'

'An unusual name, what does it mean?'

'"Ora" means "light". And she became my guiding light. My parents told me when I was older that they noticed my eyes were not as those of their other babies had been when they were born. They were afraid that something was wrong, but said nothing to my siblings. They took me to the Temple on the eighth day, to do that which was required by the law for boys. The priest asked them what my name was to be. My father said my name was to be Yoram.'

Looking at my father, the priest said, 'You know what that name means, don't you?'

'Yes,' my father replied, 'it means "God will raise him up".'

'And you feel that's an appropriate name for him?' enquired the priest.

Without saying anything more, the priest did what was required of him, and walked away. My mother heard him say, half under his breath, 'He's going to need someone to raise him up, but it won't be God; he doesn't hear sinners.'

The girl broke in, 'But why? Why did he say that? That's a dreadful thing to say to your parents!' There was anger in her voice.

Looking at her, it became clearer to me that she had come from a sheltered background.

'Haven't you heard it said? Most of the teachers of the Law believe that being born blind must mean that either my parents were sinners in some gross way and were being punished by God with a blind child, or I had somehow sinned while in my mother's womb, and this was my punishment.'

She looked at me, and I could see that she was thinking about being blind and not focusing on her own problems.

I smiled at her. 'I think his attitude was bad, but his understanding of God's Law was what has been taught for a long time. Most parents are left to get on with life and the stigma of bringing up a blind child. Now they knew what they had suspected was true – I was blind.

'My father was an honest man. He could think of nothing that he had done that should have caused this to happen to me. But he carried the guilt, feeling it must have somehow been his fault. He was determined right from the start to do all he could to help me live as normal a life as possible. He trusted my mother completely and entertained no thought of her being unfaithful to him. I don't think it even crossed his mind. He loved her and she was a very upright woman, well respected in our village. But this was soon going to change, at least in the eyes of those not close to us.

'Mother was distraught and inconsolable for days, so my sister told me when I was older. She said that mother would nurse me with tears running down her face, shaking her head and saying to herself, "No, it can't be. He is my beautiful baby. As his name is, so shall it be – God will raise him up. Oh, dear God, let it be so."

The girl was listening intently so I carried on with my story, hoping it would continue to distract her from the thought of killing herself.

'My older brother James, the first-born, had married and left home before I was conceived. Ora said that she noticed his visits home became less frequent after I was born. The elder of my sisters, Deborah, was also married and lived with her husband a two-day journey away on foot, so we didn't see her very often. But Ora said Deborah lived up to her name, which means "to speak kind words", and when she was able to visit, she would bring some consolation to my mother.'

I paused and removed the leather water bottle from my belt and offered the girl a drink. 'You must be thirsty.'

Taking the bottle, she took a long drink before handing it back.

'Thank you, I was very thirsty,' she said, and a slight smile came to her lips.

'Please, may I know your name?' I asked gently. 'But if you'd rather not tell me, I'll understand.'

She looked down at her feet for a moment, then, raising her head, she said, 'My name is Anat, and my mother tells me that means "to sing". That's a hollow joke! I haven't felt like singing for a long time.' She diverted her eyes back to her feet.

I kept silent to see if she wanted to say anything else about herself.

She looked up. 'Please go on. Tell me what it was like to live in the dark all the time.'

'Like I said, I didn't know I was in the dark, because I had never lived in any other way. As a baby, it was hard for my parents, not only living with the stigma, but also just having to watch their new baby grow without making eye contact with them, as their other children had done.

'Ora adored me. She didn't feel the humiliation that my existence had brought to my parents. She'd carry me about and take care of me. This was a great help to my mother, and some of the old spark of her personality came back. Ora told me I very seldom cried, and I would run my fingers through her hair and feel her face with my fingers, often pushing a grubby one into her mouth, just after I had been playing in the mud.

'Ora truly became my guiding light. As I learned to walk, she would hold my hand and take me out of the village and into the fields. We would lie in the grass and she would tickle me on the nose with a daisy she'd picked. She said I would giggle and grab the flower and sniff it almost up my nose.'

'But you couldn't see them,' Anat interrupted. 'That must have been so hard for you.'

'Well, not really. I could smell them. I could feel the smooth texture of the petals and the furry hairs on the stem. I didn't know what seeing was. My world was smell and sound, touch, feel and taste. Having my Ora as my guide, my world grew. I could smell how far we were from home! I could tell the times of the day by the sounds in the air and the sun on my head. I bumped into things if others had moved them in our house without thinking, but it was normal for me, and as a young child I knew nothing else. Father made a big fuss over me, and when I heard his footsteps coming along the path after his day's work I would run out of the door to greet him. He would scoop me up and cover my face with his whiskery kisses. I would bury my face in his tunic, and breathe in the smell of the olive grove where he worked. At the right season, I would reach my hand into his front pocket, where he would purposely hide a ripe olive for me to find and eat.'

Recounting these events filled my mind again with the sounds and smells of those times. But I looked at this girl in front of me, this slip of a woman. What had driven her to be out all night away from home? Had she thought of the risk she had taken, for there were bad men about who would have taken advantage of her? Why was she desperate enough to consider throwing herself to her death?

So wrapped up in her own life trauma, she didn't see the beauty all around her. I knew that I mustn't get so wrapped up in telling her my story that I forgot her fragile state of mind.

Chapter 2

'So, you didn't realise you were blind?' Anat asked. 'But there must have come a time when you realised you were different from other people around you?'

'I remember, even when I was very young, say about four or five, a question would come to my mind as to why I always went out with someone holding my hand while others seemed to go about on their own. But, and I guess it was because of the love and care of my parents, and of course my big sister Ora, I didn't dwell on it long. My young mind couldn't grapple with such complex understanding. And, as I said, I knew no other world.

'I think the time it really began to dawn on me was when I came home from a walk with Ora. There were voices coming from the house as we approached the door. Someone was speaking to my father, and it was plainly about me. I heard the visitor say, "What are you going to do with him as he gets older? He'll never be anything but a blind beggar. He won't even have a Bar-Mitzvah, as he will never be able to read the Holy Scriptures for himself. Ora won't be able to babysit him for the rest of her life – you need to think about her future as well. Why, she is old enough to be married now, and you should be looking for a good husband for her."

'My father answered the visitor. His voice was firm, but wobbled slightly, as he was observably fighting to control his emotions. "I think it is time for you to leave this house. He will not beg. He is not of a dull mind, and is quick to learn. I can teach him to recite the Law and know the scriptures. As for Ora, when the time for her is right, she will have the freedom to marry."

'"The leaders of the synagogue may have something to say about that," replied the stranger. "It's a shame on us all when you bring him along on the Sabbath, but we bear it with grace. If you push for him to have a Bar-Mitzvah, they may decide to put you out of the synagogue altogether. Be reasonable, I'm only saying this to you for your own good. Others have said it, but behind your back."

'I didn't understand what it was all about, and I felt Ora's hand grip mine more firmly, and she pulled me away from the door and round to the back of the house. "Ora, you're going too fast. Why didn't you let me go into the house to see Abba?"

'She sat down on an old wooden bench that was behind the house and pulled me close to her, wrapping her arms tightly round me in a warm hug. She was crying. I pulled away a little, and with my fingers I wiped a tear from her cheek. "What is it, Ora? Don't cry. Yoram loves you. Everything will be all right when that man has gone away," I said with childish understanding.

'She pulled me back close to her and stroked my hair. "No, Yoram, it won't be all right, even when 'that man' has gone, but Abba will find a way to make it the best he can for you."

'"What's 'blind'? What did he mean by me being a blind beggar?" I had stood up as I asked her these questions, for the words of the man were now going over in my head. "Why did he say I would not be able to read? And anyway, what's 'read?'" For the first time, a cold finger of fear touched my young life.

'Ora got off the bench, knelt on the ground in front of me and cupped my head in her hands. She leaned forward until her forehead touched mine. "Oh, dear little Yoram. How can I help you understand? Blind means that you can't see. And to read is what you learn to do when you look at writing on a parchment."

'"But Ora, what is 'see' and 'write'?"

'I could tell she was distressed as she searched for the words to try to explain it to me. "Well, 'see' is what you do with your eyes. You look with them, but…"

'I interrupted her. "But eyes are what you cry tears with when you are hurt or sad," I said, "like you are now. I can feel them on your face."

'I reached up again and wiped another tear from her face. "See, I've caught one!" I said, with a smile on my face.

'She held my hand, and took the tear from my fingers with her hand. "You said, 'See, I have caught one.' What did you mean by that, dear little Yoram?"

'I thought for a moment. "I meant, I caught it in my hand and was showing it to you. I could feel it – it was wet and it you rub or stroke it; it dries up and is gone… if you lick it, it tastes salty. I knew it! When you 'see' something, you know it. So Ora, I can't be blind 'cos I can see your tears on my fingers."

'"Yes, tears come from your eyes, Yoram, but your eyes are meant to do something else as well. When I open my eyes in the morning, I see things with them. I know things by looking at them with my eyes as well as touching them, or tasting them, or hearing them. Sadly, Yoram, your eyes can only cry. For some reason, they don't work as they should, so you can't 'know' with them. We call that kind of knowing, 'seeing'."'

Anat had been looking at me intently as I was speaking. 'Ora was very kind to you and must have cared so much about you. How difficult for her to have to try to explain what blindness was.'

'Close your eyes,' I said to her, and she did so. 'What do you see?'

'I can't see anything, Yoram. How can I with my eyes shut?!' There was a smile on her face as she spoke.

'Don't open them – keep them shut. Now turn your head to your left. What do you see now?'

'I don't see anything.'

'Wait,' I said. 'Where is the sun?'

'Well, it's in front of me.'

'Ah! You see it with your eyes closed,' I said.

'Well, no. But yes! I see what you mean!' She laughed and opened her eyes.

'You said, "I see what you mean!" Our eyes are another way of understanding our surroundings, our world. I had a world that I understood, but now I was beginning to understand that there was a larger world that was beyond my understanding, that I couldn't reach, because my eyes didn't do what other people's eyes did. Anat, this "unblind" world had dimensions that I could not understand, and my lack of understanding would make it impossible for me to live in it as freely as others could. I had so much to learn about what I was unable to learn! So much to see about what I couldn't begin to see! That day, behind the house with Ora, became the crisis point for me, and in some measure for Ora as well.

'Because of the conversation she had overheard, she was awakened to her womanhood in a way that she had not been before. She was still kneeling in front of me, and she pulled my head on to her shoulder and held me tight for a very long time. While we were embracing in this way, my father came round the back of the house looking for us.

'The visitor had gone and he had seen Ora pull me away from the door. He walked over to where we were huddled on the ground, dropped to his knees beside us and hugged us both with his strong arms. His smell of olive trees calmed my little world. I was beginning to see that I couldn't see.'

Chapter 3

Eye hath not seen, nor ear heard, neither have
entered into the heart of man, the things which
God hath prepared for them that love him.
1 Corinthians 2:9 (KJV)

Anat stood up. I was afraid she would walk back to the
edge of the rock, but she only stretched herself and then
asked if she could have another drink of water. I got to my
feet and handed her the bottle. She drank from it and
handed it back, then sat down again. The sun had moved
round, so I changed my position and sat on a boulder the
other side of her where there was some shade. I said
nothing, waiting for her to ask if she wanted to hear any
more.

'What did your father do after that, and where was your
mother while all this was going on?'

'My mother had gone to visit some lifelong friends who
lived on the other side of the village. Father had taken the
day off work to look after me, enabling her to go. Abba
picked me up and carried me into the house with Ora
walking beside him. He sat me down on a low stool by the
table, and Ora sat on a bench on the opposite side. Going
over to the large stone pitcher that had water in it, he filled
three cups for us to drink. Bringing them over, he sat them
down on the table, and then sat beside Ora.

'Reaching over the table, he took my hand in his. "I'm
sorry you heard some of what that man was saying,
Yoram. There's a lot you're too young to understand right
now, but what I want you to know, more than anything

else, is that you are loved and cherished by your mother and me."

'"And me," chipped in Ora.

'"But Abba, why did he say those thing about me? Why doesn't he like me? What does a 'blind beggar' do?" I asked, with a shiver of that cold fear touching me.

'"I'll do all that I can to see that you never have to beg. Push that thought right out of your head," Abba said, firmly.

'"I'll try, Abba, but what is a beggar, anyway?" I insisted.

'"A beggar is someone who for some reason is unable to work, and the only way he can get money to live on is to sit by the roadside or at the Temple gate and ask that people be kind to him and give him money. You will never have to do that," Abba said with determination.

'I remember asking him, "What's reading? What does it do?" He didn't answer straight away; I guess he was trying to think of a way of explaining it to me so that I could grasp it. I heard him get up and walk across the room, and rummage in the box in which he kept dry sticks for lighting the fire. He came back to the table and placed three sticks down. With a knife he cut a small notch on the end of the first one, and handed it to me. "Can you feel the notch I have just cut on the end of this stick?"

'I felt it, and told him I could. He picked up the next stick and cut two notches in its end, and handed it to me. "Can you feel the two notches on this one?" I felt it, and said that I could. He then took the last stick and cut three notches on it, and again, handed it to me to feel. I told him there were three notches on it. He picked all three up and rolled them together in his hands, then placed them in a row in front of me on the table.

'"Now the stick with one notch is yours, the one with two notches is Ora's and the one with three notches is mine. You understand?"

'"Yes, Abba, that's easy to understand," I said, and before he could say any more I reached out and felt the end of one of the sticks. "This one is Ora's because I can feel two notches on it," I said, as I handed it to Ora. Then I felt another and found one notch and put it down near myself and handed the last one to Abba. "This one's yours!"

'"Wonderful, Yoram. Now how did you know which one was yours?" he asked, as he squeezed my hand.

'"I could feel the notches like you said, and the one with one notch on was to be mine."

'"And that's reading, Yoram, that's reading!" Abba shouted joyfully. "The notches I cut into the sticks are a bit like writing – marks that mean something. When you feel the marks you can read which one is which. The hard bit for you, my dear Yoram, is that the marks that people make on parchment don't stick out nor are cut in, so you can feel them with your fingers. They are marks that can only be read by people using their eyes. We can understand the marks and read them because our eyes tell us what they are. Sadly, your eyes don't work, and so you can only read marks that you can feel with your fingers."

'I was quiet for a little while as I tried to understand what he was saying to me. "Why can't they make the writing marks on sticks, so that I can read them with my fingers, Abba?"

'"I'm sorry, Yoram, but for writing to tell us many things, there are many differently shaped marks, and it would be impossible to cut them small enough to be felt with your fingers, and you would have to have parchments as big as trees to get even a small amount on."

'His voice sounded weary as he spoke these words to me, and I used my eyes for the only thing that they could do, and cried. I could see that because I could not see, my world would be forever small, compared to most people who could get understanding through eyes that worked.

'Abba picked me up and sat me on his knee. "I will do all I can to help you grow and understand, my little man. We will find a way of doing our own writing so that you can read it, and I will read to you all the writing marks that I see with my working eyes. We love you, Yoram. Whatever happens, remember we love you."'

Anat looked at me. 'Your father must be a wonderful man. I wish my father would have held me and spoken to me like that. I wish he would explain to me why he says things have to be like they have to be – if they really have to!' She bent down and picked a stalk of grass and rolled it between her fingers. Then, looking at me again, she continued, 'As you began to understand that there would be things that you couldn't understand, did it make you angry? Did you think it was so unfair that you could not do what Ora could do?'

'I think that overhearing my Abba's conversation with the visitor focused things that I must have been thinking about for some time. Questions that, up until then, I hadn't been able to put into words. So when it happened I wasn't angry, rather more bewildered and afraid. But the love and kindness of my parents and my sister Ora helped me. Abba's words somehow gave me hope. As for thinking it was unfair, I can't really say. Because Ora was my guiding light, I knew she was sharing this mysterious sense of sight with me. Her eyes were my eyes, and as she shared her seeing world with me, my world grew along with hers.

'When I thought of the visitor, I did feel hurt and was angry with him. He did seem to be so unfair. If he had so much understanding and was so clever, why did he think it wrong to share it with me? That made me feel I was no good. I think that's what made me cry more than anything else. It was a little whisper in my mind that said, "You're no good; you're worthless," that made me sad. But the love of my family shouted louder.'

I looked at Anat and could see she was looking very fatigued. 'Anat, when did you last eat? You look done in. Do you think it would be a good thing to come home with me? You could meet my parents and have something to eat. I left before they were awake, and they may become concerned if I'm not back for breakfast.'

'If you promise to say nothing about how you first saw me, and let me leave if I want to, I'd like that. I am hungry – and I want to hear how you grew up, and most of all how you can now see.'

'Will anyone be looking for you?' I asked.

'They may be by now, as I've been away all night. We had such a blazing row and I stormed out of the house, vowing I would never return. It wasn't the first time it's happened, and I've always gone back after a few hours. They wouldn't have worried much at first, but I guess they may be a bit worried by now. But I don't care! Let them worry – if they even do!' Her last sentence was said with anger, and she stood up. 'Please, Yoram, take me to your parents' home. I'm thinking more clearly now, and I won't do anything silly,' she added.

We walked along, and she spoke for the first time about her own situation. 'They can't make me do what I don't want to do, can they? After all, I have my own life to lead. I'm over sixteen now.'

'I'm not in a position to say what "they" can or can't do, Anat. As you said to me on the rocks back there, I don't know anything about you to be able to judge. And even if I could, I'm not sure I have either the wisdom or the right to do so. What is it they want you to do?'

'My father – and mother as well – want me to marry that man! He is old, unpleasant, ugly and filthy rich! Father says if I don't, he will disown me, cut me off from the rest of the family and any inheritance I may have had coming to me. It's like I'm a farm animal, to be paired off to any man with good breeding or social standing. He is willing to pay the dowry for me to marry just so that he can move in the circles that that monster moves in. It's like I'm to be added to his trophy collection, a young filly to keep him warm in his old age!' Her voice rose as her words came out, almost tumbling over each other.

'Talk about blindness!' she continued. 'They are totally blinded by money not to be able to see who he is, and how dreadful my life would be. The only release for me would be if he died early. I wish he was dead now! But as he isn't, I felt I might as well be – anything to escape a life of a living hell with him.'

Our home was in sight, so I didn't respond to her outburst, but I was glad I knew what it was that had made her desperate enough to think of killing herself. Yes, I thought, blindness can be more than lack of eyesight.

Chapter 4

My parents were sitting outside, eating, as we arrived. Father rose to his feet to greet us. 'I see you have had a good walk this morning, Yoram, and have brought back the light of the dawn with you.' Anat blushed, but smiled at him.

'Abba, Mother, let me introduce you to Anat, who I have had the privilege of meeting on the path early this morning. She misjudged the distance of her journey and is in need of some food and drink to strengthen her for the rest of her trip.'

My mother rose and kissed her, then went into the house to bring food for us.

'Sit down, my dear,' Father said, and pulled the old wooden bench into the shade so she could sit comfortably. He poured some wine into a cup and passed it to her, then did the same for me. 'You are from Jerusalem, Anat? Which area would that be?' my father asked.

I was a bit nervous for Anat and hoped that she wouldn't feel under pressure to say anything she didn't want to say. I needn't have worried; it may have been her upbringing, for she took it in her stride and answered politely, without hesitation,

'I live with my parents on the east side of the city, not far from the Temple. My father is a merchant dealing mainly in precious stones, fine silks and quality olive oil. He travels extensively and trades with many countries of the Roman Empire. I was going to visit the home of Simon Bar-Amos in Bethany. My father trades with him, so I know his daughter well.'

I was surprised at the amount of information she was willing to tell about herself, as she had been reluctant to talk earlier. But I could see it was better for her to give more information on her terms than to be asked other questions that she might not wish to answer. 'Sir, I believe you work in the olive industry?'

I smiled to myself. *She is no fool; now she has taken control of the direction of the conversation*. But I wondered if she had realised that it was Simon's olive groves that my father managed.

'As a matter of fact, I manage the olive groves for Simon in the area you have just walked through. Most of the olive groves on the Mount of Olives belong to him. He's an honest man and a good employer. I've worked for him for many years. He was willing to let Yoram come with me to the presses, even when he had his limitation of blindness. Many others would not have been so compassionate.' Looking at me, Father added, 'Not that Yoram's blindness turned out to be a handicap for him, but more of an asset. Isn't that so, Yoram?'

Anat turned to me. 'How could that be, Yoram? How could blindness ever be an asset?'

I picked up the conversation from my father, as he went into the house to help mother with the food. 'I told you earlier, being unable to see with my eyes meant my other senses became more highly tuned than that of sighted people. I hear things others would miss; I feel vibrations in the ground that you would never notice. And my sense of smell and taste are much sharper than that of many people. This became a most useful thing as I got older, when we were pressing the olives for oil. I could smell when a batch was ready for pouring out, and taste and tell when the unwanted by-products were ready to be strained off. By taste, I could judge the quality of the oil better than others. This was a big bonus for Simon, as he graded his oil very particularly. That's probably the reason why your father trades with him.'

'That's amazing, Yoram; who would have thought that being blind could help you to work and prevent you from having to beg for a living? But we've jumped a big bit of your life. When we left that place earlier, you had only told me about how you first came to terms with being blind as a young boy, and about Ora being your guiding light and the effect that horrible man had on you. What happened between then, and how did you come to be working for Simon?'

My parents came out with our breakfast, so we ate our fill before carrying on the conversation. My mother looked at Anat. 'I thought I'd seen you before when you came along the road with Yoram. Now my husband tells me that you are friends with Simon's daughter. That's where I've seen you. I think it was about a year ago. I'd called in to take a sample of the new olive oil for Simon. His wife brought me out a drink, and you were talking with her daughter in the yard over by their well. Weren't you about to be married to a merchant's son who traded with your father?'

The colour drained from Anat's face, but she managed to keep her composure. 'I did spent time with Esther, Simon's daughter, but I think you must be mistaken about my being pledged in marriage to a merchant's son. Sadly, something so exciting has never been on the horizon for me. How is Esther? It is a while since I last visited her.'

'She's well,' Mother answered, 'but I think your timing is a bit out, my dear, for she left yesterday with her father. He suggested that she travel with him as he took some fresh olives to one of the sea ports. Only her mother will be there.'

'Oh, that's fine, I get on well with her mother too. I will be sorry not to see Esther, but seeing her mother will be a welcome break from the bustle of Jerusalem,' Anat replied.

I felt it best to break into the conversation before it became too hard for Anat not to give away something away that she didn't want to, so I said, 'Mother, if it's all right with you, I'll escort Anat over to Simon's house, so she'll not have to travel further on her own. I was telling her about my blindness as we came along the road, and she wanted me to finish the story.'

'Well, I was going as far as Mary and Martha's house, so I could walk part of the way with you,' Mother said. I noticed my father kick her under the bench. 'On second thoughts, I need to finish cleaning up here first. You young ones go on. Anat, give my greetings to Esther's mother.'

Anat thanked my parents for their hospitality, and we left on the road to Bethany. When we were out of earshot, she said, 'Thanks for interrupting; it was getting difficult. I should have realised that in any small community, everyone would know everyone else. I liked your father – he was just as I thought he would be from what you said about him. Did you see him kick your mother's foot under the bench?' She laughed as she said this, and the sound was like a brook bubbling over stones. She had become more alive.

'Will you really stay at Simon's? Is that why you came this way out of Jerusalem?' I asked her.

'It wasn't my intention to do that, but maybe it was at the back of my mind if I couldn't go through with jumping from the rocks. What do you think I should do, now you know more about me? Yoram, I really can't go back home if it means that I have to marry that old ugly man. When your mother spoke about my being pledged to be married to a merchant's son, I didn't lie to her. If it had been the son of a merchant, I would not have objected, but not to the old merchant himself.'

'I think that going to Simon's home is a good idea. If they let you stay, you will be safe from harm, and when Esther gets back you will have good company. Perhaps Simon may be able to plead your case with your father and get him to see things from your point of view. Surely he must care for your well-being, to some extent?'

'I wish that were true, but I doubt it. Money is my father's god, and everything else is dispensable in his pursuit for more. Even my mother is subject to his overriding passion for it. I was always a disappointment to him, as I was not a boy. To him, I was not only an inconvenience, but also the cause of his wife not being able to give him a son. My only redeeming feature was that, as I developed into womanhood, I was attractive to men, and that meant he could trade me in for the best connections! Just like Simon's best oil.' She was getting more and more upset as she talked and, rightly or wrongly, I put my hand on her shoulder, to show some comfort.

She stopped walking, threw her arms around me and buried her face on my shoulder. 'Oh, Yoram, why couldn't you be a wealthy merchant, then you could make it all right, just like you getting your sight back?'

She stepped back from me, and looking through tear-filled eyes said, 'I'm sorry, Yoram, I shouldn't have done that. It was totally selfish of me. Forgive me. I will be more discreet in my behaviour. But please, tell me what it's like coming out of darkness after all those years of being blind.'

We sat down on a grassy bank by a stream – a discreet distance away from each other. Her last outburst had thrown me as to what was the proper way to react. Her emotions were raw enough already without being complicated with misplaced feelings for me. I began to look at her in a new light. With the sun shining on her black hair, and her slender body silhouetted against the sky, I saw that she was a very attractive young lady. When she smiled, her face lit up, and she looked so different from the bedraggled girl I had met only a few hours before. I checked myself, and continued my story with consideration for her feelings. The Lord only knows how my own feelings and dreams had been crushed so many times in the past.

'You asked me, back at my home, what happened to me after the time my young life had been turned upside down by the thoughtless visitor. Well, it not only awakened in me the understanding that I was different because I was blind, but it also caused Ora to realise she was now a woman. One who, like you, was now able to marry. Because she had been so good to me and a blessing to my mother, I think she had spent so little time thinking about herself. The man's words stirred in her the natural thoughts and feelings of any young woman. She had adored her little blind brother so much that she had looked no further ahead for her own life.

'I think Abba was well aware of this, for when my mother came back – she was visiting Mary and Martha that day as well – he left me with Ora and took Mother off for a long walk. When they got back, Abba helped me get ready for bed while mother sat outside talking intently with Ora.

'I overheard snatches of their conversation, because as I've told you, my hearing was sharp and I could tune into different tones and block out others. Mother was comforting her over the unkind words of Father's visitor, and assured her that they would look after me in every way they could, and she was not to worry about me. Somehow, she got round to talking about how a young woman begins to want to get married herself, and have children of her own. I didn't listen much more as I was being tucked into bed by my father. He gave me the blessing and told me to be at peace and sleep well.

'From that day on, Mother would take me with her more than in the past, and she sent Ora off on errands that previously she would have done herself. Abba began to take me to work with him and explain how to look after olive trees and to get the best olives to grow. In the evenings, he would pull an oil lamp close to him on the table and get out some parchments he had, and read them out to me. I had often wondered why they bothered about lamps. What was the point of them? I liked the smell of burning oil, and had once put my finger in the flame. That hurt, and I did my best not to do that again, so I kept my hands well away from them. Now that I understood it was something to do with sight, it seemed to me that eyes only worked in the daytime. They needed light so they could see. What light was, I couldn't get my mind around. I thought it must be something like the warmth from the sun, because when the sun was shining, not only could you feel it on your face, but somehow it gave this thing called light that enabled people with working eyes to see with.

'So in the evenings, Abba would pull up the lamp and take the parchments which had these unfeelable marks on them called writing. He was very proud of these parchments, as very few people had any. They had been given to him by an old rabbi who had written on them part of the books of Moses. He began to read to me the stories of Moses. He'd told me some of these before, but now he was reading them to me from the parchments. I was captured by them, and had so many questions about Jehovah, our God.

'Mother would take Ora out and sometimes leave her to stay with a friend who had daughters of a similar age. Ora suddenly grew up. She still loved me, though, and spent as much time with me as she could. She still took me for walks out in the fields, and we would sit in the long grass. But I spent more time with my parents. Going out with Abba made my world bigger than I had ever dreamed.

'As Abba walked to the olive groves with me, he would encourage me to tell him where we were, and ask what would come next. He would say, "How far to the stream?" or, "How long will it take us to get to the olive press?" At the press, he took me around it many times, getting me to touch the racks with the large storage jars on them. Or to feel where the pile of olives would be tipped before they were placed into the press. He would ask, "How many steps to the side door? How many steps are there down to the vat that stores the pressed olives?" I was quick to learn, and very soon could make my way round the press area without bumping into anything.'

Anat interrupted me, 'Did you use a stick to help you walk along?'

'One day, at home, Abba cut two sticks from the hedge and gave me one. He carved mine with a knobbly handle, so I knew which was mine.

'"What are we going to do with these, Abba?" I asked him.

'"We are going to have a game of 'tap and see'. With these sticks we can pretend that our arms are longer and, with them, feel what is around us without bumping into anything. What do you say, Yoram, shall I start first and see how well I can do it?"

'"No, Abba, let me," I pleaded. I took the stick, and just as I would walk in the house with my hands out to touch things to get my bearings, so I walked across our yard swinging the stick from side to side and tapping anything it touched, so I could guess what it was. "That's the bench we sit on when we eat outside, and that's the tree halfway up the road. This is the gate, and now I am through the gate. I am turning towards the way we go to work." Tap. The stick hit something that I was not expecting to be there. "What's that, Abba?" I asked. "There shouldn't be anything in the middle of the road."

'"Feel it gently with your stick, Yoram, and tell me what you think it is," Abba replied. I moved the stick over the thing in my path. It moved as I pushed it. It was soft, like cloth. I lifted the stick higher and let it run over the outside of whatever it was. Then I dropped the stick and ran into the arms of my own mother who had stood in my path. "Mother, it's you!" I squealed with delight. "Abba, I can tell where I am without you holding my hand! Am I seeing, Abba, am I seeing?"

'"Seeing with your long stick arm, Yoram. You have done so very well. I think in a little while you will be able to go around our village on your own."

'I went to bed very happy that night. And my Ora had begun to spread her wings as well!'

Chapter 5

Anat reached over and picked up a broken branch that lay close by, stretching out her hand and shutting her eyes as she moved it around herself. She made contact with a tree stump and tapped it, then tried to feel the outline with the stick. She opened her eyes and said, 'I can see how it works, and it can prevent you from tripping over something, but I would hate to have only that to guide me along. It must be so hard to know which way you're going.'

'Remember, Anat, you have other senses as well, and you have to learn to use them. That's why I am now more blessed, as I have sight added to what I already had.'

'Did you learn to go out on your own?'

'Oh yes, but not until I had walked a route with my father first. He would walk behind me and let me lead him. It's amazing what you have stored in your head. I had known the way to the olive press for a long time and knew what came next, almost like a sixth sense. The first time I led my father, it was fun for me, and I did it almost without making any mistakes. I felt I could go anywhere. But, of course, that was far from the truth. Yet, it was a start. The next day I went later, after he had left. It was a bit scary at first, but I took my time and arrived at the press without falling over or making a wrong turn. Unknown to me, my mother had followed me, but out of my hearing, just to make sure I got there. We had such a celebration that day. After that, they took me into the village several times, so that I had a picture of the way in my mind, then I would do that route on my own. Before long I had a kind of map in my head of most of the village.'

'And Ora, she did leave home? How did you feel about that?'

'To put it bluntly, Anat, I was devastated. My parents did a great job of weaning me off her, and she off me. She would be away working in a field, gleaning or something like that, and I was fine with that for I knew she would be coming home and we would have time together. But the day came, about two years after that crisis point, when she broke the news to me that she would be marrying a man from the next village, Bethphage. His name was John, and he was a tanner by trade. She was excited and began making plans to set up a new home for herself and her husband-to-be. Her excitement made me excited for her at first, and she told me of their plans for the home.

'It was a few weeks later, when, with John's parents and ours, a date was set for the wedding and the details of the celebration were being drawn up, that it hit me. She would be leaving home – for good – and not coming back to live here again. I was just coming up to ten years old and Ora had turned nineteen. We had gathered at John's parents' house for this meeting, so without showing how I was feeling, I announced in the early evening that, as they had a lot still to talk about, I would begin to make my own way home. I had done this before, so they let me go. I knew several people who lived along the way, so if I had any problems I could always stop and ask someone. People were now used to seeing me making my own way with my stick.

'I came along here, about where we are now, left the path and tapped my way down to the edge of the stream. It must have been under that tree over there.' I pointed to a large oak by the water's edge. 'I walked round the other side of it and sat down with my back against it with my feet almost in the stream – and I cried – no, I sobbed, big sobs that shook my whole body. Ora was not coming back – John had stolen her from me – Abba had let her go – my world fell apart!

'I felt out of control, unable to do anything for myself. I hadn't understood the terms of darkness and light until that moment. Now I felt darkness! It washed all around me and sank deep into me. Those cold fingers of fear began to clutch at me and, I think for the first time, almost in contradiction to the coldness of the fear, but nevertheless caused by it, a hot rage exploded within me. I stood up and screamed. I threw my walking stick as far away as I could, then hammered with my fists as hard as I could on the trunk of the tree.

'When I look back, I think I came under the sovereign protection of our God, for along this very path came my father's employer, Simon. He was on his own, facing his own life-changing crisis. He heard me scream, and saw my stick flying through the air. Leaving his pack donkey he ran over to find me with bleeding hands, as I continued pounding the tree with my fists.

'"Yoram, whatever is the matter? What are you doing here on your own?"

'I shouted at him, "Go away, and leave me alone! Don't you know I'm a useless sinner that's good for nothing?"

'Simon came up to me and held me with his strong arms, so that my arms were pinned to my sides, preventing me from hurting myself any more.

'"*Let me go!*" I shouted at him, but his grip only strengthened.

'"Yoram, it's me, Simon, your Abba's master. Now calm down, stop struggling and I'll release you."

'I gave up and let my body go limp in his arms, and my legs turned to water under me. He picked me up and carried me over to his donkey. Putting me on it, he turned around and walked back the way he had come towards our house. Lifting me off, he sat me down on the bench beside the door, and sat down beside me.

'"Want to tell me all about it, Yoram? What's gone so badly wrong?" he said gently, and let me lay my head on his strong shoulder. He had the same smell as my father – olive oil.

'Slowly, between sobs, I told him the whole sorry story. I finished up by saying, "I'm no good to anybody. People say I was a sinner at birth, and will always be."'

I stopped talking and could see that Anat was crying. 'You do know how I feel, Yoram, you really do. That was just how I felt last night.' She wiped her tears with her hand and said, 'What happened when your parents got home?'

'They weren't back for quite a while, so Simon stayed with me. We talked, sort of "man to man". He didn't rebuke me, but said he understood how I was feeling. He gently helped me to see how much my parents cared for me, and they were not really treating me like I was a useless person. He explained how Ora still loved me, but as I was now a "big boy", I had to understand that life changes and we have to let people go, or we end up treating them like donkeys and trying to make them do what we want all the time.

'But the thing that got through to me most was that he had something that he wanted to tell me about himself. Something he'd told no one else in the whole world, something he had only found out that day. My young ears pricked up, and my feelings of self-worth suddenly rose a hundred times! Here was a grown-up, my own father's boss, ready to tell me something that he had shared with no one else in the whole wide world.

'"If I tell you my secret, you must promise not to tell anyone else." He paused for a moment and then added, "apart from your Abba. You may tell your Abba."

'I nodded my head and said, '"I promise, Mr Simon, I won't tell anyone apart from Abba."

'Simon carried on, "Well, you know what it's like for people to say things about you that can hurt you? And you know that some people don't want to be with you, because they think you are a sinner or unclean?"

'I nodded again. "Yes, I do know what that's like. Some people walk the other side of the road when me and Abba come along, and I did hear someone say once, 'What sinners those people are.'"

'"Well, when I heard you by the stream this evening, it made me stop thinking about myself. You see, Yoram, I've had some very bad news today, news that will probably change my life forever. A bit like you, when people find out, they may walk the other side of the road and not want to come near me. It makes me afraid of what might happen. So maybe we can help each other, as we both adjust to changes in our lives." He spoke quietly to me, and I felt that he really was afraid.

'I tried to put my arms round him and said, "I'm sorry, Mr Simon. What's the matter with you? I will help you."

'It's laughable now as I tell you, but I meant every word in a way that only a ten-year-old boy can. I felt so grown up, and needed. Here was my father's boss asking me for comfort. And I do think he was comforted by my childlike trust.

'Simon cleared his throat and said, "A little while ago, I found a patch on my body that was different from the rest of my skin. It was a bit tender to touch and it looked different. I didn't tell my wife or Esther because I thought it was just a rash that would go away in a few days. But it didn't. And now it's spread. So today I went to see a doctor who is a friend of mine, to ask him what he thought. He examined the place I showed him and then checked me all over. He looked very worried.

'"'What do you think it is?' I said to him. He said he could not be totally sure, but he had seen it before and thought it could be leprosy. Yoram, I was afraid he would say that, but he did add that there are different types of leprosy, and some are not as bad as others. I would have to come back and see him in a week's time. He said he thought it was the sort that was not catching, but most people will not believe it and so will have nothing to do with me. I will be seen as unclean, Yoram. No one will want to touch me. I probably should not even be sitting here with you."

'I held his big hand in mine. "I'll touch you, Mr Simon. We can be sinners and untouchables together." I had no idea what leprosy was or how it was feared by everyone.

"People call me 'Yoram the blind boy'. Will they call you 'Simon the leper'?" I said with the innocence of childhood.

'"If when I see the doctor next week it hasn't changed, then yes, Yoram, I will be known as 'Simon the leper'. Remember, you promised to tell no one but your Abba."

'I said, "I promise, Mr Simon, and thank you for caring for me. Will you tell Abba about me, because I don't know how, and I don't want to upset him or Ora?"

'"I think they're coming now. Yes, if you'd like me to, I'll explain it to your Abba."

'Father told me later that it was dusk when they arrived at home, and he was very relieved to see Simon with me, as he hadn't meant to be so long in coming back.

'My mother saw the blood on my hands and my dirty face, and was about to ask what had happened, but Simon got in first. "Yoram had a bit of an incident on the way home, but then he was a real man and helped me with a problem I had. He just needs a bit of a clean-up, and all will be well." He turned to me and said, "Thank you, Yoram, you have been a very big help to me this evening." Then he spoke to my father. "Nathaniel, could I talk with you? I have something on my mind that can't wait till the morning."

'Mother thought it was to do with work, so she left the men talking on the bench outside while she cleaned me up and helped me get ready for bed.'

Chapter 6

Anat was still playing with the stick. 'Why do people have to be so blind?!' she said with indignation. 'Can't they see the pain they cause others?'

'I've heard it said, "There is none so blind as those who don't want to see," but, Anat, I had to learn I was not only blind because of lack of eyesight, but blinded in so many other ways. In fact, most of us stumble along in some sort of blindness or selective seeing. So often we only see what we want to see. This came home to me a couple of years later, when I approached my Bar-Mitzvah.'

I stood, saying, 'I think we should be getting along to Simon's home.' Anat got up, and we started along the road to Bethphage.

'"Simon the leper". My father never said anything about that. But I did know that some people called him that. What was the result of his second visit to the doctor?', she asked.

'He didn't go back. The doctor, though his friend, was not careful about who he talked to, and in a conversation with a member of the synagogue he let it slip that he was concerned about someone who had come to see him with a skin complaint. In fairness, he didn't actually say it was Simon, but in the course of the conversation, the other person put two and two together and came up with the name of Simon. And he didn't keep his mouth shut! In a few days, word had got round and an angry mob gathered outside Simon's house demanding that he should go and show himself to the priest for the examination that the Law required of anyone with a skin complaint. He had no choice, so he made his way to Jerusalem to present himself to the priest. The mob followed him, at a safe distance, shouting and cursing him. He saw the priest who, following the letter of the Law, told him to come back in seven days. The mob dispersed, and he made his way home.

'My father called in to see him the next day. Simon was very low. He knew the effect this would have not only on his own life and that of his family, but also on his business. They spent the morning talking together, and when Abba got home, I was surprised when he said that Simon had asked if I would go and visit him. I felt overwhelmed that he wanted me to see him, and Abba walked back with me. When we got to Simon's house, he was out in the courtyard, sitting by the well. Abba took me to him and left us on our own. I reached out, and Simon took my hand and drew me to himself. I gave him the biggest hug that I could, and he hugged me back for what seemed like a very long time without saying a word. At first he was trembling, but slowly he became still. He placed his hands on my shoulders and held me at arm's length, as he spoke to me. "Thank you, Yoram. I needed that. I think you are the only one who really knows what I'm going through."

'I replied, "I know what it's like for people not to want me. I know how sad I feel when I can't do things. But it must be harder for you, because you've known what it's like to do things, and make them happen."

'He hugged me again. "You may be only ten years old, Yoram, but you have wisdom beyond your years. Thank you for coming to see old Simon the leper."

'"But you haven't been back to see the priest yet. He may say you are clean next week," I said with childish conviction.

'"I know that's true, but remember, I have already had this for a few weeks. I fear, Yoram, I am a leper. I will have to live outside the village, and when I come near anyone, I will have to ring a bell and call out 'unclean'. I was speaking to your Abba today and have asked him to look after the olive groves until I know what to do. I have a brother who is coming to run my business alongside his own, but we were never able to work together while we were younger, so I'm not sure how it will turn out."

'His voice cracked, and I knew he was crying. "I will have to leave my lovely wife and daughter. We have a small house that was once a shelter for my workers at another olive press; I will go and live there. They will bring me food and leave it for me at the gate." At this, he broke down and started to cry. I moved back close to him and gave him another hug.

'"I will come to visit you, Simon. Abba will teach me the way and I can come and carry food from your wife to you," I said, not really understanding the full ramifications of being a leper.

'He held me away again and said, "You have a kind heart, Yoram, and your Abba was kind to let you come, but when it is confirmed by the priest, it would not be right for you to come. You will have to stay away, my gallant young friend."

'"But I will come! I will come! Us outcasts need each other," I cried, and stamped my foot.

'"Bless you, Yoram, but I think you must do whatever your Abba says is the right thing to do. One good thing is that my olive oil business has been very good over the last few years and we do have money to take care of our needs. Thank you for coming. I will miss you very much. Now I think you must make your way back home with your Abba."

'I hugged him once more, and slowly tapped my way out of the courtyard to where Abba was waiting for me.'

Anat asked, 'My father never told me all this, Yoram, and Esther or her mother never said anything either. And it doesn't add up. When I've been to the house, I've seen Simon. He lives with them and is well and looks very fit and healthy. How does what you say fit in?'

'You forget, Anat, I am talking about ten years ago. When did you start to visit their home?'

She thought for a moment, 'Oh it must be about four years ago that I got to know Esther... but come to think of it, it's only the last year or year and a half that I've been to the house and met Simon. I first got to know Esther and her mother when they came to bring olive oil samples to my father. They said they came on behalf of Simon bar-Amos.'

'That's how it fits together, Anat. In those eight long years before you met him, Simon had been living a very different kind of life.'

'How did it affect your family, Yoram? I guess it meant that your father took on more responsibility, and so, in a way, you were all better off?' Anat asked.

'If only that were the case,' I replied. 'But nothing could have been further from the truth.'

'But why? Surely, as you've said, Simon is an upright man and he would have been grateful for the extra responsibility your father was taking on.'

'Oh, Simon was, and is, an honourable man, but his brother was something altogether different! The next week Simon went back to see the priest, and as he'd feared, he was pronounced unclean. He had hardly got out of the Temple ground before some of the mob were at his heels. They shouted at him, threw stones and quickly drove him out of the city. My father and Simon's wife met him and took him to his home. But he knew he would not be left alone for very long. They'd made preparations for the worst, and my father helped them pack what Simon would need onto his donkey, then they made their way out of the village, before any more trouble came.

'My father told me that the hardest part was when they left. At first Simon would not let Esther or his wife touch him. But his wife threw herself round him and sobbed on his shoulders. Esther joined them, and they clung together. Abba walked a little way off so they could be alone. Simon called him back after a while and they shook hands and embraced. Father told me that he assured Simon he would do all he could to help his wife and daughter and work the olive grove to the best of his ability. Simon was grateful, but was fearful as to what would happen when his brother arrived.

'Simon's brother lived up to all expectations – no good! He was as different to Simon as could be, and in all the wrong ways. Hard, uncaring and mean. He knew almost nothing about the proper care of olive trees, and yet wouldn't be told. It wasn't long before he made his presence felt and began to change the way my father worked at the olive grove. He dictated how the trees were to be pruned – in all the wrong ways – but when my father tried to point out to him that this would reduce the amount of olives that would come the following year, he was told in no uncertain terms that if he didn't like it, he could find somewhere else to work. My father put up with it for almost two years, but because of bad husbandry the crops were less.

'My father got the blame for not doing his job properly. He was accused of being lazy and also of stealing some of the best olives to make money on the side. For the sake of Simon, my father tried to reason with his brother, but it was of no use. His brother got angry and told him not to come back to work any more. He also spread lies about my father and made it very difficult for him to get other work.'

Anat broke in, 'But couldn't Simon have done something about it? Surely he could have told his brother to do things the way he wanted him to?'

'Things were more complicated than that, Anat. My father never told me, but I could tell that Simon was afraid of what his brother might do to his wife and daughter if he said too much. And as he himself was now an outcast, there was little he could do about it.'

'Did you still go and see Simon, or did your father not let you?' Anat asked.

'I did go. Simon made me stand at the gate of his property and he would talk to me from the other side. He would stand about four steps away from the gate. I felt so sorry for him – it was so unfair. He was a good man but was unable to do anything about it. Mother's friends Mary and Martha have a brother called Lazarus, and he was very good to Simon and would take food to him and help take care of Simon's wife and daughter. I think Lazarus being on the scene kept Simon's brother from doing anything inappropriate.

'It was coming up to the time of my Bar-Mitzvah and Abba was teaching me from the parchments. I was drawn to them, and hungry to learn about our history and the Law. But most of all, I wanted to know about our God, Jehovah.

'Abba took me to the synagogue every week, and I loved to hear the book of Moses being read from. Our rabbi was a good man and taught us well. The ruler of the synagogue was kind to us and would let me, after the service, touch the things in the building so that I could get an understanding of how it was set out. My mother and Ora would sit on one side while Abba and I sat with the men on the other side. Not all of the members of the ruling party of the synagogue were as gracious as the ruler, and they didn't approve of my behaviour. But in the instruction time Abba took me to, I was able to keep up with the sighted boys and quickly grasp much of the teaching. I was allowed to ask questions like all the others, and my enthusiasm gained me some respect.'

I paused and looked up into the sky. The sun was higher now, and I thought Anat should be making her way to the home of Simon. 'I think we should quicken our pace, Anat. At this rate it will be noon before we reach Simon's home.'

'I suppose we should, but I'm a bit reluctant, as I don't know if they will be pleased to see me, or how they will react when they find out I've run away from home,' she replied.

'Well, as Simon and Esther won't be home, I'm sure Susan will be glad of your company,' I said, trying to alleviate her fears as we quickened our pace.

'Anat,' I said, as we drew closer to the home of Simon, 'what would you want to do if it were left up to you? What would you change?'

We walked on, and I could see she was pondering over this thought, 'If I had my way I'd… no, if I could change anything, I would change my father's obsession with making more and more money, then we could live together with love and respect.'

She thought some more, and then added, 'I would like to be a person in my own right. Accepted as someone with a brain! Someone who has something of value to give, more than just as a possession to be owned by a man, to give him children.'

'Is that what you really feel you are, Anat? Just an object for a man to desire?' I questioned her.

'Isn't that how most men see women, Yoram? Before today, I would have said, "Isn't that how *all* men see women?" But meeting you, and seeing your father with your mother, I can see how he loves and respects her. And back there, on the rock, I saw you really cared about what happened to me. But in my family, my mother is treated by my father either as someone to exhibit to other men, or as a slave to serve him. He has no respect for her, and only treats her well because it helps his reputation to do so. He can't see she has a brain as well. She puts up with it because his money gives her clothes and things that other women could only dream of.'

As she spoke, the fire was back in her voice and she began to tremble again. 'Yoram, it's so unfair. Women have more to give than just their bodies. Given the chance, they can do just as well as men in most things.'

We turned the corner, and Simon's house was facing us. It was large, one of the biggest in the village, with its own courtyard and well. As we walked across the road, Susan came out of the door and was about to turn down the road, when she caught sight of us.

'Yoram ... and Anat! This is a surprise! What brings you both to my door today? Come in, and let me get you both a drink. Yoram, I didn't know that you knew Anat,' she said, as she stepped back into the house. 'Go through into the courtyard and I'll bring the drinks out for you.' She didn't give us time to answer her questions, and we smiled at each other as we went through to the courtyard. We sat down in the shade and I said to Anat, 'I think you will be welcome!'

She agreed. 'You're right. I guess she needs someone to talk to, with her husband and daughter being away.'

Susan came out carrying a tray with a jug of cool water and cups and sat down beside us. She filled the cups and handed them to us before she asked more questions. 'So, Anat, tell me, have you come to see Esther and stay for a few days? They're away at the moment, but should be back the day after tomorrow. Please say you can stay. I get lonely when there is no one else in the house. So how is it that you two are together? Is there something no one has told me about? How long have you been seeing each other?

Didn't Esther say something about you being married off to a business friend of your father's? My, it's a while since we saw you.'

She paused to take a drink, and I jumped in before she could ask more questions. 'I think, Susan, you could be guilty of jumping to too many conclusions. I only met Anat this morning, as we were travelling on the same road. When she told me she was coming to see you, I walked with her. All your other questions, I think Anat will be able to answer better than me.'

Susan laughed at herself, 'I did go on a bit, didn't I? Sorry, Anat, I didn't mean to embarrass you, but it's so good to see you, and I would love for you to stay.'

Anat was smiling and did not seem to be the least bit embarrassed. 'I understand, Susan. And Yoram would make a much better husband that my father's friend would. And yes, I would love to stay. In fact, I don't know what else to do.' With that, Anat began to cry.

Susan moved closer to her and put her motherly arms round her. 'Ah, my dear child, whatever is the matter? You can stay here for as long as you like.'

I took the opportunity to excuse myself. 'I think I should leave you two together. I'm glad we met this morning, Anat. I believe Jehovah has the answers for you and will show you in His time.'

I stood up ready to leave, and Anat jumped up as well. 'Must you, Yoram? You still haven't finished telling me how you got your sight back,' she said.

'That has to do with Jehovah, too, Anat. He gave me sight and He will give you insight as you need it. I promise I'll come back and finish my story.'

She kissed me on both cheeks and thanked me for my help.

'I think you need to tell Susan everything you told me, and she will be able to guide you.' I left them together in the courtyard and made my way home.

I turned off near the stream and sat once more with my back against the oak tree. Sharing my story with Anat had stirred memories afresh from that dark time in my life. I felt the rough bark of the tree that I had pounded with my fists all that while ago, and watched the water flowing in the stream. Yes, a lot of water had flown over the last ten years – and some of it very turbulent…

Chapter 7

I dropped a small stick into the stream and watched the water take it away. It swirled round some large stones breaking through the surface of the water, then for a moment was sucked under by the flow. It bobbed up again a little further down the stream, only to be dragged into an eddy round a bend. For a time it went round and round, going nowhere. A slight change in the flow of the water, and the stick was pushed out of the eddy and disappeared from my view.

I saw myself as the stick in the water. Life flows along and brings us different experiences, some we wish we could avoid. But they also shape us and bring us to a greater understanding of life.

The next 'rock' in my path had been my coming of age, my Bar-Mitzvah, and the waters of my life swirled round that one, and quickened the pace into unknown rapids.

For a Jewish boy, his Bar-Mitzvah is a big thing. This is the time when he is considered a man, in so far as being responsible for his own actions and sins is concerned. Maybe it was because I was blind, but I took it very seriously. I wanted to know the approval of the rabbi and the leaders at the synagogue. I wanted to please Jehovah, our God, the Almighty. I learned the prayers by heart and memorised as many of the scriptures as I could. I loved some of the passages from the prophet Isaiah, as he spoke about a Messiah.

One Sabbath stuck out in my memory like one of those stones in the stream. The rabbi read from the scroll of the book of Isaiah. It was like a shockwave down my spine, and I sat upright as he read:

> The Spirit of the Sovereign Lord is on me,
> because the Lord has anointed me
> to proclaim good news to the poor.
> He has sent me to bind up the broken-
> hearted,
> to proclaim freedom for the captives
> and release from darkness for the prisoners,
> to proclaim the year of the Lord's favour
> and the day of vengeance of our God,
> to comfort all who mourn,
> and provide for those who grieve in Zion –
> to bestow on them a crown of beauty
> instead of ashes,
> the oil of joy
> instead of mourning,
> and a garment of praise
> instead of a spirit of despair.
> They will be called oaks of righteousness,
> a planting of the Lord
> for the display of his splendour.
> *Isaiah 61:1-3 (NIV)*

Release from darkness – that was me! Oh, how I wanted it to be true. My mind swirled around that scripture like the little stick, and I was immersed in it – if only that could be true!

My Bar-Mitzvah came and I recited the prayer without a fault. After the service, the rabbi congratulated me and welcomed me into the synagogue as a male member. Abba hugged me, and we had a great celebration. I felt I had at last been accepted and we were no longer looked upon as outsiders, as sinners. I was floating along in the current of life, now a responsible adult.

I got up from the stream and I continued on my way home. The sun was high in the cloudless sky, but my mind was recalling the storm that had been about to break. As I walked on, I could feel again the darkness that had descended on us. It was only a week after my Bar-Mitzvah that my father came home early from the olive groves to break the news that he was no longer employed by Simon's brother. He looked for work near our home, but because of lies spread about him, he was unable to find employment locally and had to look further afield. After a few weeks he found a job working with a travelling merchant, but it meant him being away from home for weeks at a time.

My life spiralled down and my new status as one responsible for my own actions played on my mind. I was now thirteen and needed to do something to help the situation – but what? Words of the visitor three years earlier echoed in my ears: 'He'll never be anything but a blind beggar.'

With my father away, I spoke to my mother one morning. I was filling my water bottle when she came in from the backyard. It was early and she wondered what I was doing. 'Why are you filling the water bottle so early in the day?'

'I am responsible for my own actions now, Mother, and I need to do what I can to help the family. I am going to make my way to where the main road to Jerusalem cuts across this one, and I shall sit and ask for alms,' I answered her, with quiet determination in my voice.

'No, Yoram, no! That you will never do! Your Abba has always said that he would never see you beg for a living. This is a difficult time, but we will get through it.' I could tell there were tears in her eyes as she sat down, and I could hear her wiping her face in her apron.

'Yes, we will get by, but only if we each do our part, and the only part I can do is to beg,' I said with more conviction than I felt.

She protested some more, but could see that my mind was set. After a long silence, she got up and moved around the room preparing food. 'If you must, then I will at least prepare you some food,' was all she said.

With my stick and water bottle, I picked up the bag she'd put my food in and made my way out of the house. She kissed me and let me go, holding herself from crying any more while I was with her. 'May the God of our fathers keep you, and bring you safely back,' she prayed, as I made my way from the house.

As I relived that day, my thoughts went back to the girl I had just left at Simon's house. Was it only just this morning that I had seen her on the outcrop of rock, about to throw herself off? What was around the corner for her?

It was two days before I saw Anat again. I was now working back at the olive groves and had taken some fresh olives to Simon's place so that he could sample the quality, when he got back from his trip with his daughter.

I knocked on the door, only to have it opened by Esther, who had returned home the night before. From what I was given to understand, she and Anat had been awake most of the night talking. Esther let me in and took me through to the courtyard where Simon and his wife were sitting, with Anat beside them.

Simon got up and greeted me warmly. 'Good to see you, Yoram, and I see you have brought me the olives. Thank you. Sit down and I'll get the girls to bring you some refreshment.' He turned to Esther and Anat. 'We have a guest, Esther, would you be so kind?'

Both girls got up and, giggling together, went off to find me some food and drink. Simon waited until they were in the house before he spoke again. 'Anat's told us the whole story, Yoram. Poor kid, she's had no easy time of it.'

'Are you in a position to speak with her father and plead her cause?' I asked Simon.

'I can try, but she's right, I'm afraid, the most important thing in his life is making money, and other people's feelings are of little interest to him, even those of his own daughter. But I will have to let him know that she is safe, and is here with us. He may listen, but I doubt it. She can stay here if she is determined not to go back, and that will probably mean the end of any business I will have with him. He may even come and force her to go back with him.'

The girls came out with the food and drink, and sat down with us by the well.

Anat spoke first, 'Yoram, when are you going to tell me the rest of your story about how you got your sight back? None of these will tell me,' she said, as she looked around at Susan, Esther and Simon, who just smiled at her. 'They said it's your story to tell, not theirs.'

'Has Simon told you how he was cured from leprosy?' I asked her.

'Susan told me before they got back from their trip. Amazing! I've heard of this man, Jesus, but I haven't met him. I've heard my father talk about him. It seems he has caused quite a stir in the city, and he's not welcomed by the Scribes and Pharisees. My father dismissed him as a charlatan who was only after people's money. But then he would think like that! Did you meet Jesus as well? Was it He who made you see?' She was beginning to put my story together without my telling her.

'Yes, I did meet Him, but that was after seven long years of begging,' I said.

'Susan told me how Simon's brother treated your father and, reluctantly, he had to concede and let you beg. How did you cope with that, Yoram?'

I watched her face as she asked me that question, and knew that she was asking for herself as well. The others got up and left us sitting by the well, and I picked up on my story.

Chapter 8

We moved out of the sun into the shade of the house, and sat down by a low wall. Anat was much more relaxed than the first time I saw her. Having Susan and then Esther for company over these last few days had done her good. Hearing her giggling with Esther when they went for food showed that her mind had moved beyond the thought of killing herself. I wanted to tell her the rest of my story in a way that would bring her more hope.

'When I left home on the first morning, it was only a few weeks after my Bar-Mitzvah. Although I was only thirteen, I was optimistic as I set out. I was a man! I was responsible for my actions, and I would prove to the world that I could help support myself and my family. I didn't understand the stigma of being a beggar. I somehow saw myself as contributing, not begging, being somebody rather than a nobody who could only ask for people's charity.

'I was sure I would be looked upon with kindness and favour and would come back with enough money to meet our needs until Abba got back. Those who had not been supportive in the past had either changed their minds when they'd spent time with my father and mother, or they had got used to seeing me walking along with my stick. I knew Abba had not wanted me to beg, and that was still very much in my mind, but I guess a thirteen-year-old setting out on a new venture, whatever it might be, would have hope in his heart.

'That didn't last for long. I reached the spot where the roads joined and found a place to sit in the shade of a tree.

I spread a blanket on the ground, put my water bottle and food behind me, and a bowl at my feet.

'With my stick in my left hand, I had a plan. When I heard someone coming I was going to wait until they got closer, then I was going to ask very politely if they would bless me by giving me alms. I knew this was taught in the synagogue.

'I heard voices coming along the road from Jerusalem, and guessed it was four or five young men by the way they were talking. I held my nerve and waited until they were closer to me, then spoke out in a strong voice, "May you know the blessings of Jehovah as you give alms to a needy brother. Please give alms," and I held up my bowl expectantly.

'They stopped in front of me. "May you know the blessings of Jehovah as you give alms to a needy brother," one said, mimicking me in a silly voice. The others laughed and joined in, "Please give me alms!" One dropped something into my bowl.

'"Here you are, blind boy, here's your alms!" More laughter followed. I could tell by the weight of it that it was more than likely they had dropped a stone into my bowl. I was afraid and didn't know how to respond, as I realised I was defenceless before them.

'Before I had time to speak, another came up. "Oh sorry, blind boy, you can't eat that, it's only a little joke. Look, I have something much better to put in your bowl. You'll really enjoy this." I felt something drop into my bowl. It didn't rattle as it landed, and I could smell something bad.'

'"Eat it up, then," the voice said. "It's really fresh and tasty." They roared with laughter, kicked my feet and ran off down the road. I knew what it was by the smell – dog's mess!

'How to clean it out was another matter, and I didn't know what to do. I felt mortified and confused. Why would they want to do that to me? Where was the kindness of Jehovah they had been taught to show to others?

'While I was trying to think what to do, someone else reached the place I was sitting. They stopped, and before I had time to do anything about it, took my bowl from my hands and cleaned it with some water from a bottle they had with them. This was done without a word, until the bowl was given back to me.

'"It's all clean now. You don't need to worry about it soiling your fingers or any alms you may receive. I saw what they did as I was coming along the road but couldn't get to you before they left. My legs can't run any more. I'm so sorry they did that to you. Try to forgive them."

'The voice was kind, and that of an elderly lady. She went on, "I wish I could put some money in it for you, but I'm afraid I have just come from the Temple in Jerusalem and have no more left."

'I received the bowl back from her. "Thank you, it's very kind of you to help me. Please don't feel bad about not giving me any money. You have done much more than that for me. Why did you say, try to forgive them? Don't they deserve to be punished for the bad things they did? If you hadn't helped me, I would had been in real trouble."

'She sat down beside me at the side of the road. "They do need to be shown that it's wrong to do what they did, but if you carry bitterness in your heart it will spoil you more than the mess they made in your bowl."

'Her hands rested over mine, and I could feel they were old and worn by many days of hard work. Her voice was cracked but warm and reassuring, and I forgot my own troubles for a moment and wanted her to stay with me. I felt behind me and found the food mother had packed for me. "Please, will you share my lunch?" I offered, and held up the bag so she could help herself.

'"Bless you, son, you have a good heart, and I'm a bit hungry, thank you."

'She unwrapped the food from the cloth, broke off a piece of bread and gave it to me, then broke another piece for herself. We sat side by side, slowly eating for a few minutes. It was strange how I immediately connected with this unknown old lady, and I felt I could ask her anything.

'"Did someone hurt you and you had to forgive them?" I asked her.

'"When you are widowed and have no sons to look after you, you have to get on and try the best you can to survive. Many times I have been pushed away from what was rightfully mine, and got angry. There are so few who speak up for justice for a widow, and life is hard. Unless you can forgive, you are dead before you die, and your heart can become harder than your hardships."

'I was young, and I liked the soft way she talked – like a grandmother. I had lost my grandparents on both sides but had fond memories of my father's mother. This old lady reminded me of her, and as I had no visual picture of her face, the bonding was even deeper. "My name is Yoram, and this is the first time I have tried to beg," I told her. "Have you been on your own long?"

'By the tone of her voice I sensed she was smiling as she answered me. "Almost twenty years now, Yoram. My name is Elisabeth, and I guessed this must have been your first time. I come past this way often and have seen you with your father over by the olive groves the other side of Bethpage."

'I removed the stopper from my water bottle and offered it to her. She took a few sips and handed it back. "You need to keep most of the water for yourself, Yoram. Sitting here by the dusty road will make you very thirsty."

'I took a long drink and replaced the stopper. I placed it down beside me and reached up, almost without thinking, to touch her face with my fingers. She leaned forward and let me move my fingers gently over her face. It was old and wrinkled, but I felt a face that, despite hardship, was not tight and hard. The crow's feet by her eyes and the creases round her mouth spoke to me of a face quick to smile, full of kindness and peace. She took my hand between both of hers and lifted it to her lips, and kissed the tips of my fingers.

'I leaned into the folds of her clothes. They were made of a rough cloth, the sort worn by the poor, and her arm went round my shoulders and she gently rocked me. "Jehovah bless you, Yoram. You will be lifted up by Him, I sense it in my heart."

'"You know the meaning of my name!" I said with delight.

'"Yes, and do you know what mine means? It means 'God is my Oath', and, Yoram, He never breaks his word, even to an insignificant old widow like me, and blind boys like you."

'My mind went over the words from the prophet Isaiah about freedom for the captives and release from darkness. Was this what her blessing would mean for me? With my head resting on her side, I forgot I was now a man, and I spoke like a child without worrying about how my words might sound to an adult. "When you said you had no money to put in my bowl, do you mean you have no money for yourself at all or that what you have is what you need to buy food for yourself?"

'One of those bony, worn hands stroked my hair as she unashamedly answered, "Bless you, Yoram. I meant what I said, I have no more money left, but the Lord will provide. Don't worry about me. I have a little food at home, and when it has gone, He will supply me with some more. I have all I need."

'"But how, Elisabeth? Where will it come from? It's past the gleaning season!"

'"Don't you remember the story of our ancestors? When they left Egypt and were in the desert, how did they get their food?"

'"Do you mean the manna? Does God send you your own manna even now? I thought it stopped when they got to the Promised Land!"

'"In one way it did, but in other ways He sends me manna, but not like the manna they found on the ground. He will stir someone's heart to help me, or He will provide me with something I can do to earn a little money, or I will find some food left over after the market that I am allowed to take home for myself. If you keep your heart soft, Yoram, and trust Him, He will provide." She spoke with such confidence and faith that I felt peace resting on me.

'"Please, can you stay with me for a little while?" I asked. "You remind me of my grandmother."

'"I will stay for a little while, but then I must be on my way as my legs are not as young as yours, and I will need to be getting home."

'We sat side by side, with me leaning against her and her arm round my shoulders, and I felt more peaceful than I had done since my father had lost his job. A few people came by and one or two stopped and spoke to Elisabeth, as they must have known her, but they put nothing in my bowl, and I had forgotten my little speech about giving alms.

'Elisabeth was just about to get up when two men came along with pack donkeys. They were returning from the market in Jerusalem, and were in good spirits. One of the donkeys stopped just before they reached us and lowered its head to graze on some grass by the side of the road. They were in no hurry, and let the animal eat the grass.

'"Good afternoon, grandmother and grandson. You've chosen a good spot to sit in the shade of this tree. Even my donkey likes the grass you're sitting on!" said one of the travellers, and from his speech it was easy to know he was a Samaritan. "It would seem by looking at your bowl that my donkey is better off than you are. He has all this grass to eat and your bowl is empty. That just won't do." And he stooped down and dropped some coins into my bowl. Then his companion did the same.

'My adopted grandmother was quick to respond, "Sir, that is very kind of you, but I must tell you that Yoram and I are only friends, and not related in the way you have assumed."

'Grandmother was keen not to deceive them in any way, and I was impressed with her integrity. And, so it seemed, were our Samaritans. "Good lady, we thank you for your honesty, but if you will excuse me for saying so, I think our small donation could be of use to you as well as to our blind young friend here. Please accept it with our blessing."

'They reached over and shook her hand, then mine. "May your God be good to you," they said, and moved off down the road, with Elisabeth calling after them, "Oh, He really is, and may His blessing rest upon you both."

'Reaching over, I scooped the coins from my bowl and counted them from one hand to the other, "Six denarii, Grandmother!" I said, with surprise at the size of their gift to us. "That's more than two days' wages for a hired hand at the olive groves!"

'I caught her hand and pressed three of the coins into it. She began to protest. "Yoram, no! You have four and just give me two. My needs are not as great as yours and your family. Didn't I tell you we could trust Jehovah to be our provider? His manna still comes to those who trust in Him."

'She tried to give me one of the coins back, but I refused. "No, Grandmother, you have helped me so much today and have shown me more than I could have hoped to learn so quickly. Please keep half, please."

'Her skinny arm pulled me tight into her embrace, and she kissed me on the top of my head. "I am doubly blessed today! More money than I have had for a long time, and now I'm a grandmother! Blessed be our Lord and deliverer. Oh, Yoram, I'm so glad I stopped to help you today. You have made one old woman very happy. When are you going to go home? If it's not too far, let me walk back with you. I would like to meet your parents."

'And so it was. I'd done my first day's begging and I learned the truth of both the downside, shown by the boys who had abused me, and the positive side, shown by the kindness of the two Samaritan travellers. And in doing so, I gained a wonderful adopted grandmother full of faith and love.'

Anat had sat still drinking in every word I said, and her eyes glistened as she heard about the involvement of Elisabeth. 'Did she keep in touch with you and your family after that?'

'She did, and we often met at the side of the road, and she would sit with me and tell me more of her life story. It was through her that my anticipation of the coming of the Messiah grew.'

Chapter 9

It was time for me to go back to the olive groves, so I stood up and went into the house to see Simon before I went. He thanked me for the sample of olive oil and gave me instructions as to how much to press and prepare for shipping.

Anat had got to her feet, and when I emerged from the house she was standing beside the front door waiting for me. 'Yoram, can I walk a little way with you? You still haven't told me how you got your sight back!' She hesitated, then added, as if she had read my thoughts, 'Esther's coming too.'

We said goodbye to Simon and his wife and walked off towards the Mount of Olives. It was good having the company of the girls, and I was enjoying being with them. I'd known Esther for most of my life, and we had become close when her father had leprosy. I thought of her like another sister, and she had often been my guide after Ora had left home and I went to visit Simon at his small dwelling while he was banished from the community.

Esther was walking on one side of me, with Anat on the other. I could not get over how different she looked now from the girl I had seen only a few days earlier, who had been about to kill herself. She was dressed in some of Esther's clothes and her hair was well groomed, with waves of long dark hair cascading over her shoulders and down her back. Her eyes sparkled, and there was a warm smile on her face. As she walked, she moved with the elegance of the well-brought-up daughter of a wealthy family. Walking between these two, I felt I was the most blessed man on the earth!

I knew Anat wanted to hear how I had received my sight, but I wanted to find out just where she was with her thoughts and feelings towards her father and the proposed marriage. I asked her, before she prompted me to continue my story, 'Anat, have you been in contact with your parents yet? Do they know where you are?'

We walked on a few paces before she answered, 'I guessed you were going to ask me that and the answer is yes and no.'

She looked straight ahead, as she went on, 'After talking it over with Susan and Simon, we felt it was the right thing to let them know I was safe and well. So Simon sent one of his servants with a letter to let them know I was here. The servant said when he got back that at first my father was furious. My mother cried with relief when she heard I was safe, and that caused my father to calm down. He admitted he was glad to know I was safe, but still angry with me for running off on my own.'

'Are you going back?' I asked, half-afraid of what she would say.

'He gave a message to the servant, saying that he would let me stay with Simon and Esther for a few more days and then he was going to come down and see me. He didn't say he was coming to force me to go home, but just that he was coming down. I don't know what that means.'

'And if he still insists in your marrying the "ogre", what will you do?'

She stopped walking and shuddered. Esther moved round to comfort her, and we stood in the middle of the path while she regained her composure. 'What do you think your adopted grandmother would say, Yoram? Would she believe her Jehovah would want me to submit to my father and give up any chance of happiness I might have?'

'Would submitting to your father's will be less happy than throwing yourself off the cliff?' It was me who shuddered now, because in my mind's eye I could see her falling through the air like a broken bird, and her beautiful body smash on the rocks below.

'Is it wrong to have hopes and dreams of being married to a man about my own age? One who loves me for who I am and wants to build a loving home in which to raise children? Tell me, Yoram! Is that wrong?' Her voice was strong, but she was control of what she said.

I felt at a loss as to what to say, but I picked up on her mention of Elisabeth. 'Elisabeth believed that Jehovah would provide for her all she needed in His own way if she just trusted Him with all she was and had. I can't see how it can be wrong for you to have dreams of being happily married and wanting to bring up children in a secure home. But is it possible to believe that our God can bring light even into our darkest experiences? My life would say that it is. He did bring light into my blindness and set me free. So much so that as I told you when we first met, I drink in each new day and see it as a new gift from God – as Grandmother Elisabeth would say, fresh manna from heaven, just when I most need it and from the most unexpected sources.'

Esther broke in, 'You feel she should just be a doormat, and meekly do as her father so outrageously demands of her when he has no compulsion or desire to follow Jehovah?'

Now I began to think that perhaps I was not the most blessed man walking along with two lovely girls, after all, but one being blamed for all the insensitive domination of every male that ever lived in the name of religion! In the silence of my own heart, I offered up a quick prayer to the Lord, 'I need some help on this one, Lord. What do I say now. How would You answer?'

I walked slowly to the side of the path and sat down on the grass. 'Sit with me, and I'll finish my story of how I came to see. It might somehow help you see what you should do. There is more to it than just blindly following a set of rules without knowing the Rule-maker.'

Anat wasn't angry with me. She genuinely wanted to know what was the right thing for her to do. Esther, who was more indignant about the situation, felt strongly for her friend.

'Let's walk to the stream we sat by on the day I first met you, Yoram. It's more private than it is here,' said Anat.

I got back on my feet and followed them further along the path to the spot that held so many memories. She found the oak tree I'd pummelled with my fists as a child of ten. The girls took off their sandals and sat with their feet dangling in the stream. They were a couple of paces apart, and so I sat a little way back and leaned on the tree while they turned so they could keep their feet in water and at the same time look towards me.

'So you went to meet Jesus. What happened next?' Anat asked.

'Well, I didn't go looking for Jesus; He found me. It was a Sabbath and we'd left the synagogue. My parents went home, and I felt like I needed a bit of air, so I went for a short stroll. Jesus came along with His disciples, having left the Temple ground in Jerusalem.

'It's funny how if you are disabled in one way, people think you are handicapped in another! I was leaning against a tree with my walking stick in my hand, but my hearing was anything but impaired. The fisherman Peter was speaking to Jesus, as if I could not hear what he was saying, "Rabbi, why was this man born blind? Was it because of his own sins or his parents' sins?"

'I pricked up my ears to hear what Jesus said, and I loved the answer He gave: "It was not because of his sins or his parents' sins. This happened so the power of God could be seen in him."

'A tingle went down my spine. Was I going to see the fulfilment of Isaiah's prophecy in my own life?

'"We must quickly carry out the tasks assigned to us by the One who sent us. The night is coming, and then no one can work," Jesus said. "But while I am here in the world, I am the light of the world."

'I heard Him spit on the ground, and I'm told He bent over and mixed the saliva with the dirt and made a mud pack with it. I knew He was breaking one of the Sabbath laws, as the Pharisees would consider making mud to be working.

'The next thing I felt was Jesus spreading this mud over my eyes. It felt cool to my face as the sun was high in the sky. What was He doing to me in front of his disciples, who already thought that blindness at birth was caused by sin?

I felt awkward in front of this man who had healed Simon of leprosy. How was mud going to help me? What was I supposed to do now?

'I needn't have worried, I was about to find out!'

Anat pulled her feet out of the water and sat on the bank of the stream, hugging her knees to herself. 'So what did you do?'

'He told me, "Go wash yourself in the pool of Siloam."

'I picked up my stick and tapped my way along the road towards the pool. Peter's brother, Andrew, came alongside me and guided me to Siloam, and helped me get in the water.

'I'll never, ever forget what happened next. I got down on my knees and ducked my head under the water, and with both hands I splashed the mud from off my eyes. I lifted my head up out of the water and was met by a kaleidoscope of colour as the sun's rays refracted in the water droplets on my eyes. It was such a flood of sensory overload on my brain; I had to close my eyes to gain some sense of equilibrium. I screwed up my face and half-opened one eye to take another look. Blue! Sky blue! What a colour! Colour! That's what colour is!

'Opening both eyes, I turned round and looked at Andrew standing there with a massive grin on his face. His was the first face I had ever seen, and I thought he was the most handsome person in the whole world!

'I splashed in the water like a kid in a puddle after rain, and then, with Andrew leading the way, I ran back to Jesus, leaving my stick discarded by the side of the pool.

'A small crowd gathered, and some knew me, as they were our neighbours, and others who had seen me begging by the side of the road. They were totally confused and looked at me as if I had two heads. "Isn't this the man I've seen sitting along the road, begging?" said one. And others thought I must just be someone who looked like him.

'Moving closer to them, I shouted, "Yes, it's me! I'm Yoram, the blind man who you have seen sitting by the road, begging!"

'They began asking me the same question you asked, Anat: "How can that be? What happened to you? Who healed you?"

'So I told them it was Jesus, and how He had put the mud on my eyes and then told me to wash in the pool, and now I could see.'

'That's amazing, Yoram. Everyone must have been so happy for you, and just over the moon with joy at what God had done for you through Jesus.' Anat's face had traces of tears as she spoke.

'I wish that were true, Anat, but for some, this was not what they wanted to hear. To the Pharisees this was law-breaking. A group from the crowd made me go and see the Pharisees, and they gave them half a story of what had happened.

'As it was the Sabbath, the Pharisees were none too happy about anything that disturbed their interpretation of the Law of Moses, and the leading one came over and cross-examined me. You need to remember I was only beginning to get my brain around seeing for the first time. I was grinning like a demented donkey, and staring at everyone and everything. The colours were making me feel as if I was drunk with wonder.

'Anyway, the spokesman for the Pharisees asked me how was it that I could now see since I had been born blind. So I went into all the details of Jesus making mud and plastering it over my eyes and me washing it off in the pool and then being able to see. I was so happy to tell them of the most wonderful thing that had happened to me in all my life.

'Well, this put the wind up the windbags, and they were divided in their opinions as to who Jesus was. Some of the Pharisees said, "This man Jesus is not from God, for he's working on the Sabbath," while others said, "But how could an ordinary sinner do such miraculous signs?"

'They were getting quite heated about it, and I found it all very perplexing. Couldn't they see what a wonderful thing had happened to me? But for some of them, the breaking of one of their rules was more important than my sight! It was incredible!

'After arguing among themselves for a bit, they pulled me back and demanded what my opinion was about the man who healed me! I ask you – what did they think I would say about someone who had just given me sight! To me it was obvious – at the very least He must be a prophet! – and I told them so.

'My word was not enough for them, so they sent for my parents. When my father and mother got there they were shocked to see me standing there looking all around, without my stick. Seeing my mother for the first time brought tears to my eyes, and my father just stood there dumfounded. I ran over to them, and we had a family embrace.

'This was too much for some of the Pharisees and they pushed me away from my parents and demanded, "Is this your son? Was he born blind? If so, how can he now see?"

'I ask you – who was the most blind?! It's not your usual happening for a husband and wife to embrace a stranger and for them to hug the life out of each other if they're not related. Couldn't they see the joy and amazement on all our faces?!

'Father was confused by their manner and was trying to understand where they were coming from. My mind went back to the conversation I had overheard at home all those years ago when Ora had pulled me away and consoled me behind the house. I think it must have been in my father's mind too, and all the other times people had shunned us because I had been born blind. He had been afraid as to what they might do, that they might perhaps add to our isolation by throwing us out of the synagogue.

'A wearied expression was on his face as he answered, "We know this is our son and that he was born blind, but we don't know how he can see or who healed him." He looked across at me, bursting with joy at my healing, and added, "Ask him. He is old enough to speak for himself."

'So they called me over a second time. "God should get the glory for this, because we know this man Jesus is a sinner."

'I was stunned! Couldn't they see what had happened? So I replied with some force, "I don't know whether He is a sinner. But I do know this: I was blind, and now I can see!"

'"But what did he do?" they asked again. "How did he heal you?"

'Exasperated, I stared at them and pointed to my eyes. "Look! I've told you once. Didn't you listen? Why do you want to hear it again? Do you want to become His disciples, too?"

'That was it! They cursed me and said, "You are his disciple, but we are disciples of Moses! We know God spoke to Moses, but we don't even know where this man comes from."

'I couldn't let that go, and had to reply, "Why now, that's very strange! He healed my eyes, and yet you don't know where He comes from? We know that God doesn't listen to sinners, but He is ready to hear those who worship Him and do His will. Ever since the world began, no one has been able to open the eyes of someone born blind. If this man were not from God, He couldn't have done it."

'You could have cut the air with a knife! And there certainly was a clear-cut line as we stood there. Me on one side with my parents standing behind me and some of our friends behind, facing "them"!

'The Pharisees were in a bunch with hard faces and tight lips, and they trotted out the same old line: "You were born a total sinner! And you dare to try to teach us?"

'And they threw me out of the synagogue.'

Anat's face was a picture. A flash of that anger I had seen before went across her face. 'How could they do that to you? They're worse than my father! What did you do?'

'Well, they walked away in a hurry, kicking up the dust as they left. I turned round to face my parents. "I'm sorry, Father, if I was disrespectful to them and it's caused us all to be thrown out of the synagogue, but I couldn't stop myself."

'He flung his arms round me. "Look at me, son! Look at me!" He held me at arm's length and I looked him in the eye! Something I had never done in my twenty years. "If the Pharisees cannot see what I can see right now, then I am truly sorry for them – they are blind. I'd rather have you seeing than be in company with those who blamed us for you being born blind, and now wish you still were!"

'Again, as a family we embraced each other, and I just stared at each one with wonder and drank in sight of the faces of people I had known but never seen.

'My mother wanted to run home and prepare a banquet and have a big celebration, so I let them go home to make ready while I took my time and let my eyes feast on all the sights I had only heard of before!

'A short time later, I felt a touch on my shoulder, and I turned round to see for the first time the one they called Jesus . "Do you believe in the Son of Man?" he asked.

'And I just answered, "Who is He, Sir? I want to believe in Him."

'"You have seen Him," Jesus said, "and He's speaking to you now!"

'I dropped to my knees, utterly overwhelmed, "Yes, Lord, I believe!" was all I could say, and, I think, all I needed to say, and I worshipped Jesus – my Lord and Deliverer.

'As I looked up into His lovely face, He said, "I entered this world to render judgement – to give sight to the blind, and to show those who think they see that they are blind."

'I hadn't realised, but a few of the Pharisees were still around and were standing nearby. They heard what Jesus said, and came over and asked him outright, "Are you saying we're blind?"

'"You claim you can see! If you were blind, you would have an excuse but wouldn't be guilty, but as you say you can see you are guilty of what you say. Yes, you are blind." They left.'

I stood up, 'Anat, Esther, I should be getting back to the olive groves. I need to go.'

'Your story is wonderful, Yoram, but how does it answer my question? Should I submit to my father and his unreasonable demands and meekly sacrifice any chance of any happiness I could have?'

'The Pharisees knew the Law but they didn't know the Law-giver. To them, legalistic obedience to their interpretation was more important than the joy I had at being able to see. Because of that they were blind to the heart behind the Law. The Sabbath laws were given for our benefit, so that we would take time for rest and allow our minds and spirits to reflect and worship God, who is the supplier of all our needs, not our own efforts and ingenuity only. Having a Sabbath brings a rhythm to our lives that can help us see the wonder of our creator God.

'When Jesus came to me, He was "God with us", the Law-giver who loves us and wants the best for us. If I were to lose my sight again tomorrow, I would still have His light in my heart. As I have met the Law-giver I have found him to be the sinner-lover – even one born blind!

'No, I don't expect you to meekly go back to your father and just "blindly" do as he says. The Law that says, "Children, obey your parents," is good and was given for our security and happiness in the family setting. The laws of heritage were given for the balance and good of society to prevent a few strong persons from overwhelming the weak and dominating them. But if we know only the Law, and not the love of the Law-giver, we become our own god and use the good laws for our own gain, at the expense of others.

'My adopted grandmother, Elisabeth, showed me that if we first submit to the Lord, He is able to bring us through the darkness of our situation and provide us with manna that will be enough to sustain us, and we can even find joy while still in the shadows.'

She listened to me, and her eyes moistened. 'You are saying I should go back and do as he says, believing that that man will somehow bring me happiness?'

'No. I'm saying that when he comes to see you, you ask for strength to respect your father and for a way to build a bridge so that he can hear your heart. You could tell him you are sorry for any stress you have caused him by running away, and that you want to behave as a good daughter should, but you fear the man he wants you to marry is not right for you. The trusting bit is that the Lord will bring about a change in your father's heart.'

'And if it doesn't? Do I marry his choice of husband for me? Is that what you think God wants me to do?'

'I walked in darkness for twenty years before the Lord delivered me.'

'But as you said to me before, Yoram, you didn't know anything else. I do!'

'Elisabeth told me some years later – it was soon after Simon was cleansed of his leprosy – she had gone to the Temple to pray and give her offering to the Lord. She had very little left and as she got to the offering box, she stood behind those who dropped in large amounts of money – she could hear the silver coins rattling as they hit the bottom. For a moment she felt inadequate and worthless. She had only a couple of pennies to her name, and what was that compared to what she had just seen and heard drop into the box? She was about to turn away, but in her spirit she knew she could only give what she had. And as it was so small, she couldn't really halve it, so she put both pennies in, and was a bit embarrassed at the tiny tinkle they made when she let them go. She gave all she had to the Lord without knowing where her next meal would come from. Her surrender was her act of trusting that God would somehow send the manna she need to keep going.

'One of Jesus' disciples told me later, on that day Jesus just happened to be sitting watching the people give their offerings to the Lord. His comment on the old lady was that she had given more than all the rest put together, because she had given her all.'

'Did she get it back?'

'I don't know, but she didn't die till about a year later so she was sustained by the Lord, somehow. She didn't die rich, but she did die smiling.'

Nothing was said for a few minutes.

Anat stepped over to me and kissed me on both cheeks, then gave me a big hug. Standing back, she took my hands in hers and said softly, 'I will go back and wait for my father to come. I will submit to your Lord Jesus, and trust Him to help me do what He would want me to do. I'll try to drop my two penn'orth into the box and trust Him to give me His deliverance. I'm not sure I can submit to marrying the man my father wants me to, but I'll respect my father and trust that Jesus will release me from burdens I can't bear.' Tears were flowing freely now, and Esther put her arm round her.

I lifted her hands up in mine and kissed them. 'I will pray you will find His deliverance. Anat, I don't think the Lord let me stop you from jumping to your death for nothing. I hope I will see you again soon.'

I kissed her fingers again, and let them slip from my hands.

She took Esther's hand, and they walked back along the way we came.

My eyes watched as the gap between us widened, and my vision was blurred by moisture in my own eyes. Somehow, it made her shape take on a more heavenly form, and I stood watching until she walked past some trees at the bend in the road, and she was lost from my sight.

'Lord, let my eyes see her beauty again.'

The olive grove beckoned, and I obeyed.

'I am the light of the world', Jesus said.

(John 9:5, NIV)

(John 9 gives the biblical account of Jesus healing the blind man. Matthew 26:6 and Mark 14:3 mention Simon the Leper. John 11 tells of Mary and Martha and their brother living in Bethany. Mark 12:41-44 and Luke 21:1-4 give accounts of the poor widow.)

Epilogue

Time to leave the market square of Capernaum and head for home.

Yoram has delivered all his olives and is preparing for his long trip back to the Mount of Olives at Jerusalem, his eyes still bright as he looks around, missing nothing. What would he make of our modern-day market? Would he sit on the bench under the tree and chat to the young man facing chemo? Would he bring a different perspective on life and its ups and downs?

Julian the centurion scans the crowd, weighing up whether there is any situation that needs his intervention, looking to see how best to administer the law for the benefit of all. The blonde PSSO might find him interesting to talk to!

Knowing that bad things happen to good people, having lost his beloved Hannah, how would he respond to the young man on chemo? Adopting Leon gave him a heart for boys who found life hard; skateboarding teenagers would be something new!

Ruth smiles at everyone as they pass, but is saddened when one or two push by and mutter something about lazy widows. Would she find a kinship with our *Big Issue* seller, and understand where she was coming from?

Obed laughs as he jumps over a pile of crates, aware of how his own behaviour affects others, yet full of life and willing to bring a smile. He would possibly hit it off with our skateboarders and know what it's like to feel left out, and would probably buy from the *Big Issue* lady.

Funny how you see people differently when you know a bit about where they've come from.

Jesus has a Life Line for every line of Life!

Acknowledgements

A book doesn't write itself – obviously!

But I would never have sat at my laptop without the encouragement of friends and family, and the patient input of the team from Instant Apostle.

So thank you, Angela, for encouraging me to dare to start, and my wife Heather for believing I could do it and supporting me in the process. Also dear friends like Marie Claude, Gerry, Peter and Nancy, who read some of my first attempts and gave me helpful input and urged me to keep going.

The team at Instant Apostle who have made it happen; particularly thanks to Nicki for the enormous amount of time and expertise she has given to this manuscript. I am indebted to you all.